The Higher Functional Field

OXFORD STUDIES IN COMPARATIVE SYNTAX

Richard Kayne, General Editor

Principles and Parameters of Syntactic Saturation
    Gert Webelhuth

Verb Movement and Expletive Subjects in the Germanic Languages
    Sten Vikner

Parameters and Functional Heads: Essays in Comparative Syntax
    Edited by Adriana Belletti and Luigi Rizzi

Discourse Configurational Languages
    Edited by Katalin É. Kiss

Clause Structure and Language Change
    Edited by Adrian Battye and Ian Roberts

*Dialect Variation and Parameter Setting: A Study of Belfast English
and Standard English*
    Alison Henry

Parameters of Slavic Morphosyntax
    Steven Franks

Particles: On the Syntax of Verb-Particle, Triadic, and Causative Constructions
    Marcel den Dikken

The Polysynthesis Parameter
    Mark C. Baker

The Role of Inflection in Scandinavian Syntax
    Anders Holmberg and Christer Platzack

*Clause Structure and Word Order in Hebrew and Arabic: An Essay in
Comparative Semitic Syntax*
    Ur Shlonsky

Negation and Clausal Structure: A Comparative Study of Romance Languages
    Raffaella Zanuttini

Tense and Aspect: From Semantics to Morphosyntax
    Alessandra Giorgi and Fabio Pianesi

Coordination
    Janne Bondi Johannessen

Adverbs and Functional Heads: A Cross-Linguistic Perspective
    Guglielmo Cinque

A Handbook of Slavic Clitics
    Steven Franks and Tracy Holloway King

XP-Adjunction in Universal Grammar: Scrambling and Binding in Hindi-Urdu
    Ayesha Kidwai

Multiple Feature Checking and Grammatical Functions in Universal Grammar
    Hiroyuki Ura

The Higher Functional Field: Evidence from Northern Italian Dialects
    Cecilia Poletto

THE HIGHER FUNCTIONAL FIELD

Evidence from Northern Italian Dialects

CECILIA POLETTO

New York   Oxford
Oxford University Press
2000

Oxford University Press

Oxford   New York
Athens   Auckland   Bangkok   Bogotá   Buenos Aires   Calcutta
Cape Town   Chennai   Dar es Salaam   Delhi   Florence   Hong Kong   Istanbul
Karachi   Kuala Lumpur   Madrid   Melbourne   Mexico City   Mumbai
Nairobi   Paris   São Paulo   Singapore   Taipei   Tokyo   Toronto   Warsaw

and associated companies in
Berlin   Ibadan

Published by Oxford University Press, Inc.
198 Madison Avenue, New York, New York 10016

Library of Congress Cataloging-in-Publication Data
Poletto, Cecilia, 1962–
The higher functional field : evidence from northern Italian
dialects / Cecilia Poletto.
p.   cm.—(Oxford studies in comparative syntax)
Includes bibliographical references and index.
ISBN 0-19-513356-0; ISBN 0-19-513357-9 (pbk.)
1. Italian language—Dialects—Italy, Northern.   I. Title.
II. Series.
PC1841.P65   2000
457'.1—dc21   99-20704

1 3 5 7 9 8 6 4 2

Printed in the United States of America
on acid-free paper

A Chicco e Dado con amore

Preface

The original project for this book about agreement and subject clitics in northern Italian dialects dates back about six years; it was supposed to be the English version of my doctoral thesis. Since then, I decided to widen the database
of my research, which was originally restricted to just fifty dialects, belonging
mainly to the northeastern area, to include several northwestern dialects and
Rhaetoromance. Moreover, the development of the theoretical framework had to
be taken into account and integrated into the analysis.

With the help of Paola Benincà, Richard Kayne, and Laura Vanelli, who co-
operated in the project that started in 1990 and involved devising a syntactic atlas
of northern Italy, I have been able to extend and deepen the empirical domain of
my investigation. The database on which this work is now based includes more
than 100 dialects, extending its scope across both northeastern and northwestern
Italy, which have been extensively tested by using the same questionnaire to col-
lect comparable data. The geographical domain of this inquiry has been so interesting because the dialectal varieties spoken throughout this area seem to share a
fundamentally homogeneous basic grammar and lexicon. They tend to differ in a
minimal way, and this fact becomes fruitful once we have made the preliminary
hypothesis that microvariation is not at random, or at best is a purely lexical
phenomenon.

This book is set within the comparative linguistic perspective that has recently
emerged from the work of Richard Kayne and Paola Benincà (among others), who
have investigated microvariation in syntax and developed it into a powerful tool
for observing clusters of properties that are linked together in a complex and interesting manner.

In my attempt to account for dialectal variation, I have not based my explanations merely on the different parametric choices made by different dialects, as
the variation patterns that have been observed are too narrow and detailed to be
explained in terms of parameters (as they are conceived in the current generative

theory). I have endeavored to explore an alternative method of accounting for microvariation, using it to prove that syntactic structure is much more complex than has been assumed until now. Different dialects only have different moving or merging possibilities for the same elements, such as the inflected verb or the complementizer, though the syntactic structure and constraints at work are assumed to be always the same. The general picture that has emerged from this investigation is certainly provisional, as it is based on a limited sample of dialects; it is expected to change as our knowledge of this linguistic area improves. The project involving the drawing up of a syntactic atlas for northern Italy is still continuing, and it seems to me an exciting challenge to be able to provide a systematic account of what at first sight would appear to be no more than wild variation; it also proves that dialectal variation is not a random procedure at all but follows well-determined general principles and can be described in terms of implicational generalizations, which in turn can be accounted for by linguistic theory, thereby improving our knowledge of the i-language.

The new phenomena that I discovered caused me to change part of the analysis I had proposed in my thesis and urged me to more deeply investigate certain aspects, such as subjunctive and verb second sentences, which I had neglected in my earlier studies. My interest in subject clitics and agreement patterns is reflected in the second and sixth chapters, whereas the central part of my work focuses on verb movement and the left-peripheral positions of the sentence and the complementizers and particles that occur in this syntactic domain. This book offers a methodical investigation of subject clitics in declarative clauses, which show that what has been assumed until recently to be a single agreement projection actually consists of a complex set of different functional layers. I have extensively examined several contexts in which the left periphery of the sentence structure is activated, namely, main and embedded interrogative sentences, verb second clauses (in those dialects that display these properties in a generalized fashion), and subjunctive clauses. The distribution of complementizers, subject clitics, and sentence particles, as well as the behavior of the inflected verb in these types of structures, shows that the Comp domain is a set of functional projections with distinct features and checking requirements. Moreover, the position of preverbal nominal subjects is identified as a SpecC position with topic properties, whereas the position of preverbal quantifier subjects displays a number of A´ properties. Examination of the left periphery in several different types of clauses unveils the number and type of CPs activated in each sentence type, which all display two fundamental properties: (1) activated CPs do not need to be adjacent, and (2) they are activated by means of a bottom-up procedure; that is, the higher CPs can be activated only when the lower ones are.

The complex structure I provide here may also serve as a basis for comparing the structure identified in northern Italian dialects with other Romance and non-Romance languages and to test whether the two properties in the activation of distinct CPs have a more general basis.

Padova, Italy   C. P.
November 1998

Acknowledgments

This book is the result of a ten-year study that has involved a large number of people. I would like to thank my first linguistic mentor, Guglielmo Cinque, who managed to instill in me his fascination for research into language diversity and unity. His rigor and precision in handling data and his intuition about far-reaching hypotheses have been a valuable model. The person I have to thank most for having made me a dialectologist is Paola Benincà, whose ideas and inspiration are present throughout all the work I have been doing in these years. I am aware of the fact that I would have never written this book if it had not been for her constant help and support. I also wish to thank her for being a sensible friend and a generous linguist, as well as for teaching me the real meaning of teamwork. I also benefited from the support of other friends from the Linguistics Department of Padova: Laura Vanelli, who has spent many long hours discussing with me all the problems regarding the phenomena at the interface with phonology, as well as a great many pragmatic questions; Teresa Vigolo, who has been my consultant for etymological issues; and Alberto Mioni and Alberto Zamboni, the former and present directors of the Centro di Dialettologia, and now the Istituto di Fonetica e Dialettologia, who have given me the opportunity to continue with this work. Many other linguists have visited during these past few years to discuss matters of data and ideas with me at length: Richard Kayne encouraged me to begin this undertaking and suggested many of the solutions I have adopted here. I have treasured the time we spent looking for interesting phenomena in the questionnaires, and I have modeled my view of grammatical variation on his insightful observations. Raffaella Zanuttini has inspired me with her analytical way of viewing facts and has helped me clarify my hypotheses. It was a real pleasure to have them here at our June meetings. Manuela Ambar, Adriana Belletti, Anna Cardinaletti, Alessandra Giorgi, Maria Teresa Guasti, Nicola Munaro, Hans Georg Obenauer, Mair Parry, Jean-Yves Pollock, Luigi Rizzi, Ian Roberts, Alessandra Tomaselli, Christina Tortora, and Massimo Vai have all been a direct or indirect source of inspiration for me.

Many thanks also go to all the informants of the ASIS (Atlante Sintattico dell'Italia Settentrionale, the Syntactic Atlas of Northern Italy) project who have kindly given us their gratuitous collaboration; they are just too numerous to mention here. I also want to thank Daria Valentin, for her invaluable help while collecting data on Rhaetoromance varieties.

And finally, I want to thank my two children, Federico and Davide Chiariotti, to whom this book is dedicated. Their presence constantly reminds me of how wonderful and precious and concrete life is.

Contents

1   Introduction   3
  1.1.   Aim of this Work   3
  1.2.   The Theoretical Framework   4
  1.3.   The Varieties Examined and Survey Methods
         Employed   6
  1.4.   Previous Analysis of Subject Clitics   9

2   Preverbal Subject Clitics in Declarative Contexts   11
  2.1.   Introduction   11
  2.2.   Two Tests for SCL Positions   18
  2.3.   More SCL Positions   22
  2.4.   One More Position   30
  2.5.   Subject Clitic Climbing Inside the
         Agreement Field   32
  2.6.   The Agreement Field   35

3   Interrogative Sentences   41
  3.1.   Introduction   41
  3.2.   Subject Clitic Inversion   42
  3.3.   Variation in Main Interrogatives   55
  3.4.   Theoretical Implications of Split Interrogative CP   80
  3.5.   Embedded Contexts   83
  3.6.   Conclusion   86

4   Rhaetoromance Verb Second: A Split-CP
       Perspective   88
  4.1.   Introduction   88
  4.2.   Rhaetoromance V2: Data   89

4.3. Left Dislocation: The Declarative-Interrogative
       Asymmetry   91
4.4. Different Degrees of Focalization   95
4.5. Embedded V2   98
4.6. Subject Positions   102
4.7. A Brief Comparison with Germanic V2   106

5 Subjunctive Clauses: The Modal Field   108
5.1. Introduction   108
5.2. Disjunctive Clauses   110
5.3. Optative and Counterfactual Clauses   115
5.4. Complementizer Deletion and Verb Movement
       in Italian   118
5.5. Complementizer Deletion in the Northern
       Varieties   131
5.6. Suppletive Imperatives   133
5.7. Conclusion   137

6 Subject Positions   139
6.1. Introduction   139
6.2. Subject Positions and Case Checking   140
6.3. Subject Positions in Nondeclarative Contexts   153
6.4. The Subject in CD Contexts   164
6.5. Conclusion   166

7 A Brief Summary   168
7.1. Introduction   168
7.2. Some General Properties of Functional Structure   173

Notes   177

Bibliography   193

Index   205

The Higher Functional Field

ONE

Introduction

1.1 AIM OF THIS WORK

The aim of this book is to investigate the syntax of the upper portion of the functional sentence structure on the basis of comparative data collected from the domain of a hundred Romance varieties in northern Italy. This geographical choice is justified by the fact that the dialects spoken in this area are quite homogeneous from a lexical, morphological, and syntactic point of view. They represent an ideal ground for analyzing microvariations in syntax, as the grammatical systems compared do not differ very much from one another. Thus, this is as near as we can get to a controlled scientific experiment, in which grammatical systems that differ only on the basis of a single feature are compared. In this manner, the single varying feature may be isolated and studied through controlled experiments, as there are no other factors to interfere with the definition of the phenomenon under investigation, while the rest of the grammar remains constant. This book is not intended as a typological study, describing the simple distribution facts of a given phenomenon, but rather it aims to determine which phenomena are correlated and in what way these relationships can be encoded into syntax. Therefore, this book does not report all varieties of the data investigated but focuses only on those data that are relevant to the analysis of the empirical domain mentioned above.

Chapter 2 analyzes the distribution of subject clitics, showing that they consist syntactically and morphologically of four types; that is, they occupy four distinct and nonadjacent positions. Chapter 3 presents an overview of all interrogative structures found in NIDs and analyzes them in terms of a split-CP perspective. Subject clitic inversion (SCI) is analyzed as verb movement in most dialects and as a morphological effect in other dialects. Chapter 4 focuses on the analysis of Central Rhaetoromance dialects, which have maintained their primitive Romance V2 structure, making it possible to examine the higher portion of the sentence structure and allowing interesting possibilities for comparison with the Germanic verb second phenomenon. Chapter 5 extends the analysis to hypothetical, disjunctive counterfactual clauses and to suppletive deictic and nondeictic imperatives. In all of these constructions, the verb moves to a higher position than the one occupied by the verb in indicative clauses. In addition, an analysis of complementizer deletion in standard Italian is given. Chapter 6 provides an overview of subject distribution in all the structures discussed so far, that is, indicative declaratives, interrogatives, hypothetical, counterfactual and optative clauses, and V2 contexts. I present a hypothesis regarding the positions that a preverbal subject may occupy. In addition, I claim that the subject position in the NIDs (and in standard Italian as well) is located higher than the position of wh-elements and that QPs and DPs occupy different positions. The final chapter contains a brief summary of a few of the possible research perspectives that an analysis of northern Italian dialects opens up. Much work is still to be done on the subject positions and on the exact nature of the relationship between the complementizer and verb and operator movements inside the CP layer.

1.2   THE THEORETICAL FRAMEWORK

In general, I adopt the minimalist theory proposed in Chomsky (1995) and make diverging assumptions only for the following points; first, the number of functional projections proposed here is much greater than that proposed in Chomsky (1995), and second, the notion of features with strong and weak values is used here in a simpler manner than in the minimalist approach, as the difference between interpretable and noninterpretable features is not exploited. It is simply assumed that some features are strong in certain dialects, and must be checked before being spelled out, and weak in others; therefore the latter do not need to be checked in the syntax but only at LF. Furthermore, it is assumed that the strong features of any functional projection may be checked (and the FP in question "activated") when its specifier or head position is occupied by a phonetically realized or empty element.

This work owes a great deal to Cinque (1999) and Rizzi (1997). In both of these works, the split-IP hypothesis first proposed in Pollock (1989) has been developed so that the IP and CP layers are expanded to contain several FPs, each checking a single semantic feature.[1] Cinque's work on the IP structure exploits evidence relating to adverbial positions, verb movement, and morphology in order to hypothesize a very rich set of FPs that correspond to different semantic features (several types of aspect, mood and modality, and tense). Rizzi does the same for the CP structure, expanding it on the basis of evidence drawn from left dislocation, topicalization, complementizer deletion, and so on. Following the same line of reasoning, I deal mainly with the number and properties of FPs in northern Italian dialects and, more generally, with the way sentence structure articulates and the kinds of relationships that may be established among them. Therefore, although analyzing SCLs, this book only marginally deals with the pro-drop theory (cf. Poletto 1993b, 1996, for data and discussion on this topic).

I analyze the distribution of subject clitics in declarative, interrogative, verb second, and various types of subjunctive clauses in a comparative perspective, under the assumption that the set of functional projections is always the same in all the dialects examined.

The hypothesis that all languages have the same set of FPs has been one of the major issues of recent discussions in generative literature. I do not make claims in this regard. The assumption made in this work is much weaker: all northern Italian dialects have the same set of functional projections, as they are all very closely related languages, both from a genetic and a typological point of view.

The analysis concerns the number and type of FPs that make up both the IP and CP layer and the boundary between the two. This raises the issue of the existence of a distinction between two syntactic layers, IP and CP. Because inflected verbs may move to the CP layer (as is demonstrated further on) in certain cases, such as interrogatives and verb second clauses, this raises the question of whether it would be useful to maintain a distinction between the two layers or whether functional structure should be considered as one single set of FPs, each encoding a different semantic feature. This issue has already been discussed in the literature, starting with Grimshaw's (1991) proposal of extended projections, which are taken to define some structural segment including a lexical head and a set of contiguous functional projections related to the lexical head. Grimshaw (1997) considers both IP and CP as "extended projections" of the verb, although they are still kept separate. Rizzi (1997) explicitly admits that IP and CP are two distinct layers but does not give any argument in favor of his hypothesis.

In other words, the distinction between IP and CP is not based on verb movement, since the inflected verb can move up to the CP layer in certain contexts (see above), but rather on another difference—the fact that inside the IP layer the head of a projection may be activated through movement of the lexical verb or the merging of an auxiliary, which is still a verbal element. Hence, verb movement can be substituted by the merging of another verb, which has certain peculiarities (such as the lack of a thematic grid) that make it an auxiliary. Within the CP layer, the head of a projection is activated again through movement of the lexical verb or the insertion of a complementizer (or a subject clitic, as is discussed in chapters 2 and 3), which is not a verbal element at all. It should be noted, however, that certain semantic features are present in both the IP and CP layer: agreement with the subject is present in both, and some relationships between the projections that encode the same feature must be established since there is evidence that heads merged in the lower IP projection can target the higher projection in CP for movement (cf. chapter 2, section 5.1).

If we follow this line of reasoning, IP and CP appear as two distinct layers, and the boundary separating the two is set by the F° in which the complementizer can be merged in the structure. All projections above this head position are considered to belong to the CP layer, and all projections below it are placed inside the IP layer. However, an alternative view, considering sentence structure as a unit, is also perfectly plausible. In this case, it would be totally irrelevant to establish whether a verb moves to the CP layer or not; what should be determined is only the exact position targeted by the verb.

Therefore, although it is temporarily assumed that CP and IP are distinct, I attempt to determine the exact location and the semantic feature of each FP with respect to all other FPs. Moreover, it becomes evident in the course of the discussion that the distinction between IP and CP is not what is needed to account for many relations at a distance among certain nonadjacent projections; nevertheless, they appear to constitute a sort of "circuit" with respect to the features they encode in the syntax and movement of elements such as subject clitics. These sets of projections are referred to as "fields." Chapter 2 considers an "agreement field," which includes several different kinds of subject clitics, whereas chapter 3 considers an "interrogative field," that is, a set of nonadjacent projections whose specifier positions host wh-items.

1.3   THE VARIETIES EXAMINED AND SURVEY METHODS EMPLOYED

Although this is not intended as a typological study of northern Italian dialects, it surely has certain peculiar properties with respect to current work on generative syntax. Why microvariation may be useful in improving our knowledge of syntax has already been mentioned: dialectology is a privileged field for testing whether our hypotheses about the interplay between UG and variation are correct. Nevertheless, a considerable amount of fieldwork is necessary, as it is often difficult to sort out the jungle of different dialects, which quite often reveal what at first sight may be perceived as random variation.

For this reason, a systematically ordered list of the varieties examined is presented here. Other dialects were also investigated for single phenomena in order to check the descriptive generalizations. The dialects analyzed in this study were chosen to cover the northern Italian territory, and closer investigation was done for varieties that were already known to exhibit particularly interesting features, such as Central Rhaetoromance V2 or Northern Veneto and Eastern Lombard wh in situ. This survey may not appear to be equally distributed across the map of northern Italy because the selection of dialects to be investigated was made on the basis of a previous study, which indicated that in certain areas dialects tended to differ much more than in others. This is mainly due to historical, social, and economic reasons and does not concern us here. Instead, the important point for this survey is to achieve an adequate empirical coverage. The choice of locations to be investigated was made with the intention of creating a tighter survey network in places where greater variation was expected, whereas the survey was less concentrated in those areas where less variation was known to occur. In some cases, this choice was made on the basis of practical difficulties, such as the presence of a reliable informant in a given village. A list of the survey locations is presented below, grouped together according to their geographical and typological characteristics.

Veneto

Venezia	Altavilla Vicentina
Portogruaro	Cereda
Jesolo	Coneda
Motta di Livenza	Belluno
Pramaggiore	Tignes d'Alpago
Padova	Cencenighe Agordino
Bastia di Rovolon	Cesiomaggiore
Arsiero	Verona
Tezze sul Brenta	Rocca Pietore (Rhaetoromance)
Rovigo	Laste (Rhaetoromance)
Loreo	

Trentino Alto Adige

Rhaetoromance

Badiot: S. Leonardo, Corvara, S. Vigilio di Marebbe
Gardenese: Ortisei, Selva
Fassano: Pera di Fassa, Alba, Campitello, Moena
Trentino: Trento, Cles (Val di Non), Castello (Val Lagarina)

Friuli Venezia Giulia

S. Michele al Tagliamento	Cordenons
Cesarolo	Sutrio
Teglio Veneto	Palmanova
Aquileia	Clauzetto
Remanzacco	Forni Avoltri
Moimacco	Collina
Gorizia	Veneto variety: Trieste

Piedmont

Torino	Pontivrea
Riva di Chieri	Borgomanero
Novi Ligure	Bollengo (Ivrea)
Poirino	Borgofranco d'Ivrea

Piedmontese-Provençal

Rodoretto di Prali

Lombardy

Eastern Lombard

Monno	Rovato
Malonno	Lonato
Vione	Bergamo

Northern Lombard

Livigno   Albosaggia (Sondrio)

Western Lombard

Milan   Bagnolo S. Vito
Como   Pavia
Lecco Vaprio d'Adda

Emilia Romagna

Romagnolo

Forlì   Cesenatico
Cesena

Emilian

Piacenza   Bologna
Guastalla   Casalmaggiore
Carpi   Bondeno

Tuscany

Fiorentino (city dwellers)   Colle Val d'Elsa
Incisa val d'Arno

Liguria

Central Ligurian

Chiavari   Savona
Genoa   Cicagna

Western Ligurian

Imperia   Oneglia
Alassio

Alpine area

Favale di Malvaro   Cairo Montenotte
Borghetto di Varo   Carcare
Altare   Calizzano

Cinqueterre

Monterosso

Italian Switzerland (Northern Lombard)

Bellinzona	Comano
Locarno	Brione s. M.
Cevia (Valle Maggia)	Montagnola (Lugano)

In the first phase of the survey, informants were asked to translate a questionnaire of about 350 sentences from standard Italian into their own dialect. The questionnaire was the same for all varieties. In the second part of the survey, informants were asked to give their grammatical judgments on dialect sentences that had previously been translated into their own dialect in order to test the generalizations made on the first set of data. When all the data of the first questionnaire had been examined, special questionnaires were drawn up for each individual variety that presented interesting phenomena, thus submitting them to closer investigation and determining the conditions of linguistic variation. The data presented here are drawn from the ASIS database (Atlante Sintattico dell'Italia Settentrionale, i.e., the Syntactic Atlas of Northern Italy) and were gathered in collaboration with Paola Benincà, Richard Kayne, and Laura Vanelli.

Following the tradition of all syntactic work on northern Italian dialects (from Brandi and Cordin 1981 to Zanuttini 1997), the survey data were not transcribed into a phonetic alphabet, as this is not necessary for our syntactic analysis. Some of the data used here may be consulted on the Internet in the IPA version.

1.4. PREVIOUS ANALYSIS OF SUBJECT CLITICS

Chapter 2 describes the proclitic subject clitic system of NIDs. Chapter 3 deals with data concerning interrogative sentences where enclitics occur. Before entering into this topic, a brief presentation is given of previous analyses of subject clitics (SCLs). Kayne (1975) first noted that standard French SCLs differed from object clitics on the basis of the following data:

(1) a. Il mangera de la viande et boira du bon vin.   Standard French
         he will-eat some meat and will-drink some good wine
         'He will eat some meat and drink some good wine'.

     b. *Paul les lit très vit et relit soigneusement par la suite
         Paul them reads very rapidly and rereads carefully immediately afterward
         'Paul reads them quickly and then reads them again more carefully'.

Example (1) shows that SCLs may be omitted in a coordination structure, whereas object clitics cannot. As a result, they occupy different positions.

Benincà (1983) analyzed the SCL *a* in Paduan dialect, demonstrating that it has different properties from third- and second-person singular subject clitics:

(2) a. A vago mi.   Benincà (1983: 8)
         SCL go I
         'I am leaving'.

b. *El riva Giorgio
SCL comes Giorgio
'Giorgio is coming'.

c. A no te parli mai.   Benincà (1983: 12)
SCL not SCL speak never
'You never speak'.

d. *El no parla mai
SCL not speaks never
'He never speaks'.

Benincà suggests that 'a' is not a true SCL and that it occurs in a left peripheral position, which she calls 'Top'. The present study follows from Benincà's original observation that not all subject clitics are alike and that some of them may interact with the theme/rheme structure.

Rizzi (1986b) analyzed Trentino subject clitics as Infl elements, under the assumption that they were heads and not specifiers, as in the case of French subject clitics, since they occurred after the postverbal negative marker, cooccurring with a DP subject, and had to be repeated in a coordination structure like (1a). The same proposal was made by Brandi and Cordin (1989) for Fiorentino and Trentino subject clitics. In the present framework, it is not possible to adopt Rizzi's assumption that SCLs are generated inside Infl (or in a split-infl framework in AgrS°). As shown by Belletti (1990), the inflected verb moves in Italian to AgrS°; therefore, the verb should adjoin to the subject clitic, yielding the order verb–subject clitic, which is exactly the opposite of that which is usually found in declarative clauses.[2] Later in this book, it is shown that it is not possible to give a unique answer to the question of the subject clitic position.

The comparative work in Renzi and Vanelli (1983) shows that the paradigm of SCLs for the six persons is not homogeneous. Their work investigates thirty dialects from the northern Italian territory and formulates a number of descriptive generalizations on the distribution of subject clitics across the verbal paradigm. Chapter 2 shows that it is not possible to squeeze all SCLs for the different persons into one single position and that their distribution differences force us to assume different solutions for different types of SCLs. In chapter 2, I attempt to show that the agreement field (the set of FPs where SCLs occur) is very complex in the NIDs and that it includes four distinct positions for SCLs and one position for the inflected verb (the lowest one).

TWO

Preverbal Subject Clitics
in Declarative Contexts

2.1 INTRODUCTION

This chapter analyzes the syntactic distribution of SCLs in the hundred varieties of the corpus. The following hypothesis is presented: in NIDs, it is possible to isolate four classes of SCLs on the basis of the set of morphological features they encode. Each class is merged in a distinct syntactic position. Several syntactic tests (illustrated in section 2.1.2) are used to prove that four distinct positions are necessary. A few of these tests are already known in the literature and concern the coordination and relative order of SCLs with respect to negation. Others are totally new, for example, those regarding the interaction between SCLs and C°. Section 2.2 considers the position of the preverbal negative marker and SCLs. The Zanuttini (1997) typology of preverbal negative markers is adopted, and analysis is restricted to "strong" preverbal negative markers, analyzed by Zanuttini as heading an independent NegP projection (p. 24).

It is shown that if the type of preverbal negative marker is kept constant, the position of SCLs with respect to negation does not vary randomly but depends on the type of SCL: two classes of SCLs occur higher and two occur lower than the strong preverbal negative marker. Moreover, it is shown that the two prenegative types interact with CP elements and are sensitive to theme/rheme restrictions, whereas the postnegative types are not. Prenegative SCLs may occur in two positions, which will be distinguished on the basis of the different results they give for (1) coordination tests, (2) the compatibility with respect to wh-items, and (3) the possibility of signaling the whole sentence as new information.

Postnegative SCLs are also shown to occur in two distinct positions on the basis of the following tests: (1) they behave differently with respect to coordination, and (2) they behave differently with respect to inversion (an analysis of subject clitic inversion is given in chapter 3).

As a consequence of the analysis of SCLs, I claim that the AgrS projection has to be split into a set of four FPs, corresponding to each of the SCL classes. Moreover, I show that an additional position needs to be postulated for the inflected verb (which moves higher than T° yet lower than the SCL positions). These five positions are defined as the "agreement field," namely, the set of FPs in which subject features are syntactically encoded.

There are interesting data that show that SCLs can move from a lower to a higher position within the agreement field. The arguments in favor of this hypothesis are discussed in section 2.5. The closing section of this chapter contains a few speculations about the structure of the agreement field that has been found in these dialects. I show that the hypothesis about the agreement field accounts for Renzi and Vanelli's (1983) descriptive generalizations that examined the number and distribution of SCLs across the verbal paradigm in thirty dialects. Moreover, the analysis of the agreement field occupied by SCLs and the verb is an interesting basis for comparative work with the structure of other languages and with that of the agreement projections inside the DP structure, an issue that will be left for future research.

2.1.1 Four Morphological Types of Subject Clitics

In the dialects examined it is possible to distinguish four morphological classes of SCLs. The first class of subject clitics does not encode any subject feature at all, as it is an invariable for all persons. The table in (1) illustrates the fact that these clitics never vary according to the person:

(1) 1 2 3 4 5 6
     a a a a a a

Invariable SCLs are found in many Veneto, Lombard, and Emilian varieties and may cooccur with other types of clitics [as in (2b)]:

(2) a. A vegni mi.   Lugano (Swiss Lombard) (Vassere 1993)
        inv. SCL come I
        'I come'.

     b. A ta vegnat ti.
        inv. SCL SCL come you
        'You come'.

     c. A vegn luu.
        inv. SCL come he
        'He comes'.

     d. A vegnum.
        inv SCL come
        'We come'.

     e. A vegnuf.
        inv. SCL come
        'You come'.

   f. A vegn lur.
      inv. SCL come they
      They come'.

The second class of SCLs encodes a deictic feature, as it only has two forms: one used for the first and second person (singular and plural) and one for the third person (singular and plural):

(3) 1 2 3 4 5 6
     i   i   a   i   i   a

This type of SCL is sensitive to the +/–third-person distinction or, better, to the distinction between the deictic persons who are present in a conversation (first and second person) with respect to those who are absent (third person). This class of SCLs does not encode any singular versus plural distinction. Therefore, this type is defined as "deictic SCLs."[1] Deictic clitics are found in Friulian and Piedmontese varieties. They may also co-occur with other types of SCLs (but never with invariable clitics; cf. section 2.5.2.3 for all possible co-occurrences among different types of SCLs).

(4) a. I mangi.   S. Michele al T. (Friulian)
        deict. SCL eat (I)
        'I eat'.

     b. I ti mangis.
        deict. SCL SCL eat (you)
        'You eat'.

     c. A l mangia.
        deict. SCL SCL eat (he)
        'He eats'.

     d. I mangin.
        deict. SCL eat (we)
        'We eat'.

     e. I mangè.
        deict. SCL eat (you)
        'You eat'.

     f. A mangin.
        deict. SCL eat (they)
        'They cat'.

In the sections that follow, where the syntactic status and position of the four types of morphological clitics are examined, it is shown that deictic and invariable clitics need to be distinguished on the basis of a number of factors, although they constitute a single class with respect to other syntactic phenomena. The class that includes deictic and invariable clitics is referred to as "vocalic clitics" throughout the discussion.

    The third class is the one that encodes only person features, and it is generally realized only for second singular (in all dialects) and third singular (in a few dialects, especially with auxiliaries). This class does not generally realize the first person (singular and plural).[2,3]

(5)   1   2   3m   4   5   6
      –   t + V   V + l –   –   –

This class is clearly sensitive to a person feature, which nevertheless cannot be defined as a general person feature as it only occurs in second- and third-person singular. The distinction that is observed here may be expressed by a [+/–hearer] feature. The second-person singular is the marked form specified as [+hearer], and the third-person singular masculine is the unmarked form of the opposition and is specified as [–hearer]. Clitics of this class do not encode any [speaker] feature, as there are no first-person clitics in the paradigm. Section 2.5.2.2 presents a possible hypothesis to account for the absence of first-person clitics. Moreover, this type of SCL does not encode any number features. The person clitic occurs to the right of the deictic clitic in the second- and third-person singular [cf. (4)]. This class of SCLs is referred to as "person clitics."

The fourth type of SCL is generally instantiated by a consonant plus a vowel. It encodes person, number, and gender features and has the following distribution:

(6)   1   2   3f   4   5   6m   6f
      –   –   l + a –   –   (l) + i   l + e

This type of SCL realizes a [-hearer] feature that has already been seen for person SCLs, though it also encodes number and gender features. Hence, those persons that include a [speaker] specification are again excluded from the paradigm.[4] It ought to be noted that third-person masculine is not instantiated by this type of SCL. All other third-person clitics are formed by the same consonant *l* (that expresses the person feature) and by a vowel that expresses the number and gender distinction. In all cases, the vowel follows the consonant. This class of SCLs thus expresses—in addition to person features—a [+/–plural] and a [+/–feminine] distinction. An example of this type of system is Venetian:

(7)   a. La magna.   Venice
         SCL eats
         'She eats'.

      b. I magna.
         SCL + masc. eat
         'They eat'.

      c. Le magna.
         SCL + fem. eat
         'They eat'.

This type of subject clitics will be defined as "number clitics" to distinguish them from the class of person clitics that do not encode number and gender features but only person features. Person and number SCLs exemplified in (5) and (6) have similar though not identical properties and form a unique class with respect to several syntactic phenomena. They therefore are defined as agreement clitics in the following discussion, as opposed to vocalic (deictic and invariable) SCLs. Subject clitics can thus express several different features, depending on their form:

1. They may be invariable.
2. They can express a [+/–deictic] feature.
3. They can express a [+/–hearer) feature.
4. They can express [–hearer) and, in addition, a [+/–plural] and [+/–gender] feature.

The distribution of the four morphological types across the different persons is summarized in the following table:

(8)	1	2	3	4	5	6
Invariable	+	+	⊦	+	+	+
Deictic	+	+	+	+	+	+
Person	–	+	+	–	–	–
Number	–	–	+	–	(+)	+

The first-person singular and plural are never realized with an unambiguous clitic; they may be expressed by a deictic clitic, which nevertheless does not distinguish it from the second person (either singular or plural). It therefore appears that the [speaker] feature has no specific morphological counterpart within the domain of SCLs. I return to this observation in section 2.4, where I propose a syntactic explanation for this gap.

2.1.2   Preliminaries on the Tests Used

It is possible to distinguish between different positions for SCLs according to their position with respect to other elements. The SCLs are always the first element of the clitic cluster; in none of the varieties examined were they preceded by an object clitic (either accusative or dative). However, differences were noted in the preverbal negative marker, which may appear either before or after the SCL. Thus both orders SCL-neg and neg-SCL are found.

The data appear to be complicated by the existence of at least two types of preverbal negative markers, as Zanuttini (1997: 24) shows. Several NIDs have two preverbal negative morphemes, one before and one after direct and indirect object clitics:

(9)   a. I **n** te **n** dan nent u libru.   Cosseria (Ligurian) (Parry 1997b:
                                                                          251; Zanuttini 1997: 17)
       SCL neg OCL neg give 3plur neg the book
       'They do not give you the book'.

       b. E **n** te **n** capisc.   Carcare (Ligurian)
       SCL neg OCL neg understand
       'I do not understand you'.

Zanuttini proposes to capture the difference between the two by syntactic position: one type of negative marker, which can occur after object clitics, is adjoined to the F° occupied by the inflected verb and is defined as a weak negative marker. The second type of negative marker, which always occurs before object clitics, is an independent head and is always located in a NegP higher than the position of the inflected verb, defined by Zanuttini as a "strong negative marker." Zanuttini's work shows that the preverbal negative markers that obligatorily co-occur with a postverbal negative marker are of the first type, that is, a weak negation, whereas preverbal negative markers that occur without other negative elements can be either weak or strong.

To establish the relative order of SCLs with respect to negation, we have to keep the type of negative marker constant. As SCLs are always higher than weak negative markers, only preverbal, strong negative markers, which occur only in the head of NegP, are considered in the survey of dialects presented here. Hence most Piedmontese, Lombard, and some Emilian dialects have to be excluded, and our discussion is limited to the eastern part of the domain and to some Ligurian and Tuscany dialects. Several Friulian varieties show complementary distribution between certain SCLs and the negative marker. They also are not considered here for the moment. On the basis of this test, it is seen that SCLs need to be split into prenegative and postnegative types.

The second test is coordination. This test was used by Kayne (1975) to show that French SCLs are different from object clitics, as SCLs can be left out in a coordination structure whereas object clitics have to be repeated in the same sentence:[5]

(10) a. Il mangera de la viande et boira du bon vin.   Standard French
          he will-eat some meat and will-drink some good wine
          'He will eat some meat and drink some good wine'.

      b *Paul les lit très vit et relit soigneusement par la suite
          Paul them reads very rapidly and rereads carefully immediately afterward
          'Paul reads them very rapidly and rereads them carefully'.

Kayne interprets this difference as a consequence of the different structural position that SCLs occupy with respect to object clitics. As SCLs are located higher in the structure of the sentence, they may be omitted in a coordination that involves a verb with its object. Object clitics are located lower in the structure and cannot be left out in such a coordination.

I do not attempt to analyze coordination structures (cf. Kayne 1994) but only assume Kayne's (1975) conclusion that differences of the type illustrated in (10) correspond to distinct structural positions. In other words, the fact that a SCL has to be repeated in the second conjunct of coordination but another does not is interpreted as a consequence of their different syntactic positions; the SCL that has to be repeated occupies a lower position that is included in the coordinated part, whereas the SCL that can be omitted occupies a position that is outside the coordinated structure. This conclusion remains valid even within an asymmetric theory of coordination, which assumes that the coordinating conjunction is a head with the first conjunct in its specifier and the second conjunct in its complement position. The conclusion assumed here applies even when the two coordinated members do not belong to the same syntactic category, as the test compares distinct classes of SCLs, and the differences found among those classes need to be explained, whatever theory of coordination is adopted.

Three types of coordination are exploited here (cf. Benincà and Cinque 1993 for a detailed discussion of different coordination types). The first type coordinates two inflected verbs with their nominal objects, as exemplified by the standard Italian example in (11):

(11)　Mangio patate e bevo caffé.　　　　　　　　　　　　Standard Italian
　　　　eat potatoes and drink coffee
　　　　'I eat potatoes and drink coffee'.

This structure has been traditionally referred to as "VP coordination," but within the split Infl hypothesis adopted here, it is not clear which structural portion of the sentence is involved. Therefore, this test is referred to with a neutral term, namely, "type 1 coordination."

The second type of coordination includes two distinct inflected verbs that have the same nominal object, such as in (12) ("type 2 coordination"):[6]

(12)　a.　Uso e sciupo sempre troppa acqua.　　　　　　Standard Italian
　　　　　use and waste always too much water
　　　　　'I always use and waste too much water'.

　　　　b.　uso [e_i] e sciupo sempre [troppa acqua_i]

Here, the portion of the sentence involved seems smaller, as it contains only the two inflected verbs but not their objects. Nevertheless, Kayne's (1994) LCA prohibits coordination of two heads. Therefore, Kayne proposes that (12a) has the structure in (12b) with an empty object. Hence, a sentence like (12) has the same structure as (11) and is a case of XP coordination. I show that our data are an interesting confirmation of Kayne's proposal.

The third type of coordination is the one exemplified in (13) (cf. Benincà and Cinque 1993) for an analysis of this structure):

(13)　a.　Leggo e rileggo sempre lo stesso libro.　　　　Standard Italian
　　　　　read and reread always the same book
　　　　　I read and read always the same book'.

　　　　b.　Leggo e leggerò sempre lo stesso libro.
　　　　　read and will-read always the same book
　　　　　'I read and will always read the same book'.

Benincà and Cinque (1993) treat (13a) and (13b) as analogous because they involve coordination of the same verb with different tense or aspect specifications.[7] It may be noted that this type of coordination is different from the previous one, although in both cases two inflected verbs have been coordinated. Here, the two verbs share most semantic features: in (13a) the aspect prefix *ri* (meaning repetition) has been added into the second conjunct, and in (13b) only the verbal tense has been changed. As Kayne (1975) noted, object clitics may be omitted in the second conjunct only in this third structural type [showing that its structure is different from (10) above]:

(14)   a. Jean les lit et relit sans cesse.   Standard French
       Jean them reads and rereads incessantly
       'Jean reads and rereads them incessantly'.

     b. Jean les$_i$ lit et [e$_i$] relit sans cesse

According to Kayne (1994), this type of structure is still an XP coordination, but the object clitic is not repeated because the overt object clitic licenses an empty clitic in the second conjunct, as in (14b). This is not possible if the two verbs are not sufficiently similar.

Although all cases of coordination are XP coordination (since X° coordination is excluded by the LCA), it is probable that coordination of type 1 and type 2 involve the same FP, whereas coordination of type 3 involves a different structural set of projections. We therefore have three coordinating structures that may in principle distinguish different SCL positions:

1. A coordinated verb plus a complement
2. Distinct inflected verbs coordinated with a shared object
3. The same verb coordinated with a different prefix or tense with a shared object

These tests are used to distinguish the different positions for SCLs. Three other tests are used to distinguish among various types of SCLs and confirm that SCLs occupy four different positions. The tests used to reinforce the claim based on the negation and coordination tests take into account the behaviour of SCLs in interrogative structures and the sensitivity to theme/rheme conditions.

In the next section I show that SCLs may be split into two classes on the basis of two tests, clustering with a complementizer and their position with respect to a strong preverbal negative marker.

2.2   TWO TESTS FOR SCL POSITIONS

2.2.1   Subject Clitics and Preverbal Negative Markers

The strong preverbal negative marker enables us to draw a distinction between two types of SCLs, those that appear before the preverbal negative marker (preneg) and those that appear after it (postneg), thus proving the need to assume at least two SCL positions. Many varieties appear to have a mixed behavior with respect to the order between the verb and the negative marker. The examples reported in (15) for the Basso Polesano variety can be reproduced in other varieties as well.

(15)   a. A no vegno.   Loreo
       SCL not come
       'I do not come'.

     b. No la vien.
       not SCL comes
       'She does not come'.

A striking fact emerges when examining more closely the order between SCLs and negation: the position of the SCL with respect to the negative marker depends on the class of the SCL in question. Invariable and deictic SCLs are always higher than the strong preverbal negative marker. There are no exceptions to this observation, which therefore enables us to formulate the following descriptive generalizations:

(16)   a. If a SCL belongs to the invariable class, it always occurs before the preverbal negative marker.

       b. If a SCL belongs to the deictic class, it always occurs before the preverbal negative marker.

This strongly suggests that both invariable and deictic SCLs are merged in a structure higher than NegP. As for number and person SCLs, it is generally true that they occur after a strong preverbal negative marker. The following Venetian example illustrates this point:

(17)   a. No ti vien.   Venice
       not SCL come
       'You do not come'.

       b. No la vien.   Venice
       not SCL comes
       'She does not come'.

However, there are cases in which both person and number SCLs are found to the left of the strong negative marker. Genoese and Florentine illustrate a case of prenegative person and number SCL, respectively:

(18)   a. Ti nu catti.   Genoa (Ligurian)
       SCL not buy
       'You do not buy'.

       b. La un viene.   Florence
       SCL not comes
       'She does not come'.

The fact that most dialects exhibit postnegative person and number clitics, whereas others have prenegative SCLs, could suggest the hypothesis of movement of the SCL to a prenegative position. Both person and number SCLs can be assumed to be merged in an F° located lower than NegP, as the Venetian example shows, and then may (or must) move to a prenegative position in some dialects. Section 2.5 presents two arguments in favor of this hypothesis. Let us for the moment assume that it is correct and state the following descriptive generalization:

(19)   a. If a SCL belongs to the person type, it generally occurs after a strong preverbal negative marker. In certain dialects it occurs before a strong negative marker.[8]

       b. If a SCL belongs to the number type, it generally occurs after a strong preverbal negative marker. In certain dialects it occurs before a strong negative marker.[9]

It is assumed that the agreement field contains at least two SCLs positions, a prenegative and a postnegative. The former is occupied by invariable and deictic SCLs, whereas the latter is the F° where number and person SCLs are merged.

(20) [$_{FP1}$ invariable SCLs/deictic SCLs [$_{NEGP}$ [$_{FP2}$ number SCLs/person SCLs]]]

These two positions may be distinguished on the basis of another two tests that are shown in the following sections.

2.2.2   Co-occurrence of SCL Positions

One possibility that comes to mind, showing that there are at least two SCLs positions, as I propose, is to attempt to combine the different positions and see if all types of SCLs co-occur or if there are any restrictions. Here, all possible combinations of the four morphological classes are considered. Only some of them are found in the varieties I was able to analyze.

First, invariable SCLs are compatible with both number and person SCLs, as illustrated in the following examples:

(21)   a. A l'è bela.   Loreo (Veneto)
         SCL SCL is nice + fem
         'She is nice'.

       b. A te vien.
         SCL SCL come
         'You come'.

(22)   a. A l è vegnu.   Montagnola (Lugano, CH)
         SCL SCL is come
         'He has come'.

       b. A ta vegnat.
         SCL SCL come
         'You come'.

(23)   a. A la vien.   Padua (Veneto)
         SCL SCL come
         'She is coming'.

       b. A i vien.
         SCL SCL come
         'They are coming'.

No cases were found in which an invariable and a deictic SCL co-occur.
    Second, deictic SCLs are also compatible with person and number SCLs:

(24)   a. I t manges.   Turin (Piedmontese)
         SCL SCL eat/
         'You eat'.

       b. A la ven.   Remanzacco (Friulian)

Third, number and person SCLs cannot co-occur.
    The following schema sums up the possible co-ocurrences of SCL classes found in the corpus:

(25)   invariable   deictic
    Number   +   +
    Person   +   +

The co-occurrence of invariable with number and person clitics and deictic with number and person clitics is expected if we assume an analysis such as the one illustrated in (20). It may be noted, however, that the co-occurrences observed here show only that there are two positions, not their exact location. Moreover, in the following sections I claim that the SCL positions are not only two but four and that the lack of co-occurrence between deictic and invariable SCLs, on the one hand, and between number and person clitics, on the other hand, must be due to another factor.

The data and the discussion presented here are merely speculative, as an analysis of other dialects not included in the present corpus could entirely change the picture by presenting certain co-occurrences that have not yet manifested themselves.

2.2.3   Clustering with the Complementizer

The third test to distinguish F1° from F2° suggests that there is a relation between deictic and invariable SCLs and the CP projection. Invariable and deictic SCLs necessarily cluster with the complementizer, whenever there is one. This appears to be a general fact, as none of the speakers accepted sentences like (26b) and (26d):

(26)   a. Ara ch'a vegno.   Loreo (Veneto)
        look that + SCL come
        'Look, I am coming'.

    b. *Ara che a vegno.

    c. No so sa vegno.
        not know if + SCL come
        'I do not know whether I will come'.

    d. *No so se a vegno.

The complementizer and the invariable or deictic SCL are perceived as a single unit and cannot be separated. This relation holds only for prenegative SCLs; the same does not appear to be true for number and person clitics (the postnegative ones).

Number and person SCLs may also be clustered with the complementizer, though the process is totally optional:

(27)   a. Ara che el vien.   Loreo (Veneto)
        look that + SCL comes
        'Look, he is coming'.

    b. Ara ch'el vien.

The difference between (27a) and (27b) has to do with the speed of the pronunciation: a more "allegro" utterance is produced in (27b), whereas more accurate and slow speech produces (27a). The difference between (26a) and (26b) is one of syntax and yields ungrammaticality if the process of clustering does not apply. This test points to the same direction as the test with negation: prenegative SCLs necessarily cluster with the complementizer, whereas the process is only the result of allegro speech for postnegative SCLs.

The most natural analysis of data like (26) is one of adjunction.[10] Because I adopt Kayne's (1990) theory that prohibits right adjunction and because the order is complementizer + subject clitic, the only way to analyze the cluster is to assume that the SCL merges in a position higher than the complementizer and that the complementizer moves to adjoin to the SCL, as illustrated in (28):

(28) $[_{C°} ch_i + SCL   [_{C°} t_i [IP]]]$

This amounts to admitting that

1. The CP layer is not a single projection but a set of FPs.
2. The complementizer moves inside this domain.
3. Deictic and invariable SCLs are merged inside the CP and not in the IP layer.

Arguments are provided for all three assumptions in the course of the discussion in this and the following chapter. In particular, this chapter provides evidence for the claim in 3. It is shown that deictic and invariable SCLs are sensitive to typical CP elements as wh-items and that invariable SCLs are also incompatible with focalized and left-dislocated XPs ; these two facts receive a natural interpretation if we assume that the two types of SCLs are located inside the CP layer. In chapter 3, I provide evidence for the claims in 1 and 2; it is shown that in some dialects three CP levels are activated in main interrogative clauses and that the complementizer moves from the lowest to higher positions. Therefore, the hypothesis illustrated in (28) is assumed, thus postponing the discussion of the arguments in favor of the three claims in 1, 2, and 3. The structure in (20) can thus be rewritten as (29):

(29)   [CP invariable SCLs/deictic SCLs [NEGP [IP number SCLs/person SCLs]]]

In (29) FP1 corresponds to CP (although which CP it corresponds to becomes clear in the course of the discussion) and FP2 corresponds to IP, as number and person clitics are located lower than NegP, which is currently assumed to be part of the IP projections. On the basis of this hypothesis, from now on invariable and deictic clitics are referred to as CP-SCLs, and number and person SCLs are referred to as IP-SCLs.

2.3   MORE SCL POSITIONS

After having examined the arguments in favor of two SCLs positions, one in IP and the other in CP, I discuss the syntactic behavior of each morphological class.

2.3.1   Invariable SCLs

Invariable clitics occur before a strong negative marker and cluster with complementizers, as illustrated above.

2.3.1.1 Theme/Rheme Relations

Invariable SCLs are the only clitics that express a theme/rheme distinction. Beninčà (1983) first noted that invariable clitics are found in sentences that convey new information or in exclamative contexts. More precisely, she reports that invariable clitics may be used to indicate that the whole sentence is new information; hence, the whole sentence is a rheme.[11]

(30) a. A piove!   Padua
          SCL rains!
          'Look, it's raining!'

      b. E vvu venite!   Florence
          SCL SCL come!
          'You are coming!'

This is not compatible with a focalized element or with wh-items, but is compatible with yes/no questions:

(31) a. A ve-to via?   Beninčà (1983: 24)
          SCL go-you away?
          'Are you going away?'

      b. *Dove a zelo ndà?
          where SCL is-he gone?
          'Where has he gone?'

      c. *A dove zelo ndà?
          SCL where is-he gone?

(32) *EL GATO a go visto.[12]
       the cat SCL (I) have seen
       'I have seen the cat'.

Moreover, invariable clitics are not compatible with left-dislocated items:

(33) *Co ti, a no voio ndare.
       with you SCL not want to go
       'I do not want to go with you'.

One could hypothesize that this fact may not depend directly on the position of SCLs but may be seen as a result of morphology; only those clitics that have completely neutralized their agreement features may be reanalyzed as rheme markers. However, whatever the morphological requirements for an SCL to become a rheme marker might be, it seems plausible that it also occupies a position corresponding to the syntactic features it checks. As invariable SCLs are probably merged inside the CP layer, the most natural hypothesis to account for the data in (30)–(32) is to assume that 'a' occupies a position inside the CP layer that has to do with theme/rheme conditions. Beninčà (1983) suggests that invariable SCLs occupy a TOP position and saturate the left periphery of the sentence.

   In a perspective that splits the left-dislocation position from the focus position, as that proposed by Rizzi (1997) and adopted here also, this fact may appear quite surprising at first sight, as the presence of an invariable SCL seems to prevent wh-, focalized, and left-dislocated items from being realized. However, this is not so strange if we consider the meaning of invariable SCLs. Because they indicate that the whole sentence is new, they cannot be compatible with wh-items or focalized items, as they represent new information in contrast with the rest of the clause, which must be old information. Supposing that left-dislocated items roughly correspond to old information, in contrast to the rest of the sentence, which is new information that concerns the left-dislocated item. The incompatibility shown in (33) derives from the fact that part of the clause is new and part of the clause is old information. In other words, invariable SCLs are incompatible with all structures that split the sentence into two parts, a new and a given one. As for the syntactic counterpart of this semantic requirement, one could imagine that invariable SCLs are able to move through the head of the CP projections where wh-items occur (see chapter 3) to the head of FocusP, and then to the head of the left dislocation position, thus preventing wh-, focalized, and left-dislocated items from occurring in the sentence

(34) $[_{LDCP} SCL_i [_{FocusCP} t_i [_{WhCP} t_i [IP]]]]$

This amounts to admitting that the invariable SCL is a sort of expletive for the LDP, FocusP, and interrogative CP, as it realizes the default feature of each of these projections and not the marked value that is realized when a wh-, focalized, or left-dislocated item enters its SpecC position. In other words, identifying the whole sentence as new information means that all the projections that split the sentence into a "given" and a "new" part must be activated and occupied by the SCL, which prevents the merging of wh-, focalized, and left-dislocated item. When all these positions are occupied by the invariable SCL, the meaning of the sentence corresponds to totally new information.

2.3.1.2 Type 1 Coordination

To support the analysis of invariable SCLs as CP elements, I use the test of co-ordination of type 1, which is illustrated in section 1.3 and repeated in (35):

(35) Mangio patate e bevo caffé.   Standard Italian
      eat potatoes and drink coffee
      'I eat potatoes and drink coffee'.

As expected by our analysis, which assumes that invariable SCLs are very high in the structure, they are left out in the second member of a type 1 coordination:

(36) A canto co ti e balo co lu.   Loreo
      SCL sing with you and dance with him
      'I sing with you and dance with him'.

We can therefore formulate the following generalization:

(37) Invariable SCLs may be omitted in a type 1 coordination.

This distinguishes invariable SCLs from all other SCL classes, as is seen in the next section, and confirms the idea that the invariable SCL not only expresses a theme/rheme distinction but also occupies a distinct position in the sentence structure, which differs from all other SCL types.

2.3.2   Deictic SCLs

As noted, deictic SCLs partially resemble invariable SCLs, as they both occur before the negative marker and cluster with the complementizer. It has been assumed that they also occur in the CP layer as invariable SCLs. However, as they do not encode theme/rheme distinctions and are shown to possess distinct syntactic properties, they are analyzed as occupying a position different from invariable SCLs.

2.3.2.1   *Interaction with Wh-items*

The first test, showing that deictic clitics are not merely a morphological class but also have special syntactic properties, concerns the interaction with several different types of wh-items. Deictic SCLs are compatible with certain wh-items and they are incompatible with others:

(38)   a. Se (*a) fanu?   S. Michele al T. (Friulian)
           what SCL do + they?
           'What are they doing?'

       b. Do (*a) vanu?
           where SCL go + they?
           'Where are they going?'

Moreover, in the same dialect, deictic SCLs necessarily occur together with another class of wh-items (essentially the wh corresponding to 'when' and wh–complex phrases):

(39)   a. Quant *(i) mangi-tu?   S. Michele al T.
           when i eat + you?
           'When are you going to eat?'

       b. Quantis caramelis *(i) a-tu mangiat?
           how many sweets i have + you eaten?
           'How many sweets did you eat?'

The occurrence of deictic clitics in wh-structures splits the class of wh-elements in two; monosyllabic wh-items do not tolerate the presence of a deictic SCL, whereas other wh-items do. A more detailed description is given in chapter 3, where it is hypothesized that wh-items can occupy several positions in the CP structure (each of these corresponding to a different semantic interpretation) and that monosyllabic wh-items, which are most probably weak pronouns, can only occupy positions located lower than deictic SCLs. For now, let us simply note that the phenomenon is restricted to the deictic class and is not found (at least to my knowledge) with number or person clitics, which are always compatible with all types of wh-items.

The fact that wh-items interact with deictic SCLs is predicted by our analysis, which assumes that deictic SCLs are located inside the CP layer. Anticipating what will be proposed in chapter 3, it is assumed here that deictic SCLs are located higher than the position where monosyllabic wh-items occur (and higher than subject clitic inversion), though lower than where wh-phrases occur:

(40) [_{CP} wh   [_{CP} deictic SCL   [_{CP} wh . . . [IP]]]]

Number and person SCLs do not show any effect of the type described here, and this is predicted by the hypothesis that they occur inside the IP layer. In the two sections that follow, two further arguments in favor of the hypothesis that deictic SCLs are located inside the CP layer but lower than invariable SCLs are considered.

2.3.2.2   *No Theme/Rheme Distinctions*

The position of deictic SCLs is assumed to be lower than that of invariable SCLs, which probably move from a FocusP to a LDP. As expected, deictic SCLs are perfectly compatible with dislocated items, as is shown in (41):

(41)   A ciasa o soi già laat.   Palmanova (Friulian)
       at home SCL am already been
       'I have already been at home'.

This test shows that invariable and deictic SCLs are two different types of elements. Deictic SCLs are not sensitive to theme/rheme distinctions and are therefore kept separate from invariable SCLs. This probably has to do with the fact that deictic SCLs still encode a subject feature, (the [+/–deictic one) and cannot be reanalyzed as pure topic particles.

2.3.2.3   *Type 1 Coordination*

It has been suggested that deictic SCLs occur in a position lower than invariable SCLs; the type 1 coordination test shows that this is correct. In a type 1 coordination, deictic SCLs cannot be omitted in the second conjunct of the coordination structure:

(42)   a. I cianti cun te e i bali cun lui.   Cervignano (Friulian)
          SCL sing with you and SCL dance with him
          'I sing with you and dance with him'.

       b. *I cianti cun te e bali cun lui

As mentioned in section 2.1.3, it is assumed that whenever an SCL is repeated in a given type of coordination and another is not, the one that is repeated occupies a lower position than the one that can be omitted. Hence, as expected, deictic SCLs are located lower than invariable SCLs.

We can therefore postulate two distinct prenegative positions, one that is included in the coordination (forcing the clitic to be repeated) and one that is excluded (where the clitic does not need to be repeated).

On the basis of the data discussed in section 2.3.1 and above, I assume a structure described in (43):

(43) [$_{LDCP}$ [$_{CP}$ deictic SCL [$_{IP}$]]]
         invariable SCLs   deictic SCLs

Invariable SCLs occupy a high position in the CP layer. If the hypothesis pre-sented in section 2.3.1 is correct [cf. (34), repeated here as (44a)], invariable SCLs move from the lowest position where wh-items are realized to a left-dislocation position, moving through all the projections that split the sentence into a theme and a rheme. Deictic SCLs occur higher than weak wh-items but lower than wh-phrases, as is shown in chapter 3 [cf. (40), repeated here as (44b)]:

(44)   a. [$_{LDP}$ SCL$_i$ [$_{whP}$ t$_i$ [IP]]]

          b. [$_{WhCP}$ wh [$_{CP}$ deictic SCL   [$_{WhCP}$ wh . . . . [IP]]]

If weak wh-items are located lower than deictic SCLs, the starting position from which invariable SCLs move to LD° is lower than the position where deictic clitics occur:

(45) [$_{LDP}$ inv SCL$_i$ [$_{CP}$ deictic SCL [$_{whP}$ t$_i$ [IP]]]]

As shown in (45), deictic SCLs interfere with invariable SCL movement, and this accounts for the incompatibility between deictic and invariable SCLs, which in fact never co-occur. This incompatibility is not due to the fact that they occupy the same structural position but rather to the fact that one interferes in the move-ment path of the other.

2.3.3   Number and Person SCLs

2.3.3.1   *Coordination Tests*

I now examine the syntactic behavior of number and person SCLs. In section 2.2 they are assumed to be merged in the IP layer, as they occur after the preverbal negative marker in most dialects of the corpus and because they do not cluster with complementizers. I now start from the assumption that number SCLs occur in IP, and I examine their behavior with respect to interrogative sentences and to type 1 and type 3 coordination.[13]

As for type 1 coordination, number and person clitics should behave as deictic SCLs, as they are located even lower in the structure. If it is true that higher ele-ments can be left out from the coordinated portion of the sentence, whereas lower elements must be included, we predict that SCLs located lower than deictic clitics always have to be repeated in a coordination of type 1. Hence, both number and person clitics would need to be realized in both conjuncts of a coordination struc-ture of type 1. This prediction is confirmed by the fact that no variety I was able to examine shows deletion of number or person SCLs in coordination structures of type 1. Examples like the following are ungrammatical in all varieties tested:

(46)   a. *La magna patate e beve vin   Venice
            SCL eats potatoes and drinks coffee
            'She eats potatoes and drinks coffee'.

b. *Ti magni patate e bevi vin
SCL eat potatoes and drink wine
'You eat potatoes and drink coffee'.

The examples in (46) are given in the Venetian variety, but I have not found dialects in which a sentence corresponding to (46) is accepted. This confirms the proposed hypothesis.

Type 1 and type 2 coordination cannot be exploited for investigating whether there are any additional differences within the group of postnegative SCLs, as all clitics of this group must be repeated in such structures. However, we can exploit type 3 coordination. Let us repeat the type of coordination we are considering:

(47)   Leggo e rileggo sempre lo stesso libro.   Standard Italian
        read and reread always the same book
        'I read and reread always the same book'.

It is possible to distinguish between two types of postnegative SCLs on the basis of this test: person SCLs must be repeated in type 3 coordination, whereas this is not the case for number SCLs, as shown by the contrast among (48), (49), and (50).

(48)   a. *Ti lesi e rilesi sempre el stesso libro   Venice
           SCL read and reread always the same book
           'You read and reread always the same book'.

        b. Ti lesi e ti rilesi sempre el stesso libro.
           SCL read and SCL reread always the same book
           'You read and reread always the same book'.

(49)   a. *Nisun l'ha e avarà vist la Maria . . .   Cornuda (northern Veneto)
           nobody SCL has and will + have seen the Mary
           'Nobody has seen and will see Mary'.

        b. Nisun l'ha e l'avarà vist la Maria . . .
           nobody SCL has and SCL will + have seen the Mary

(50)   La lese e rilese sempre el stesso libro.   Venice
        SCL reads and rereads always the same book
        'She reads and rereads always the same book'.

In many dialects, person SCLs behave as illustrated in (48) and (49).

The contrast between person SCLs in (48a) and (49) and number SCLs can be directly accounted for by splitting the postnegative domain into two positions, as in (51):[14]

(51)   [NegP   [NumbP SCL [PersP   [IP . . .]]]]

In (51), both number and person SCLs are located lower than negation. However, to explain the difference between (48) and (49), on the one side, and (50), on the other, I have split the position of IP-SCLs into two, one of number and one of person (however, it must be kept in mind that person clitics never express the [speaker] feature; I come back to this point in section 2.4.) This type of structure has been proposed by a number of authors (Shlonsky 1990 and Tortora 1998, among others) on the basis of several independent arguments. Moreover, it has often been noted that agreement is a complex category and that the idea of splitting it into its single components (as number and person) is indeed plausible. I do not analyze here all the arguments that have been proposed to justify the existence of two projections, one encoding number and another encoding person features; instead, another argument in favor of the hypothesis in (51) is presented in the next section.

An apparent counterexample to structure (51) is represented by the fact that number and person SCLs cannot co-occur, and this fact is not immediately accounted for by the analysis proposed in (52). However, number SCLs also show person and gender features. Therefore, it may be plausible to assume that number SCLs are merged in the same position where person SCLs occur and then move higher to check a number and (in a certain number of dialects) a gender feature. If both types of SCLs are merged in the same position, they cannot co-occur, although number SCLs move higher whereas person SCLs do not.

As a final remark, it ought to be noted that sentences corresponding to (48a) and (49a) are indeed grammatical in some dialects. One example is Paduan:

(52)   Te lesi e rilesi sempre el stesso libro.   Padua
       SCL read and reread always the same book
       'You read and reread always the same book'.

If we compare the dialects of Venice and Padua, we obtain a minimal pair for second-person singular; in Paduan the sentence corresponding to (48a) is grammatical, and the second-person SCL may be omitted in the second conjunct of a type 3 coordination.[15] Again, we face the problem of which type of SCL goes in which position. It appears clear that person SCLs in some dialects need to occur lower than in others, as the contrast between (48a) and (52) shows. This problem is discussed in section 2.5, where arguments are provided for a movement analysis of SCLs.

2.3.3.2   The test of Inversion in Interrogative Contexts

Venetian person SCL *ti* also differs from number SCLs and from its Paduan counterpart *te*, as it is not omitted in interrogative sentences; number SCLs (and Paduan person SCL) display a phenomenon known as subject clitic inversion, in which the subject clitic cannot occur preverbally but is replaced by a postverbal form, as in (53a). The Venetian *ti* behaves like object clitics because it occurs in a preverbal position when the inflected verb moves to C° in interrogative main clauses, as shown in (53):

(53)   a. *Cossa ga-stu?   Venice
          what have + SCL
          'What's the matter with you?'

       b. Coss' ti ga?
          what SCL have?
          'What's the matter with you?'

The possibility of maintaining a preverbal position when the inflected verb moves to C° correlates with the coordination data (cf. chapter 3 for an analysis of subject clitic inversion in terms of V to C in the dialects discussed here). Venetian third-person pronouns admit inversion and can be left out in a coordination of type 3:[16]

(54) a. Cossa ga-lo?   Venice
          what has he?
          'What the matter with him?'

      b. Cossa se che'l ga?
          what is that he has?

      c. *Cossa el ga?
          what he has?

(55) La lese e rilese sempre el steso libro.
      SCL reads and rereads always the same book
      'She reads and rereads always the same book'.

Hence, we can hypothesize that Venetian third-person SCLs and Paduan second- and third-person SCLs are located higher than Venetian second-person SCLs. The two types of SCLs differ with respect to deletion in the second conjunct of a type 3 coordination and the preverbal versus postverbal position in main interrogative sentences. We therefore adopt the structure presented in (51) and split the post-negative agreement field into two positions. Subject clitics may appear in four distinct positions, two of them located above the strong preverbal negative marker and two below it. Section 2.5 discusses the problem of person SCLs that seem to occur in a position higher than Pers°, as in Paduan. It is suggested that they are moved from Pers° to a higher position.

2.4   ONE MORE POSITION

In this section, two problems that have been noted in the course of the chapter are discussed. The first regards the gap in the paradigm that is noted in section 2.1.2, namely, that there are no SCLs that morphologically distinguish first-person SCLs. We have seen that first-person SCLs occur in the deictic class but are never mor-phologically distinct from second-person SCLs. The only dialects that have dis-tinct first-person SCLs are Franco-Provençal varieties, which have a system similar to French. As noted, these dialects do not have true subject clitic heads but only weak pronouns, as Cardinaletti and Starke (1999) report for standard French. Therefore, they are not considered here as a relevant counterexample to the gen-eralization that there are distinct first-person SCLs in NIDs.

The second issue for which I intend to provide a solution is the position of the inflected verb. Specifically, I intend to answer this question: as SCLs occupy the projections corresponding to AgrS, does the inflected verb remain in T° or is there an additional position that hosts it?

It is possible to show that the T° position is not where the inflected verb occurs in the NIDs by examining the position of temporal adverbials. Cinque (1999) shows that temporal adverbs are located in SpecT position and that the inflected verb in standard Italian moves higher than temporal adverbs. As the same is true for NIDs, it is not possible to assume that T° is the landing site for the inflected verb. However, SCLs occupy the positions corresponding to AgrS, so there appears to be no structural space for the inflected verb.

The hypothesis I make here solves this problem and provides an explanation for the gap in the SCLs paradigm. First, let us assume that the [+/−speaker] distinction is indeed encoded in the syntax and that it is located lower than the [+/−hearer] position. In northern Italian varieties this is the position occupied by the inflected verb, which is why no SCLs encode this distinction. I propose to modify structure (52) in the following way:

(56)   [NegP   [NumbP SCL [HearerP SCL [SpeakerP V   [TP . . .]]]]]

Structure (56) explains why there are no first person SCLs and provides a landing site for the inflected verb. Moreover, if we adopt a general theory of features as that proposed in Cinque (1999) (who assumes that an FP can be marked with a + or − value for the semantic feature it encodes), it is not easy to see how person, which is obviously a complex feature, can fit into such a framework. If we intend to maintain the hypothesis that each FP can only be marked for a positive or negative value, the most natural solution would be to assume that the morphological concept of "person" does not correspond to any single FP where all six persons (or even more in certain languages) are mapped but that more "basic" distinctions are reflected into the syntactic component, and their combination results in the interpretation of first, second, or third person.[17] This is what we see in (56).

Independent evidence in favor of this hypothesis is provided by the following facts. It is well known in the descriptive literature on northern Italian dialects that certain Lombard, Trentino, and Rhaetoromance dialects have an agglutinated SCL located to the right of the verb, and that this occurs only for some persons. In the Rhaetoromance variety of S. Leonardo, for instance, the first-person singular verb has an agglutinated vowel *i*, which is neither etymologically justified nor an epenthetic vowel (which in this variety is *e*). Benincà and Vanelli (1975) discuss the problem of first-person singular morphology in all Romance varieties that have lost all final vowels except *a*. They note that in most varieties the vowel adjoined to the verb to reestablish a symmetrical number of syllables with other persons of the paradigm coincides with the epenthetic vowel.[18] This does not apply to Lombard, Trentino, and as mentioned above, certain Rhaetoromance varieties. Benincà and Vanelli interpret this non-epenthetic vowel as a first-person pronoun, which has been agglutinated to the right of the verb in the dialects in question.

There is a natural interpretation of these facts within our framework: the cluster-inflected verb + first-person SCL is derived through verb movement to the Speaker° position and adjunction of the verb to the left of the [+speaker] SCL. In the Rhaetoromance variety mentioned above, this happens only with the first-person singular, which realizes the + value in the [+/−speaker] opposition.[19] Hence, one may assume that in Rhaetoromance the verb stops in the Speaker° position and adjoins to the first-person SCL. In other varieties, where no subject clitic appears to the right of the inflected verb, it may be assumed that the verb has been moved by substitution into the Speaker° position and not by adjunction to the SCL (cf. Roberts 1993c).

It is interesting to note that verb movement to SCL positions is attested even for the higher Hearer° position in other varieties. As Benincà and Vanelli (1975) mention, certain Lombard dialects show an agglutinated pronoun even for first-person plural and second-person singular and plural (respectively, *n*, *t*, and *f*).[20] Again, the analysis that comes to mind is verb adjunction to the subject clitic, which moves in these Lombard dialects not only to the Speaker° head but even higher inside the SCL domain.

Another case of agglutination of a subject clitic that may be interpreted as verbal adjunction is that found in Livinallongo and examined in Benincà (1995a), who shows that a vocalic clitic of the deictic class is found to the right of the inflected verb. Benincà explicitly considers verb movement to a position where the subject clitic is located. In the structure I have adopted here, it appears that the verb moves to different positions for the various different dialects. It adjoins to the Speaker° position where the speaker feature is realized in the Rhaetoromance variety of S. Leonardo, whereas it rises to the Hearer° position in Lombard and rises even further, to the deictic position, in Livinallongo. It is not possible to consider each single dialect and determine which position the verb moves into or whether it adjoins to a SCL or if it moves by substitution into this position tout court. However, data about agglutinated SCLs show that verb movement inside the agreement SCL field is possible and opens up interesting opportunities for an analysis of interrogative inversion, which is discussed in the following chapter.

2.5   SUBJECT CLITIC CLIMBING INSIDE THE AGREEMENT FIELD

The structural tests that have been examined in the previous section show that there are four distinct positions for SCLs. However, they also show that there is variation among dialects with respect to the following cases: first, it has been assumed that number and person SCLs are merged in two agreement positions (one encoding number and the other encoding hearer features) after the preverbal strong negative marker, and this claim is justified both by data from northeastern and northwestern dialects. However, in many varieties, number and even person SCLs occur before the negative marker. Second, in section 2.3.3, the type 3 coordination test is used to distinguish between number and person SCLs. However, I have presented the case of Paduan dialect in which person SCLs behave like number SCLs, in the sense that they may be omitted in the second conjunct of a type 3 coordination. So far, I have simply overlooked these counterexamples to the hypothesis that each morphological SCL class is merged in one single position.

To account for these cases, I suggest that SCLs are able to climb up inside the agreement field from the position in which they are merged to a higher position. Independent evidence in favor of this hypothesis may be found in both northeastern and northwestern dialects. I consider one case for each of the two groups.

Let us consider the following examples taken from the Polesano dialect of Loreo, a Southern Veneto (northeastern) dialect:

(57)   a. N' i vien mina.   Loreo
             not SCL come not
             'They are not coming'.

        b. *I ne vien mina
             SCL not come not

(58)   a. I m'ha dito che n'i vien mina, sato.   Loreo
             SCL to-me has told that not SCL come not, know + you
             'They told me that they are not coming, you know'.

        b. I m'ha dito ch'i ne vien mina, sato.
             SCL to-me has told that + SCL not come not, know + you

The pattern illustrated in (57) shows that the basic position of the SCL is to the right of the negative marker, and this is the only possible position in a main declarative sentence. In embedded sentences, however, it is possible (though not obligatory) to move the SCL to the left of the negative marker, as in (58b). It therefore appears that the presence of a C° head realized by the complementizer permits raising of the SCL to a prenegative position.[21] It ought to be noted that the constraint on the embedded status of the sentence (where movement applies) appears to be the opposite of verb movement in V2 languages. Hence, the movement of the SCL must in some sense depend on the complementizer in the opposite manner to verb movement. In other words, the movement of the SCL must be parasitic of the existence of the complementizer. As we have seen in section 2.2, cases of interaction between the complementizer and SCLs are frequent in the northern Italian domain, but only for the deictic and invariable classes. There are two possible explanations for the order found in (58b): either the SCL moves, or the position of the negative marker is different in (58b) with respect to (58a). As the negative marker remains the same (i.e., in both cases it is followed by a postverbal element) and there is no independent reason to postulate that *ne* moves higher in these contexts, I analyze (58b) as SCL movement to a prenegative position.

One can imagine various target positions for the SCL; the first could be an adjunction to the negative element *ne*. However, this would not explain why movement occurs only in embedded contexts, as the position adjoined to the preverbal negative marker should be available in both main and embedded sentences. Moreover, it appears that the SCL is necessarily clustered with the complementizer, as are deictic and invariable clitics (cf. section 2.2.1.2).[22]

(59)   a. I m'ha dito ch'i ne vien mina, sato.   Loreo
             SCL to-me has told that + SCL not come not, know + you
             'They told me that they are not coming, you know'.

        b. *I m'ha dito che i ne vien mina, sato

One can therefore make the hypothesis that the prenegative position to which the SCL moves is occupied by deictic or invariable SCLs, which in fact are necessarily clustered with the complementizer.[23]

This hypothesis may also explain why the phenomenon is restricted to embedded contexts in these dialects. The entire set of CP projections is already present only in embedded contexts since the main verb selects a CP projection, not an IP. The SCL is therefore free to move higher than its usual position in IP. This argument is dealt with in further detail in chapter 3, where the interaction between CP and SCLs is examined.

Let us now turn to a second case of movement found in the Tuscany variety of Incisa Valdarno, which is a slightly different case from Polesano dialect examined above. Here, we do not find a constraint on the embedded versus the matrix character of the sentence, although the CP projection is most probably involved in the movement of the SCL. Second-person SCLs may move to a prenegative position only in the case of questions or exclamative contexts.[24]

(60)   a. *Te tu un mangi   Incisa Val d'Arno (Florentine-Tuscany)
           you you not eat
           'You are not going to eat'.

        b. Te un tu mangi.
           you not you eat

        c. Te tu un mangi?
           you you not eat?
           'Don't you want to eat?'

        d. Te tu un mangi!
           you you not eat!
           'You are not going to eat!'

As the ungrammaticality of (60a) shows, a person SCL cannot be found in the prenegative position if the sentence is a declarative one. However, this is possible in interrogative and exclamative contexts. This appears to suggest that in the Incisa dialect, a C° position permits rising of the SCL only if it is activated by some independent strong feature, such as in interrogative or exclamative clauses. It may be noted that although the contexts that trigger SCL movement are partially different in the Loreo dialect and in the Incisa dialect, in both cases it is an active C° that triggers movement of the SCL. In Polesano it must be a phonetically realized complementizer; in Florentine it must be a C° with strong (interrogative or exclamative) features. In main declaratives, where the CP projections are probably not even projected in non-V2 dialects, movement of the SCL is ungrammatical.

There is another piece of data that could help us understand what is at issue here. The same speakers that find (60c and 60d) acceptable give the following judgments:

(61)   a. Che mangi?   Incisa Val d'Arno
           that eat?
           'Are you eating?'

  b. *Che tu mangi?
     that you eat?

  c. Tu mangi?
     you eat?

In (61), the person SCL is in complementary distribution with the complementizer, realized in yes/no questions in Tuscany dialects. The complementary distribution between the SCLs and the complementizer suggests that either they are in the same position or that the SCL has passed through the position where the complementizer is realized. Thus, the prenegative status of SCLs in interrogative and exclamative contexts has to be interpreted as movement of the SCL to the CP position, activated by exclamative or interrogative features. The prenegative status of SCLs in these contexts is thus a case of movement similar to those treated by Zanuttini (1997), who proposes that in negative questions, it is the negative morpheme rather than the inflected verb that rises to C°, where it realizes the strong features in C°. In the Incisa Valdarno dialect, it would be the SCL and not the negative morpheme that moves to the interrogative or exclamative C° to check the strong features in this position. This case is analyzed in further detail in chapter 3. For the time being, it simply shows that there is an SCL climbing inside the agreement field (and even higher inside the CP domain) and that it is sensitive to features realized in the CP domain.

   Our hypothesis—that there is a position for each type of SCL and that when a SCL is found higher than its normal position, it must have moved there—is strengthened by the fact that there do exist clear cases of SCL movement to higher than normal positions. Hence, the proposal made in section 2.1 is now assumed; that is, for every semantic morphological SCL type, there is a syntactic position where it is realized, and when we find a SCL higher than its basic position, it must have moved there.

2.6   THE AGREEMENT FIELD

2.6.1   The Structure of the Agreement Field

This section examines the four SCL positions more closely to determine the structure of the agreement field and, in particular, which morphological features are realized as independent syntactic projections and which are clustered together. Let us first summarize what we have learned about the nature of these four positions.

   The agreement field has been split into pre- and postnegative subfields. The prenegative subfield is realized in CP, whereas the postnegative one is located inside IP.

   The highest position occurs before the strong preverbal negative marker; the SCL necessarily clusters with the complementizer and is the only one that can be excluded in a type 1 coordination. It is incompatible with wh-elements, focalized, and left-dislocated items because it contains features relevant for informational structure that mark the whole sentence as new. It is filled by a vocalic clitic, which is not marked for person, gender, or number. This type of vocalic clitic (generally *a* or *e*) appears with all persons and may be used as expletive and quasi-argumental subjects (see Poletto 1996 for an analysis of invariable SCLs with respect to the pro-drop theory).

The lower position is still realized before the negative marker and clusters with a complementizer but cannot be left out in a type 1 coordination. It interacts with wh-elements (it singles out two classes of wh-items) but does not contain features relevant for informational structure. It marks a deictic feature, as is used for first, second, fourth, and fifth person (and marks the strong value of the [+/–deictic] opposition) or for third person, and in this case it marks the weak or default value [–deictic]. Both positions can be left out in a type 3 coordination.

On the basis of these arguments, I propose the following structure:

(62) $[_{LDP}$ inv SCL_i $[_{CP}$ deictic SCL $[_{FP}$ t_i [IP]]]]

1. Invariable SCLs move to a LD° position from a focus position, saturating both projections (which cannot be occupied by another element, such as a focalized or left-dislocated XP, respectively). Deictic SCLs occur higher than the basic position of invariable SCLs; anticipating the discussion in chapter 3, I have assumed that deictic SCLs occur higher than weak wh-items but lower than complex wh-items. Deictic and invariable SCLs never co-occur because deictic SCLs interfere with the movement of invariable SCLs, as shown in (62).

2. Both postnegative positions (located in IP) are always repeated in a type 1 coordination, as expected by our proposal.

3. The position of number SCLs is realized after a strong preverbal negative marker but can be left out in a type 3 coordination. This type of SCL does not occur when the inflected verb has moved into the C° domain.

4. The lowest SCL position is realized after the strong preverbal negative marker and must be repeated in a type 3 coordination. It can be occupied only by person clitics, which behave in the same way object clitics do when the inflected verb moves higher into the CP domain and encodes only a [hearer] feature.

5. In addition to these SCL positions, I propose that the inflected verb occupies a position where the [speaker] feature is realized. This solves two questions: the position of the inflected verb, which is higher than T° but lower than SCLs, and the fact that no SCLs are distinctively marked for the first person.

The whole agreement field is illustrated in (63):

(63) $[_{LDP}$ inv SCL_i $[_{CP}$ deic SCL $[_{FP}$ t_i $[_{IP}$ $[_{NegP}$ $[_{NumbP}$ SCL $[_{HearerP}$ SCL $[_{SpeakerP}$ inflV [TP]]]]]]]]]]

Apart from invariable SCLs, all other SCL classes encode some subject feature, although there is never a repetition of the same feature. However, it may be noted that the subject features realized in the prenegative field are different from those realized in the postnegative field: we find person, number, and gender lower than

NegP, whereas the higher field contains only a [+/–deictic] feature that distinguishes between the first and second person on the one hand, and third person, on the other. Hence, the type of agreement found inside the CP layer is different from the features that we see in IP. Another interesting observation is that the structure of the agreement field is not simply one of person, number, and gender, corresponding to PersP, NumbP, and GenderP, respectively, but also includes a higher position that signals the distinction between deictic and nondeictic persons; a single position for number and gender, where gender is parasitic on number; and two positions that realize the two components of person, namely, the [hearer] and [speaker] features.

Many questions could be asked at this point. I formulate them here, but I provide an answer only for a few of them in the following chapters. First, the existence of a position that simply indicates that a subject exists and the fact that this position has been labeled TOPP by Benincà (1983) because it reflects topic/focus relations, is, on the one hand, reminiscent of the extended projection principle, which states that a clause must have a subject; on the other hand, it indicates a connection between this and the fact that the subject is often the topic of a sentence, and in many languages it is treated as such. I do not speculate any further on this question (see chapter 6 for a hypothesis concerning the subject position inside the CP layer), as it would lead us too far from the empirical domain we are considering. A second interesting question regards the scattering of person into three positions (the FPs corresponding to the deictic and the hearer and the speaker features) that are not adjacent.

If the hypothesis that the prenegative portion of the agreement field is located inside the CP layer is correct, the agreement subdomain contained in CP has fewer feature specifications than the one located in IP, although it does not appear to be a direct "impoverished version," or a rough copy of the features realized in IP, because it also contains distinct features. The feature that expresses new or old information realized in the higher position in CP has nothing to do with the number and gender features realized in the higher position in IP. Thus, the two agreement subdomains are not copies of the same agreement instantiation because they appear to encode independent features. At the same time, they must have something in common as the SCL movement from the IP positions to the CP agreement positions attests.

2.6.2 Speculations on the Agreement Field

On the basis of morphological and syntactic evidence, we have hypothesized the existence of four SCL positions, each realizing a specific morphological feature of the subject. One could ask whether there is other independent evidence for this proposal, how it could reflect on the general framework, and what we gain by splitting the structure of AgrS in such a complicated way. In addition to the tests illustrated above, which force us to postulate the existence of four positions, there is a strong argument in favor of the idea that subject clitics belong to different classes. The complex set of FPs I have proposed directly accounts for Renzi and Vanelli's (1983) generalizations on the distribution of SCLs across the verbal paradigm. Renzi and Vanelli note that not all the NIDs have a complete set of SCLs for all persons and that the distribution of the SCLs across the verbal paradigm can be described in the form of implications. They formulate nine descriptive generalizations in their work. The first three are discussed here (the others concern the doubling phenomenon with DPs and are not considered here):

(64)   a. If a variety has only one SCL, this is the second-person singular.

   b. If a variety has two SCLs, these are the second-person singular and the third person.

   c. If a variety has three SCLs, these are the second-person singular and the third-person singular and plural.

We can represent these generalizations in the following schema:

(65)
	1.	2.	3.	1pl.	2pl.	3.pl
a.	/	+	/	/	/	/
b.	/	+	+	/	/	/
c.	/	+	+	/	/	+

So there are dialects that have only a second-person singular pronoun, dialects that have only second-person singular and third-person singular, and dialects that have second-person singular and third-person singular and plural. If a dialect has third-person singular, it also has second person; if a dialect has third-person plural, it also has second- and third-person singular.

If we compare the pattern of the table with the morphological classes of SCLs, we find an interesting analogy: the SCLs that are more frequently realized, namely, second and third persons, are those that morphologically encode person and number features. The persons that are less frequently realized, namely, first-person singular and plural and second-person plural, are generally expressed by a SCL that does not encode person and number features; it may be invariable for all persons or change on the basis of a deictic feature that encodes a distinction between first- and second-person, on the one hand (i.e., the deictic ones), and third persons, on the other (i.e., the nondeictic ones).[25] Let us repeat the table, reporting the four classes of SCLs and their distributions with respect to the persons:

(66)
		1	2	3	4	5	6
a.	Invariable	+	+	+	+	+	+
b.	Deictic	+	+	+	+	+	+
c.	Number	–	–	+	–	–	+
d.	Person	–	+	+	–	–	–

It may be noted that generalization (64b) corresponds to (66d), which illustrates the person SCL class, and (64c) corresponds to (66c), which describes the distribution of number SCLs.[26] There is a partial overlap between the two tables: the second descriptive generalization corresponds to the realization of the person SCL class, whereas the third corresponds to the realization of the number clitic class.

What can be said about (64a), that is, the first generalization on the realization of second-person singular? One could hypothesize that certain dialects only realize the marked value in the opposition [+/–hearer]—namely, the +, hence second person—and do not mark the default value of the opposition, namely, the [–hearer], corresponding to the third person (without any plural or gender features). It therefore appears evident that Renzi and Vanelli's (1983) generalizations may be expressed in terms of our hypothesis simply by stating that a given dialect has a given class of SCLs or it does not. All three generalizations thus correspond to different morphological types of SCLs, and, it is more interesting to note, the implication goes hand in hand with the syntactic positions of SCLs. It may be noted, in fact, that the first classes that are realized are those located lower in the structure proposed here. Thus, a dialect like Venetian has only person and number SCLs, hence those SCLs are merged in the IP layer.

Most dialects realize the marked opposition of the lowest SCL class, whereas several dialects realize the unmarked value of the [+/hearer] opposition as well. Certain dialects realize only the IP positions. This suggests that Renzi and Vanelli's (1983) generalizations can be directly encompassed by our hypothesis on the syntactic layering of SCLs, providing it is assumed that the syntactic projections of the agreement field are occupied by starting from the lowest position up to the highest one.[27] The condition that states the necessity of occupying lower positions before realizing higher positions is interesting in a wider perspective, if one considers the general issue of determining whether all languages have the same inventory of syntactic projections (as Cinque 1999 proposes) or simply the same inventory of features (as Giorgi and Pianesi 1997 hypothesize). Following Cinque's hypothesis, we see that the number and type of FPs are encoded in UG, which also determines the layering of the FPs. If Giorgi and Pianesi are right, UG encodes only semantic features in a given order, and languages differ in the way they encode semantic features on one projection or on more projections: they press more features inside the same syntactic node or scatter them within a set of FPs. On the basis of this framework, we can add an interesting restriction, that is, that scattering has to start from the lower FPs. This means that there are languages that scatter only the lowest of a given set of features, namely, those corresponding to person; languages that also realize the number feature, and languages that also realize the deictic feature as independent FPs. A condition that restricts scattering is not something unexpected, and one would also expect that there is a number of other conditions that rule the system. The assumption that the scattering process of semantic features starts from the lowest feature is compatible with the recent minimalist view that the structure is built in a bottom-up fashion and that it is created through the merging of elements contained in the numeration.

We can therefore formulate the condition on scattering of the agreement features:

(67)   Features have to be scattered by starting from the lowest one.

Let us suppose, for instance, that the difference between standard Italian and the NIDs involves the scattering of the persons, number, gender, and deictic features of the subject and that Italian has only one position where all these features are realized but the NIDs realize a more complex structure. We could ask how scattering takes place and whether there are any subsets of features that remain inside a single projection while others are scattered.

An apparent exception to condition (67) is the fact that number and gender features are collapsed onto a single projection, whereas the deictic feature is projected higher on a distinct FP. I have not found any data that lead in the direction of splitting number and gender into two distinct projections. This is not the case for person, which is probably realized in two positions, one for the hearer feature and one for the speaker feature. So it appears evident that although the features are scattered in a bottom-up fashion, some features are more tightly connected than others. In other words, certain subsets of features are treated as a single unit. However, the fact that number and gender do not scatter but the deictic feature does is not a problem for condition (67), although it has to be accounted for by our representation of the features that may be scattered. The NIDs show that the morphological features encoded in the syntax through the SCL system are not simply gender, number, and person, as they are known from traditional grammar, but that we have to analyze which morphological features are relevant for the syntactic operation of scattering in more detail. If it should turn out that number and gender are associated even in other language groups (see Shlonsky 1997 for an analysis of Hebrew in this sense), as they are in the NIDs, this would mean that number and gender need to be considered as a unit, at least in the verbal system, because they are typical nominal agreement features.

As a concluding remark, I point out that there is an alternative interpretation of condition (67), which can be conceived of as a very general fact about the way in which functional structure is built up: it is possible to build up higher projections only if the lower ones have been projected. When the lower projections are not there, their higher ones are obviously not accessible.

THREE

Interrogative Sentences

3.1 INTRODUCTION

Let us now turn to the higher section of the agreement field that we identified while examining different types of SCLs in chapter 2. As we saw, two SCL positions are realized lower than NegP and clearly within the IP layer, and two are realized higher than NegP in the CP layer. This chapter discusses the structure of the CP layer in main and embedded interrogative clauses. I provide a detailed analysis of the interaction between wh-elements and deictic SCLs and of the phenomenon known as subject clitic inversion (from now on SCI) or interrogative inflection in descriptive grammars on NIDs. I claim that SCI can be interpreted either as movement to a low C° position or as a pure morphological phenomenon that is not related to syntactic movement of the inflected verb to a higher position than that of declarative clauses, and the choice between the two analyses depends on the dialect chosen.

I provide several tests to distinguish the dialects in which SCI is still V to C and those in which it does not imply V to C. I propose a comparison between SCI and deictic SCLs, on the one hand, and the agreement in Comp phenomena found in the German languages, on the other hand (cf. Haegeman 1993; Shlonsky 1998; Tomaselli 1990; Vikner 1995; Zwart 1993). I take into account dialectal variation in interrogative main clauses and show that the different structures can be accounted for only in a split-CP perspective. This involves the exact distribution of the CP projections in interrogative clauses and the elements that can fill the CP positions. Wh-items are split into different classes and are shown to occur in different positions.

The chapter is organized as follows: in section 3.2, I analyze subject clitic inversion (SCI) and ascertain whether the verb movement in question does or does not involve the CP layer in a given dialect; in many dialects, SCI is a case of residual V to C movement (these languages were V2 in the medieval period, as shown by Benincà 1995b), but in others it is not.

41

Section 3.3 contains an overview of the possible interrogative structures that have been found in the sample of dialects examined. For some of these, a split-CP perspective is necessary to account for the various morphemes that occur in main interrogatives. There are dialects in which three distinct CP projections are activated (in the sense that they contain three visible heads) in main interrogative sentences. Moreover, if all NIDs have the same set of functional projections, comparative evidence is provided to show that four distinct projections may be activated in main interrogatives. Each of these four CP projections involved in interrogative structures corresponds to a different interpretation of the interrogative sentence.

In section 3.4, I discuss some theoretical problems raised by the adoption of a split-CP analysis concerning the definition of the limit between the IP layer and the CP layer and the possibility of maintaining Rizzi's wh-criterion and its connection with V to C movement.

Section 3.5 briefly illustrates embedded interrogatives, whose structure is much more homogeneous than that of main interrogatives in the northern Italian domain. I claim that only the highest projection found in main interrogatives may be occupied by a wh-item in embedded clauses.

3.2   SUBJECT CLITIC INVERSION

In this section, I consider interrogative subject clitic inversion (SCI), a structure that is widely represented in the sample of dialects examined. This is the most conservative interrogative structure and one that was used by most varieties until the past century (cf. Poletto 1998). However, this structure is gradually being lost by many varieties and replaced by various structures, as will be seen in section 3.3. The aim of this section is to provide a detailed analysis of the way SCI occurs and to show that SCI corresponds to syntactic movement of the inflected verb inside the CP domain in some dialects, although it has lost this property in others. This is an empirical claim, and it needs to be shown for each and every northern Italian dialect. As it is not possible (for reasons of space) to examine each single dialect and classify it into one type or the other, I simply discuss a few arguments in favor of the hypothesis of V to C movement taken from a number of varieties in which verb movement is particularly clear. In addition, I provide some general criteria for determining whether SCI corresponds to a case of V to C or not in a given variety. The first argument is the restriction to main contexts: SCI occurs in main interrogatives but not in embedded interrogatives in the majority of the dialects I have examined:

(1)   a. Cossa fa-lo?   Cereda (Central Veneto)
         what does-he?
         'What does he do?'

      b. No so cossa che el fa.
         (I) not know what that he does
         'I do not know what he does'.

c. *No so cossa (che) fa-lo
(I) not know what does-he

d. *Cossa (che) el fa?
what (that) he does?
'What does he do?'

As shown in (1), SCI is restricted to main contexts [cf. the ungrammaticality of (1c)]. Moreover, SCI must occur when it is permitted [cf. the ungrammaticality of (1d)]. This immediately recalls verb movement processes such as V2 that exhibit asymmetry between main and embedded contexts and has been treated in the literature as implying V to C. The standard analysis for V2 is that the verb can only move to C in main clauses because only in this context is the C position free; in embedded sentences, C is already filled by a complementizer and V2 is excluded.[1] Later, I present three empirical arguments in favor of the hypothesis that the SCI corresponds to V to C when it is restricted to main contexts. Before doing so, however, I provide the three criteria that distinguish the dialects in which SCI is still V to C, as well as dialects in which SCI has lost this syntactic property. The first criterion, which shows that SCI is V to C in a given dialect, is the fact that it is restricted to main interrogative sentences and obligatory when possible. As expected, provided that these dialects are not verb second languages, SCI never occurs in declarative clauses (neither main nor embedded) in this set of dialects, as shown in (2):

(2) a. El fa cusì.   Padua
SCL does so
'He does so'.

b. *(El) fa-lo cusì
(SCL) does-he so

c. I dise che el fa così.
SCL say that SCL does so
'They say that he does so'.

d. *I dise che (el) fa-lo così
SCL say that (SCL) does-he so

It may be noted, however, that in many dialects the context of inversion is not restricted to main interrogative structures at all; it very often occurs in counterfactual (3a), hypothetical (3b), exclamative (3c), and disjunctive clauses (3d), as noted in Benincà (1989):

(3) a. Fusse-lo rivà!   Scorzè (Central Veneto)
were-he come!
'Had he come!'

b. Vinisi-al tio pari, o podaresin là.   Clauzetto (Friulian)
came-he your father, we could go
'If your father came, we could leave'.

c. Quanto belo se-lo!   Padua
how nice is-it!
'How nice it is!'

   d. Sedi-al puar o sedi-al sior, no m'impuarte.   Clauzetto
      be-he poor or be-he rich, not to me-interests
      'I do not care whether he is rich or poor'.

This recalls the case of subject inversion in English, which occurs in main interrogative sentences and in a few of the contexts exemplified in (2). As the English
case is treated as residual V2, and hence is a case of V to C movement, we have to
assume that for all the varieties in which we see that counterfactuals, disjunctive,
hypothetical, and some exclamative contexts (cf. Benincà 1996 for a detailed
analysis of exclamative contexts) show SCI, this phenomenon has to be interpreted
as V to C movement. On the basis of the similarity between English and NIDs, I
consider the fact that SCI occurs in the contexts shown above as a second criterion for determining V to C.

The asymmetry between main and embedded clauses exemplified in (1) is
not found in other dialects: in the Trentino dialect of Rovereto and in several
Romagnolo varieties, SCI is possible in embedded interrogatives and also in declarative clauses. Moreover, in Romagnolo, the SCI process is embedded under a
complementizer:

(4)   a. Chi ch a fasi-v?   Forlì (Romagnolo)
         what that SCL do-you?
         'What are you doing?'

      b. I m a chiest chi ch a fasi-v.
         SCL to me have asked what that SCL do-you?
         'They asked me what you are doing'.

      c. A n lisi-v mai di livar.
         SCL not read-you never some books
         'You never read books'.

The SCI process is optional in these dialects, as the grammaticality of the following sentence shows:

(5)   Chi ch a fasi ades?   Forlì
      what that SCL do now?
      'What are you doing now?'

Several facts show that SCI is not V to C movement in the Romagnolo dialect of Forlì; the first is that it co-occurs with the complementizer. Nevertheless, this is not a very strong argument within a split-CP analysis, as the complementizer could occur in a higher C° and the SCI in a lower C° (see the discussion
below on Piedmontese data). However, SCI also occurs in interrogative embedded contexts and is possible in all declarative clauses, which undoubtedly shows
that the process is not peculiar to some restricted contexts. As Romagnolo is
not a V2 language, it will be assumed that SCI is not V to C movement in this
dialect.

In summary, the three criteria I propose for determining whether a V to C
analysis is correct for a given dialect are the following:

1. Main versus embedded asymmetry
2. Presence of SCI in other typical V to C contexts (cf. English hypothetical clauses)
3. SCI not generalized to declarative clauses

I now focus on the dialects for which SCI is a restricted phenomenon, such as those exemplified in (1) to (3). Several authors (cf. among others Fava 1998) consider SCI as a sort of morphological process of interrogative inflection that does not have any syntactic correlate. However, this approach cannot be considered correct, as the data discussed in (1)–(3) would lack explanations. Moreover, SCI is not a sort of "interrogative mood," as it also occurs in counterfactual clauses, exclamative clauses, and so on.

Hulk (1993) hypothesizes that SCI occurs in AgrS°; the SCL moves from the SpecT position and incorporates into the inflected verb. This can take place only in main interrogatives, in which I is endowed with strong [+wh] features, and not in embedded interrogatives, in which it is the C° position that contains the [+wh] feature. The empirical reasons for believing that SCI is indeed verb movement are given below. For the moment, I only point out two theoretical reasons for not assuming this analysis. The first is that SpecT is considered to be an A position in Romance languages. Hulk assumes that SpecAgrS is an A' position, but she needs a lower position (which is not SpecVP) to host the SCL. In the present framework, I follow the approach of Cinque (1999) in assuming that SpecT is the position that hosts temporal adverbs rather than subject DPs. Moreover, incorporation of the SCL to the inflected verb is achieved through a right adjunction procedure, which is excluded by the framework adopted here (cf. Kayne 1991, 1994).

A similar analysis has been proposed by Sportiche (1997), who assumes that SCI is not verb movement in the syntax in Romance but a type of inflection that is licensed by covert V to C movement at LF. Therefore, SCI occurs only when covert V to C movement is triggered by independent reasons; in the syntax of main interrogative sentences, the verb does not move higher than in declarative sentences. In what follows, it is shown that V to C movement occurs in the syntax and not at LF, at least in the majority of the NIDs examined.

It has recently been proposed by Munaro (1997) that SCI does not always imply movement to a C° position but that the movement only reaches the highest projection inside the IP layer, a position where the sentence type is defined.[2]

At this point, I take the following approach: I propose that SCI is both a morphological and a syntactic phenomenon. Though SCI may be treated as a morphological process of affixation (see section 3.2.2), as proposed by Fava (1993) and Sportiche (1997), it always implies syntactic movement of the inflected verb to a higher position than that of the inflected verb in declarative sentences.

I need to prove that two claims are correct, namely, that SCI corresponds to syntactic verb movement and that the verb reaches the CP layer. To show that SCI indeed corresponds to syntactic movement of the verb, I examine some very clear cases of verb movement. The first case involves movement of the verb higher than a focus morpheme in the Rhaetoromance variety of Pera di Fassa, which is not a V2 variety in declarative sentences. In this dialect, it is possible to use an focus marker (*pa*, etymologically derived from the Latin *post*; cf. Pellegrini 1972), which is an independent morpheme with the following distribution:

(6)   a. O'la pa tu vas?   Pera di Fassa (Rhaetoromance) (Benincà 1995a: 67)
         where interr. marker SCL.go?
         'Where on earth are you going?'

      b. O'la vas-to pa?
         where go-SCL interr. marker?

      c. *O'la pa vas-to?
         where interr. marker go-SCL?

      d. *O'la tu vas pa?
         where SCL go interr marker?

The particle *pa* can be found either to the right or to the left of the inflected verb. If the order is *pa*-V, the SCL appears before the verb, whereas if the order is V-*pa*, the SCL occurs as an enclitic. Under the assumption that the position of the interrogative marker remains constant, the data in (6) can be interpreted as verb movement. If the verb remains to the right of the interrogative marker, only a proclitic is possible. If the verb moves higher than the interrogative marker, an enclitic must be used. In other words, the distribution of proclitic versus enclitic SCLs corresponds to two distinct verb positions; only when the verb has moved higher than the interrogative marker can (and must) an enclitic be used.[3]

It may be noted that the data from the dialect of Pera di Fassa only prove that SCI is a case of verb movement; they do not tell us where the verb moves. The position to the left of the particle could be C° or a lower position between *pa* and C° but still inside the IP layer. This depends on how we analyze the structure and where we locate the particle *pa*. It is plausible to assume that the particle is located inside the CP domain and not below, as it does not occur in embedded interrogative sentences, where a complementizer is obligatory:

(7)   a. Co l fas-to pa?   ·   Pera di Fassa
         how it do-you interr. marker?
         'How do you do it?'

      b. Dime co che tu l fas.
         tell-me how that you it do
         'Tell me how you do it'.

      c. *Dime co l fas-to (pa)?
         tell-me how it do-you interr. marker

The semantics of *pa* is discussed in further detail in section 3.4. For the moment, I only show that it occurs in the CP area. Let us consider the following data, which illustrate another possible structure of main interrogative sentences in the Fassano variety of Pera di Fassa:

(8)   a. Olà che tu vas?   Pera di Fassa
         where that you go?
         'Where are you going?'

b. *Olà che vasto (pa)?
   where that go-you (interr marker)?

c. *Olà vasto che (pa)?
   where go-you that (pa)?

In (8), the wh-item *olà* "where" is followed by a complementizer and SCI is impossible, either with or without *pa* [cf. (8b/c)]. Here, it must be noted that *pa* and the complementizer can never be combined. It should be possible, a priori, to find structures in which the complementizer and the interrogative marker are combined without SCI. This is not the case.[4]

(9) b. *Olà che pa tu vas?   Pera di Fassa
        where that interr. marker you go?
        'Where are you going?'

     c. *Ola pa che tu vas?
        where interr marker that you go?

Neither of the possible orders is grammatical; *pa* can never be combined with a complementizer.

The possible structures for interrogative sentences in Fassano are the following:

(10) a. Olà vasto?   Pera di Fassa
         where go-you?
         'Where are you going?'

      b. Olà vasto pa?
         where go-you interr.marker?

      c. Olà pa tu vas?
         where interr marker you go?

      d. Olà che tu vas?
         where that you go?

A main interrogative sentence can be expressed in four ways: (1) by simple SCI, (2) by SCI followed by *pa,* (3) by *pa* followed by a proclitic and the verb, or (4) by a complementizer followed by a proclitic and the verb. Not all possible combinations are attested to, and the excluded possibilities are the following:

(11) a. Complementizer-SCI

      b. SCI-complementizer

      c. Complementizer-*pa*

      d. *Pa*-complementizer

      e. *Pa*- SCI

Therefore, *pa* can be combined with SCI, whereas the complementizer cannot. *Pa* and the complementizer cannot be combined, SCI and the complementizer cannot be combined, but *pa* and SCI are compatible. This distribution of the various elements in Fassano main interrogatives is immediately accounted for if we assume that *pa* is a specifier, whereas the complementizer is a head. The verb can rise through *pa* but not through the complementizer, which blocks head movement to the CP layer. The structure I propose is the following:

(12) $[_{CP} [_{C°} V + SCL [_{CP} pa [_{C°} che]]]]$

Fassano interrogative structures can be accounted for by assuming that *pa* occupies a specifier position located below the C° head that is the landing site for verb movement. The verb can move through the head, of which *pa* is the specifier, and reach the higher C°, thereby explaining why the order SCI-*pa* is grammatical. The complementizer occupies a C° head position located lower than SCI, whereas the specifier of the CP is occupied by *pa*. Therefore, the complementizer and SCI are never compatible because the complementizer blocks verb movement to the higher C projection where SCI occurs [this excludes the ungrammatical structure (11a) and (11b)]. *Pa* and *ch* never co-occur because of a doubly filled comp filter, which could be rephrased in minimalist terms by assuming the following "minimization procedure": if the head already realizes a strong feature, there is no need for the specifier to realize the same feature.[5] This excludes the ungrammatical structure (11c) and (11d). As for the impossibility of (11e), the order *pa*-SCI, this is directly accounted for by the fact that the SCI position is higher than the position of *pa*. Hence, the structure in (12) accounts for both the grammatical and the ungrammatical data in (8) to (11).

Another interesting piece of evidence in favor of this analysis may be found in Badiotto (a V2 Rhaetoromance dialect spoken in a valley near Fassa) imperative clauses. *Pa* can also occur in imperative clauses (in alternative to other imperative particles, each of which is interpreted with a different semantics; see Poletto and Zanuttini 1998):

(13)   a. Faal pa!   S. Leonardo
          do-it particle
          'Do it!'

       b. Faal ma!

       c. Faal poe!

Suppletive imperatives with a subjunctive verb and a complementizer are grammatical if other particles are chosen but are ungrammatical if the particle *pa* is used:

(14)   a. Ch al vagnes ma ince os cumpagn.   S. Leonardo
          that SCL comes particle also your friend
          'Your friend may come in, too'.

       b. Ch al vagnes poe ince os cumpagn.

       c. *Ch al vagnes pa ince os cumpagn

Example (14) shows that the incompatibility between the complementizer and the particle *pa* is replicated in Badiotto imperative clauses. Moreover, the true imperative form in (13) can rise higher than *pa*, as already noted for Fassano interrogative clauses. In Poletto and Zanuttini (1998, sec. 2.2), *pa* is analyzed as a focus particle, which assigns focus to the entire sentence in certain dialects or to an XP in others (see section 3.4 for a contrastive analysis of the different usage of *pa* in different dialects). This particle signals emphatic affirmation or negation in Badiotto, whereas it is used to focalize a wh-item in Fassano. If *pa* is indeed a focus particle, we have one more argument in favor of the idea that it is in the CP layer, where the Focus phrase is traditionally encoded in Romance languages (see Ambar 1988; Rizzi 1997) as part of the focus/topic organization that is realized inside the left periphery of the sentence. We can conclude that the data in (6) prove that SCI corresponds to verb movement and that the data in (7)–(14) show that the focus particle *pa* is located in the CP layer.

Another argument in favor of a V to C analysis is provided by an Eastern Lombard variety, the dialect of Monno. This variety shows a form of "do-support" (or better, "fa-support"), which is fairly similar to the English phenomenon (cf. Benincà and Poletto 1998 for a detailed discussion of the data and theoretical implications for the treatment of English do-support):

(15) a. Come fa-l comportas?   Monno (Eastern Lombard)
         how does-he behave-himself?
         'How is he behaving?'

      b. Quata fe-t majan?
         how much do-you eat-of it?
         'How much are you going to eat?'

The support verb has an enclitic SCL to its right; the Monno dialect is a particular case of SCI that is limited to a support verb and does not apply to all verbs. As in English, fa-support is necessary in main interrogative sentences; it does not occur in embedded interrogative contexts, where the wh-item is followed by a complementizer, or in declarative sentences:

(16) I ho domandà col che l'ha fat.   Monno
      (I) to-him have asked what that he has done
      'I asked him what he did'.

(17) M'domandio . . .   Monno
      I myself ask . . .
      'I am wondering . . .'

Moreover, it does not occur with auxiliaries and modals, although it occurs with 'fa' itself:

(18) Qual e-t cercà fo?   Monno
      which have-you found out?
      'Which did you choose?'

(19) Che fa-l fa?   Monno
      what does-he do?
      What is he doing?

As in English, do-support cannot occur with the subject. In (20) a complementizer follows the wh-item. This, incidentally, shows that although do-support is not possible, the subject-wh must move to the CP domain (as proposed by Rizzi 1991), and cannot remain in SpecAgrS, as has been proposed by many authors (cf. Benincà and Poletto 1998 for a discussion on this point):

(20)   Chi che l'ha magnada?   Monno
       who that it-has eaten?
       'Who ate it?'

Monnese fa-support is interesting for its insight into SCI, just because it is similar to the English do-support phenomenon. The latter is analyzed as a movement of the dummy verb into the C° position; the fa-support phenomenon found in Monnese is amenable to the same analysis. Fa-support can thus be considered as a case of verb movement to the C° position in interrogative main clauses. As fa-support exhibits SCI, I conclude that at least for this variety SCI is indeed a case of movement of the inflected verb and that the position to which the verb is moved is the C° position, not a lower position.

A third argument for assuming that SCI corresponds to verb movement inside the CP domain comes from the variety Rodoretto di Prali. Coordinated interrogatives with 'or' have the following form in this dialect:

(21)   L'achatà-tu ou qu' tu l'achatte pa?   Rodoretto di Prali (Piedmontese-
       It buy-you or that you it buy not?   Provençal)
       'Do you buy it or not?'

If coordination implies symmetry, that is, that the two coordinated items are the same part of the sentence structure (i.e., that it is impossible to coordinate an IP with a CP), we are forced to assume that SCI is in the CP domain, as the second member of the coordination shows a complementizer. [6]

Let us sum up the evidence presented here to show that SCI corresponds to V to C movement. Three arguments have been presented. First, in Rhaetoromance dialects, SCI crosses the particle *pa*. Second, certain Eastern Lombard varieties show a do-support phenomenon that is strikingly similar to English, which is generally considered to be V to C. Finally, in certain dialects coordinated interrogatives show SCI in the first conjunct and a complementizer in the second. As coordinated conjuncts have the same structure, we are forced to assume that SCI is on a par with the complementizer in CP.

It has been pointed out to me that these three arguments only prove that the verb is moving to C in these structures and not that SCI occurs in the CP layer. It might well be the case that SCI occurs in IP every time the inflected verb is forced to move higher to the CP layer in the syntax or at LF. This is true, as I have proved only that the mechanism of SCI requires V to C movement in the syntax (and not at LF, as assumed by Sportiche 1997), and I have not shown that SCI is V to C itself. At this point, it becomes quite difficult to distinguish between the two hypotheses on an empirical basis; therefore I leave the question open. What can be shown is that in the NIDs, enclitics are not the same class of elements as the proclitic SCLs examined in chapter 2. This is the issue discussed in the next section.

3.2.1   The Mechanism of Subject Clitic Inversion

Having established the fact that SCI requires verb movement to the C° position, I now examine the enclitic SCL series and how enclisis is formed. The process of enclisis can be treated in two ways: the first hypothesis considers the enclitic series to be identical to the proclitic series. On the basis of this idea, we hypothesize that the enclisis process is derived through movement of the inflected verb that adjoins to the left of the subject clitic on its way to the C° position. A similar proposal was made for French SCI by Rizzi and Roberts (1989). They assume that enclitics and proclitics are the same entity and that enclisis occurs when the verb has moved higher than the SCL, which in turn adjoins to the right of the verb. According to Kayne's (1994) framework, right adjunction is banned, and the only possibility is left adjunction. Hence, we would have to assume a second analysis, namely that it is the verb that adjoins to the left of the SCL before the complex moves upward. This is straightforward for northern Italian dialects, in which all SCLs are heads and not specifiers. It might be a problem for French (at least standard French), in which SCLs are not heads but specifiers. The same applies for the recent analysis of Cardinaletti and Starke (1999), who treat French subject pronouns as weak pronouns, an intermediate stage between tonic pronouns (which have a full DP structure) and clitics, which do not have the higher functional projections of the DP structure. Because the verb, being a head, cannot left-adjoin to a specifier, we might be forced to assume two distinct pronominal series even in standard French, namely, a proclitic series, consisting of weak pronouns that occupy a specifier position, and an enclitic series, made up of heads that the inflected verb adjoins to when moving upward in main interrogative sentences. This idea would imply that enclitics and proclitics are not the same entity and could be located on different positions and have different statuses.

A third possible analysis of the SCI mechanism is a purely morphological one, which considers SCI as a different form already listed in the lexicon and used only when the syntactic conditions it requires (as V to C movement) are satisfied. From an empirical point of view, it is not a simple matter to distinguish an analysis of SCI as affixes that occupy a given functional head and trigger verb movement from an analysis of SCI as an inflected form that can be used only when its features can be checked by verb movement. Fava (1998) provides arguments based on the phonological and morphological processes in certain Veneto dialects and shows that the form V + SCL is currently formed in the lexical component and not in the syntax. In fact, the data that I discuss later are compatible with both options. I do not focus here on the morphological side of the question of whether SCI is formed as an affixation process in the syntax through verb movement or whether it already exists in the lexicon as a fixed form. Rather, I concentrate on the syntactic side of the analysis, to prove that enclitics and proclitics are not the same entity in northern Italian and that, therefore, SCI is not formed by moving the verb through the positions of proclitic SCLs and adjoining it to the left of the proclitic SCLs in turn. In other words, what is important here is not the morphological process that creates the sequence V + SCL but rather the syntactic properties of the complex form. Even though the form is created in the lexicon (or at a lower level in IP, as Hulk 1993 and Munaro 1997 assume), what interests us here is the path that the verb is forced to take when the complex form V + SCL is used.

I now discuss the arguments that exclude an analysis of enclitics as proclitics to which the verb has left-adjoined. This analysis is illustrated in (22):

(22)   [$_{CP}$ V + inv. SCL [$_{CP}$ V + deict. SCL [$_{NumP}$ V + numb. SCL [$_{PersP}$
        V + hear. SCL]]]]

Structure (22) represents the structure of the agreement field with the four types of SCLs. As has been shown in chapter 2, SCLs occupy four positions: two of them are located higher than NegP in the CP layer and two are in IP. If we assume that the enclisis process is due to left adjunction of the inflected verb to the SCL, we have to postulate that the verb moves through the SCL positions as in (22), adjoining to the left of each of the four SCLs and taking the SCL with it when it moves to a higher position inside the agreement field. A number of predictions follow from this hypothesis: first, if we consider enclitics and proclitics as the same entity, they would have to show the same morphology and the same person distinctions. Second, if enclisis is formed through head-to-head movement and left adjunction to the SCLs, we should find more than one enclitic on the verb. Third, the pro-drop conditions under which SCL occurs should be the same; this would mean that if a proclitic SCL in a given dialect is found with quasi arguments or expletives, its enclitic counterpart also has to be found with quasi arguments and expletives.

The second hypothesis (which could be extended to standard French, as we have seen above) considers the enclitic series as bound morphemes that appear on the verb when it reaches a syntactic position located higher than the usual position of the inflected verb. [7] The order V + SCL can be formed in the syntax through movement of the verb to a given F°, as originally proposed by Pollock (1989), or alternatively be formed already in the lexicon, provided the complex form checks the features of a given head in the syntax, as assumed by Chomsky (1995).

Following this line of reasoning, we would have to postulate a projection that is activated only when the inflected verb + SCL moves to it. If the verb does not move to this position, the bound morpheme cannot occur. The structure of such a sentence is the following:

(23)   [$_{CP}$ inv. SCL [$_{CP}$ deict. SCL [$_{AgrC}$ V$_i$ + SCL [$_{NumbP}$ t$_i$ [$_{PersP}$ t$_i$]]]]]

Here, the name AgrCP has been assigned to the projection that the complex form V + SCL has to reach because it has subject agreement features but is probably already located inside the CP domain, as discussed in the previous section. [8] The reason for using this term is determined by the fact that an agreement affix or morpheme, such as an enclitic, is connected to a CP projection, in the sense that the verb has to move to C when the agreement morpheme is there. This recalls the hypothesis, suggested by several authors (cf. chapter 4 for references on V2), that the feature in V2 languages that forces verb movement to C° is precisely that of agreement. Agreement in Comp phenomena have been studied by Haegeman (1993) and Shlonsky (1998), who include subject clitics inside the CP layer. Therefore, the term is extended to define the position that the inflected verb has to reach when it has the complex form V + SCL.[9]

On the basis of this hypothesis, enclitics differ from proclitics: enclitics form a single entity with the verb, which acquires a number of features that have to be checked in a position inside the CP layer. What interests us here is once again not so much the way in which the complex form is put together but its syntax, that is, the final position the form has to reach. As mentioned in the previous section, when the form V + SCL is used, the verb is forced to reach the CP layer for most of the dialects that have retained the form. For other dialects, such as the Romagnolo variety of Forlì, examined in (4), the form V + SCL does not require any special movement of the V + SCL form to the CP layer and may be used in all contexts, including embedded interrogatives and declarative clauses.

Let us examine the first hypothesis and attempt to keep the proclitic and the enclitic series together. At first glance, the hypothesis in (22) would appear to be quite plausible. A cross-linguistic argument shows the connection between proclitics and enclitics. Neutralization of person features occurs along the same pattern. It is noted in chapter 2 that first and fourth persons are always represented by the same SCL morpheme in NIDs, and the same is true even for enclitic SCLs: the two morphemes are identical.[10] Moreover, when observing the distribution of enclitic SCLs, it is possible to note that they follow the same pattern already reported by Renzi and Vanelli (1983) for proclitics; the most frequently realized persons are second and third singular.

Although these facts point in the direction of keeping proclitics and enclitics together, there are arguments that show that this might have been true in the past but is no longer the case in most modern varieties, as the proclitic and enclitic series are not identical either in form or in number (see Poletto 1998 for a detailed description of the diachronic path of enclitics). Hence, the structure in (22) is probably not correct for most northern Italian varieties. As has been frequently noted before, the structure that has to be assigned to SCI is an empirical question, which needs to be discussed for each variety. However, it is not possible to consider each dialect here; therefore, I present some general criteria that may help us to discriminate between the two hypotheses illustrated in (22) and (23) for a given dialect. A given dialect is defined as having changed from (22) to (23) if there are differences

1. In the form
2. In the number between proclitic and enclitic SCLs series
3. In the pro-drop conditions under which the SCL occurs
4. In the cooccurrence between a proclitic and an enclitic SCL

If a dialect presents some or all of these characteristics, it has to be analyzed as illustrated in (23), and (22) is excluded. Thus it is not possible to assume that (22) is the correct structure for SCI and that we have to resort to a structure like (23).

If proclitics and enclitics do not show any morphological difference and never co-occur, it may be plausible to assume that (22) is the correct structure for SCI, as it most probably was in the past. Morphological differences between the enclitic and the proclitic series that can be observed in many varieties are exemplified in (24):

(24	1	2	3	4	5	6
a.	a	a te	el/la	a	a	i/le
b.	ia	to	lo/la	ia	o	li/le

Example (24a) represents the proclitic series in the Veneto variety of Loreo, and (24b) represents the enclitic series. The two series are not identical in form. Only the third- and sixth-person feminine are the same; all other persons are different.

Differences in the number of SCLs realized in one series or the other are exemplified in (25):

(25)	1	2	3	4	5	6
a.	/	te	el/la	/	/	i/le
b.	i	to	lo/la	i	o	li/le

Example (25) represents the two series in Paduan: the proclitic series (25a) does not have a form for the first, fourth, and fifth, whereas the enclitic series (25b) has all six forms.

For other varieties, the pro-drop conditions that force the realization of a SCL differ with respect to the proclitic versus enclitic character of the SCL:

(26) a. Piove.   Montesover (Trentino)
           rains
           'It is raining'.

        b. Piove-l?
           rains-SCL
           'Is it raining?'

(27) a. Al plof.   Collina (Friulian)
           SCL rains
           'It rains'.

        b. Plof?
           rains?
           'Is it raining?'

For the Trentino dialect of Montesover, quasi arguments do not show any SCL in declarative clauses, and the SCL emerges in the enclitic series. The opposite is found in the Friulian dialect of Collina, in which it is the proclitic series that realizes a SCL with quasi-argumental subjects, whereas the enclitic series has no morpheme for quasi arguments. This is not expected if the two series are one and the same element.

Enclitic and proclitic SCLs co-occur in other varieties, as in (28):

(28) a. sok *a l* a-*lo* fait?   Rodoretto di Prali (Piedmontese-Provençal)
           what SCL has-SCL done?
           'What has he done?'

b. *la* baɲ-*la*?   Pra del Torno (Provençal)
   SCL rains-SCL?
   'Is it raining?'

If two elements co-occur, it is clear that they cannot be considered as one and the same entity. Cases like (28) might be a potential problem for our analysis of V to C in main interrogatives. However, the fact that a SCL occurs preverbally is not uncommon because object clitics also do the same, although it is clear that the verb is moving to a higher position (as mentioned earlier about the Monnese do-support case and the Fassano raising of the verb over a focus marker). Therefore, this problem is left open, as it implies an analysis of object clitics that cannot be given here. I limit myself only to pointing out that the problem could be solved by assuming that object clitics [and also SCLs in cases like (28)] may move to some very high position in the CP layer and that this position might be the same as that used in the Tobler-Mussafia phenomenon.

We can conclude that in the varieties that show the distinctions between proclitics and enclitics illustrated above, it is not possible to assume (22) as the structure for SCI, where the proclitic and the enclitic series are the same. The fact that the two series are not the same does not mean that SCI has to be treated as a purely morphological phenomenon of interrogative inflection. The hypothesis proposed here for the varieties that show the distinctions exemplified, from (24) to (28), considers SCI to be a lexical phenomenon that corresponds to syntactic movement to an AgrC position. The correct structure for these cases is (23), where the enclitic series is considered to be agreement morphemes that check their features in a projection located quite high in the structure, most probably within the CP domain. Thus, SCI may be analyzed in most dialects as a morphological signal for verb movement to a position within the CP domain, a position that we have called AgrC. As I assume an expanded CP structure, the next task is to locate the AgrC projection inside the CP layer more precisely. To do this, we first have to establish what the positions inside the CP layer are and, in particular, which of them is involved in main (and embedded) interrogative structures and can be filled by wh-items by the verb or by interrogative particles. In this chapter, I consider the interrogative structure. Chapter 5 takes into account data about several structures in which a subjunctive verb is used: counterfactuals, disjunctive, hypothetical, and suppletive imperatives.

3.3   VARIATION IN MAIN INTERROGATIVES

3.3.1   Introduction

In this section, I examine the structure of interrogative main clauses in a number of northern Italian dialects (NIDs), giving an account of the variation data from a split-CP perspective. The idea that there may be more than one CP projection (at least in certain constructions or certain languages) has been around for many years in terms of CP recursion. Here, it is assumed that the CP projections visible in the NIDs are not cases of CP recursion; rather, each CP has different syntactic properties that correlate with different interpretations of the elements inside the CPs.

The proposal I present here provides an answer to a question that was left open in chapter 2: why deictic SCLs interact with wh-elements. In the NIDs it is possible to identify up to four active C° heads in interrogative structures, each containing a different type of lexical head (a complementizer, the verb, a focus marker, a deictic clitic, etc.) which triggers a different interpretation of the question when it is activated. The structure I propose is the following:

(29) $[_{CP1}$ ch´ $[_{CP2}$ SCL $[_{CP3/AgrCP}$ SCI $[_{CP4}$ pa/ch/lo]]]]

As for the position of wh-items, these could be placed in the specifier positions of the complementizer and the deictic SCL, as well as that of the SCI position. However, I am assuming here that the doubly filled Comp filter is active in the CP domain and that it can be relaxed only in the cases of Spec-head agreement between the specifier and the head (see fn. 5). The mechanism of Spec-head agreement can be exploited only when the specifier and the head share the same features. It is plausible to assume that the deictic SCL does not have any interrogative features, as it only realizes certain subject features. On the other hand, it is also plausible to assume that the form verb + SCL has indeed some interrogative or maybe operator feature,[11] as its occurrence is restricted to structures in which there is an operator.

It is not clear whether the complementizer has interrogative features or not. If the criterion we use to postulate that Spec-head agreement is possible is purely morphological, the complementizer cannot undergo a process of Spec-head with the wh-item because it does not show any specialized form for interrogative sentences in the majority of the dialects examined here. If we assume that the interrogative features may also be abstract, the complementizer will be able to undergo the process of Spec-head with a wh-item. The discussion that follows leaves this question open, as it is irrelevant for the analysis being proposed in this section. I come back to it in section 3.5. For the sake of concreteness, I represent the structures with Spec-head agreement between the complementizer and the wh-item:

(30) $[_{CP}$ wh $[_{CP}$ ch´ $[_{CP}$ wh $[_{CP}$ SCL $[_{AgrCP}$ wh V+SCL $[_{CP}$ pa/ch/lo]]]]]]

Here, I attempt to prove that we need several CPs because there are four distinct heads filled by different elements (section 3.3.3.), and moreover, we need several specifiers where the wh-items move, depending on their interpretation. We see that some CPs specialize for a particular interpretation, whereas the SCI projection (AgrC) is interpreted as a true request of information, which I will refer to as "out-of-the-blue interrogative" (but see section 3.4).

3.3.2   An Overview of Dialectal Variation

Among the varieties examined here, there is variation in the structures used to express main interrogatives. The first type of interrogative sentence I present is found in Ligurian and Lombard varieties:

(31)   a.   Unde i van?   Caserta Ligure (Ligurian)
             where they go?
             'Where are they going?'

    b. Dund i van?   Alassio (Ligurian)
       where they go?
       'Where are they going?'

    c. Se fan?   Milano (Lombad)
       what do?
       'What are they doing?'

    d. In duè ta veet?   Vaprio d'Adda (Lombard)
       where you go?
       'Where are you going?'

Here, there is no apparent variation with respect to declarative clauses because the SCL occurs in a preverbal position and no complementizer surfaces. The only indication that this is an interrogative sentence is the presence of the wh-item in SpecC for wh-questions and rising intonation in yes/no questions. It is not possible to insert a DP subject between the wh-item and the SCL, and this could be taken as an indication of the fact that the verb is indeed moving to C°, even though SCI is not present:

(32) a. *Unde Mario (l) va?   Caserta Ligure
          where Mario (SCL) goes?
          'Where is M: going?'

      b. *Dund Mario (l) va?   Alassio
          where Mario (SCL) goes?

      c. *Se la Maria (la) fa?   Milano
          what the Mary (SCL) does?
          'What is M. doing?'

      d. *In duè la Maria (la) va?   Vaprio d'Adda
          where the Mary (SCL) goes?
          'Where is M. going?'

However, it will be shown in chapter 6 that the subject position for DPs is higher than wh-elements and that this is why the sequence wh-subject DP is excluded.

Therefore, dialects like Milanese do not provide any overt evidence that the verb is moving to C or that interrogative sentences have a particular syntax apart from wh-movement. Thus, it would be plausible to admit that in Milanese only one CP projection is activated, and it hosts the wh-item in its specifier position and no overt morpheme in the C° position.

The structure of several dialects that display simple SCI also require a single CP, as already discussed. Most of these exhibit main/embedded asymmetry and the possibility of using inversion in other structures in which V to C applies:

(33) Cossa fa-lo?   Padua (Central Veneto)
      what does-he?
      'What is he doing?'

This structure has been discussed in detail in section 3.2 and constitutes the most conservative type of structure in the NIDs.

Another very common structure is similar to embedded interrogatives, in which a complementizer follows the wh-item and a proclitic SCL appears before the verb:

(34)   Cossa che te fa?   Portogruaro (Veneto-Friulian)
        what that you do?
        'What are you doing?'

This is an innovation found only in those dialects that also have the same phenomenon in embedded contexts; as shown in Poletto and Vanelli (1994), a sentence like (34) is possible only in dialects in which an overt complementizer is realized in embedded questions (see section 3.5 on embedded questions).

This structure may be used as an out-of-the-blue interrogative, as in the variety exemplified in (34), or (in other varieties) it may have a particular interpretation that is discussed in section 3.3.4. Sentences like (34) can still be analyzed as having a single CP projection, as they differ from structures like (32) and (33) only in the realization of the $C°$ head, which is not overtly realized in (32) and occupied by the inflected verb in (33).

Another possible structure has already been presented in the previous section to show verb movement in SCI contexts. This is a structure in which a particle appears to the right of the V + SCL complex in the sentence. The conditions under which the particle (*pa*) may occur vary across dialects. In some varieties, *pa* is obligatory in the case of an out-of-the-blue interpretation, as in Gardenese (a V2 Rhaetoromance dialect) for both yes/no and wh-questions. If the particle is absent, the interpretation is that of a rethorical question, or the question is interpreted as a request for more information (see below):

(35)   a. Ciuldì ciant-el (pa)?   Selva di Val Gardena (Rhaetoromance)
           why sings-he interr. marker?
           'Why is he singing?'

        b. Ciant-el (pa)?
           sings-he interr. marker?
           'Is he singing?'

For other varieties, such as Badiotto, *pa* is obligatory only for wh-questions in order to achieve the out-of-the-blue interpretation:

(36)   a. Ula vas-t (pa)?   S. Leonardo di Badia (Rhaetoromance)
           where go-you pa?
           'Where are you going?'

        b. Vas-t (pa) a Venezia?
           go-you (pa) to Venice?
           'Are you going to Venice?'

In wh-questions, an out-of-the-blue interrogative requires the presence of *pa* and its absence triggers a rhetorical interpretation, whose exact meaning is discussed in section 3.3.4. In yes/no questions, the opposite is true; the presence of *pa* makes the question rhetorical and its absence corresponds to an out-of-the-blue question. In other varieties, such as the Fassano dialect considered in section

3.2, *pa* always makes the sentence a rhetorical question for both wh- and yes/no questions.[12]

(37) a. Vasto (pa)?   Pera di Fassa
         go-you interr. marker?
         'Are you going or not?'

      b. Che asto (pa) fat?
         what have-you interr. marker done?
         'What (on earth) have you done?'

As we have seen, SCI corresponds to verb movement to a given position. We therefore need to postulate two positions: one in which SCI applies and one for the marker *pa*. Both positions are activated in main interrogative sentences in Rhaetoromance dialects. This type of structure supports the idea of splitting the CP projection into several FPs, as two distinct interrogative strategies are adopted (SCI and the occurrence of the particle *pa*). In section 3.4, I analyze the semantic contribution of this particle to wh- and yes/no questions in Fassano, Gardenese, and Badiotto, the three Rhaetoromance dialects considered above, arguing that the particle marks different values of a Focus position for different dialects. On the basis of the evidence described in section 3.2, *pa* is presumably a CP element and precisely the specifier of a low CP position, which can also be occupied by the complementizer (which alternates with the particle, as the doubly filled Comp filter prohibits simultaneous occupation of both the specifier and the head of the same projection if they do not undergo a Spec-head agreement process). The structure of sentences like (35)–(37) is as follows:

(38) [$_{AgrCP}$ wh [$_{AgrC°}$ V + SCL] [$_{CP}$ pa]]]

In section 3.2, I attribute the name AgrC to the projection that the form V + SCL has to reach in order to check its features because of the similarity between the complex form V + SCL, which is used only when an operator occupies a SpecC position, and the phenomena of "agreement in Comp" connected to V2 in the Germanic languages. I do not pursue this comparison any further here, as it implies an analysis of the relation between subject and topic, which is beyond the scope of this work.

Rhaetoromance data provide evidence that more than one projection is activated in main interrogative clauses. Other dialects also show that this claim is correct, and they reveal the structural makeup of another part of the CP layer. Friulian and Emilian dialects show an interesting sequence of proclitic and enclitic SCLs:

(39) a. Quant a van-u a Pordenon?   S. Michele al T. (Friulian)
         when a go-they to P.?
         'When are they going to P.?'

      b. Ks a fen-i?   Bologna (Emilian)
         what a do + they?
         'What are they doing?'

      c. A vag-ia anca mi?   Bondeno (Emilian)
         a go + I also me?
         'Shall I go too?'

    d. Parchè a magna-t an pom?   Guastalla (Emilian)
       why a eat-you an apple?
       'Why are you eating an apple?'

    e. A magnom-ia l pom?   Guastalla
       a eat-we the apple?
       'Are we going to eat the apple?'

    f. Chi an vo-t mia vedar?   Guastalla
       who a not want-you not see?
       'Who don't you want to see?'

In some Friulian dialects (the variety examined here is the one spoken in S. Michele al Tagliamento), a deictic SCL appears in front of the verb and an enclitic follows it. The presence versus the absence of the proclitic deictic SCL depends on the wh-item, as we see in section 3.3.5. Some wh-items require the presence of the deictic clitics [as in (39)], whereas others are incompatible [cf. (40)]. With a third group of wh-items, the deictic clitic is optional, though its presence changes the meaning of the sentence, as illustrated in (41). I merely record the examples here; they are interpreted in section 3.3.5.:

(40) a. *Do a van-u?   S. Michele al T.
      where a go + they?
      'Where are they going?'

    b. *Se a fan-u?
      what a do + they?
      'What are they doing?'

    c. *Quant i mangi-tu?
      how much i eat + you?
      'How much do you eat?'

(41) a. Quant *(i) mangi-tu?   S. Michele al T.
      when i eat + you?
      'When are you going to eat?'

    b. Quantis caramelis *(i) a-tu mangiat?
      how many sweets i have + you eaten?
      'How many sweets did you eat?'

(42) a. Dulà a van-u?   S. Michele al T.
      where SCL go + they?
      'Where are they going?'

    b. Dulà van-u?
      where SCL go + they?
      'Where are they going?'

    c. Coma i a-tu fat il compit?
      how have + you done the task?

    d. Coma a-tu fat il compit?
      how SCL have + you done the task?
      'How did you do the task?'

In chapter 2, it is assumed that deictic SCLs occur in the CP domain because they cluster with the complementizer in declarative clauses (see chapter 2 for an analysis of the coalescence of the complementizer with deictic and invariable SCLs). In section 3.2, I discuss a number of arguments for the idea that the form V + SCL has to check its features in the CP domain in a position located higher than the particle *pa*. Therefore, the structure of sentences (39)–(42) is the following:

(43) $[_{CP}$ wh $[_{C^\circ}][_{CP}[_{C^\circ}$ SCL $[_{AgrCP}[_{AgrC^\circ}$ V + SCL$]]]]]$

As mentioned, the doubly filled Comp filter prohibits the presence of a wh-item in the SpecC position where the SCL occurs. Therefore the wh-item must occur in a higher SpecC position with an empty head.

Another interesting structure that is more rarely found across the domain considered here is the following:

(44) a. Cossa ch'a l'a-lo fait?   Turin (Piedmontese)
         what that s.c has + he done?
         'What has he done?'

This sentence is not accepted by all speakers, who consider it old-fashioned. Nevertheless, it exists. At first sight, this structure appears quite surprising, given the analysis of SCI as V to C movement. As SCI co-occurs with a complementizer, one might well argue that the analysis is wrong and that SCI does not correspond to V to C movement but, in the best case to V, to some very high IP position or that it is simply a case of interrogative inflection, in which the verb does not move further than in declarative clauses.

Some data that might help us view the situation for Piedmontese are presented here:

(45) A venta che gnun ch'a fasa bordel.   Turin (Piedmontese)
         SCL needs that nobody that + cl do + subjunctive noise
         'It is necessary that everybody be quiet'.

(46) A venta che Majo ch'a mangia pi' tant.
         SCL need that Majo that cl eat more
         'It is necessary that M. eats more'.

These examples are discussed and analyzed in chapter 6, referring to subject positions. For now, I only point out that there are two complementizers in the embedded declarative clause. It appears that this Piedmontese variety has a complex CP structure that is also overt in embedded declaratives. Therefore the structure of examples (44) and (46) is the following:

(47) $[_{CP}$ ch $[_{CP}$ deictic SCL $[_{AgrCP}$ SCI $[_{IP}]]]]$

A higher complementizer occurs both in embedded clauses and in main interrogative clauses; the lower position is occupied by the complementizer in embedded declaratives and by the complex form V + SCL in main interrogatives. I conclude that the data in (44) show that SCI occurs in a low CP, which is the same as that usually found in embedded declarative clauses. Kayne's (1975) intuition that SCI does not target the same position realized by the higher complementizer in declarative clauses is maintained; nevertheless, SCI still targets a C° position and not an I° head.

Another structure found in the sample corresponds to a cleft sentence, which is a widespread phenomenon throughout the whole northern Italian domain. It is possible in all varieties with the same semantics as it has in standard Italian, where it is used to single out a member of a set of already known objects or as a request for repeating what had been said before. In certain dialects it has been extended and is now a substitute for out-of-the-blue interrogatives (this is especially true in the Lombard area, even in embedded contexts):

(48) a. Ch el c a fiv adess?   Albosaggia (Alpine Lombard)
         what is-it that SCL do now?
         'What are you doing now?'

      b. Al so ca chi c a l'è c a l'è ruat.
         SCL know not who that SCL SCL is that SCL SCL is come
         'I do not know who has come'.

The phenomenon of clefting is very frequent in main interrogatives when the wh-item is the subject. This is due to a peculiarity of the subject, as is seen in chapter 6.

From the set of possible structures described in this section, it is clear that main interrogative structures present quite a wide spectrum of variation. However, this is not the case for embedded interrogatives, which present a very limited set of possible variations (as we see in section 3.5). This is an interesting fact per se, which will be given a principled explanation in section 3.5. Let us now attempt to assign a structure to all these interrogative sentences and make some sense out of the variations found within the domain.

3.3.3 The C° Heads

The first three structures examined can be accounted for by postulating a single CP projection. They are repeated here as (32):

(49) a. Unde i van?   Caserta Ligure (Ligurian)
         where SCL go?
         'Where are they going?'

      b. Cossa fa-lo?   Cereda (Central Veneto)
         what does-he?
         'What is he doing?'

      c. Cossa che te fa?   Portogruaro (Veneto-Friulian)
         what that you do?
         'What are you doing?'

SCI has already been analyzed in section 3.2 as a movement of the verb to an AgrC projection for those varieties in which it obeys the criteria we have formulated. The interpretation of structures like those in (49) does not require splitting the CP projection; one may simply state that a null morpheme, the complementizer, or the inflected verb occupy the C° position. In (49c) there is no SCI, and the SCL appears to the left of the verb, as in declarative sentences. In the varieties presenting this structure, it is not possible to have a complementizer-SCI combination (which is only possible in certain Piedmontese varieties). Hence, for dialects like Milanese, Portogruarese, and Paduan we can adopt a structure in which only a single projection is activated, and it is occupied by the verb + SCL in one variety and by a complementizer (which can be null or phonetically realized) in the other. In those dialects in which only a complementizer appears and no SCI is possible, we can assume that SCI is blocked by the presence of the complementizer, which occupies the position where the verb should be when SCI occurs. An alternative analysis could be stated in terms of the head movement constraint: although the complementizer is not on the same head where SCI occurs, but is lower than SCI, it blocks SCI all the same because it prevents the verb from moving head to head to the SCI position. Hence, the complementizer position can be either the same as SCI or lower. A higher position would not be possible, as in this case we would find the combination of a complementizer followed by SCI. The two possible structures needed to explain the ungrammaticality of the sequence complementizer-SCI in the dialects in which it is excluded are the following:

(50)   a. $[_{CP}$ SCI/ch $[_{IP}$]]

       b. $[_{AgrCP}$ SCI $[_{CP2}$ ch $[_{IP}$]]]

In (50a) the complementizer and SCI occur in the same C° head and alternate for this reason. In (50b) the complementizer occurs in a C° head located lower than SCI, and this blocks verb movement to AgrC° because it must go through C2°, which is already filled by *ch*. I claim that (50b) is the correct structure on the basis of Fassano data (see below).

I now discuss the possibility of the existence of a CP projection lower than AgrC for dialects like Portogruarese [cf. (43c)]. There is an interesting piece of evidence that may help us to distinguish between the two possibilities illustrated in (50). We need to decide whether SCI and the complementizer that blocks SCI occur in the same position or if the complementizer is located below SCI in a head position, blocking the movement of the verb to the SCI position. Let us turn to the case of Rhaetoromance *pa* that we have already discussed. In section 3.2, I used data from the Rhaetoromance variety of Pera di Fassa to show that SCI is indeed a case of verb movement. I have shown that in interrogative sentences *pa* is indeed located in the CP domain, as it alternates with a complementizer. Since *pa* (and therefore the complementizer) is located lower than the position in which the form V + SCL checks its features, a structure like the one in (50b) becomes more attractive. Nevertheless, both options (50a) and (50b) remain open. If the phenomenon observed in note 9 is really a case of an agreeing complementizer, as it appears to be, we have one more argument to show that SCI is higher than the lowest CP, as SCI occurs in the AgrCP projection.

Other dialects reveal the necessity of splitting the CP projection activated in interrogative sentences, as exemplified in (39) by Friulian and Emilian data. In these examples the wh-item is followed by a deictic SCL, which is in turn followed by SCI. As deictic SCLs are autonomous heads, as shown in chapter 2, we cannot collapse the sequence deictic clitic + V + SCL into a single C° position.

The structure I propose for these examples is the following:

(51)   [$_{CP}$ wh [$_{C°}$][$_{CP}$ [$_{C°}$ deictic SCL [$_{AgrCP}$ [$_{AgrC°}$ V + SCL]]]]]

The third type of dialect I have examined is Piedmontese. The structure I assume for the Piedmontese dialects illustrated in (44)–(46) is the following:

(52)   [$_{CP}$ wh [$_{C°}$] [$_{CP}$ [$_{C°}$ ch] [$_{CP}$ [$_{C°}$ SCL] [$_{AgrCP}$ SCI]]]]

Because deictic SCLs can occur without the complementizer, we cannot assume that the complementizer and the deictic clitic can be merged into the same head. In other words, deictic clitics cannot be collapsed either with SCI or with a complementizer; they occur as independent heads, as shown for declarative sentences in chapter 2. Therefore, a structure like (52) is the most plausible analysis of examples like (44).

This means that certain varieties activate three head positions in interrogative sentences, as in (52); others activate two of them, as in (51); and still others might activate possibly one or two projections, as in (50). Thus, the variation data within the northern Italian domain show that at least three projections may be activated in interrogative sentences inside the same sentence, the highest C° containing a complementizer, a lower C° containing a deictic clitic, and an agreement projection inside the CP layer, namely, AgrC.

Some interesting facts about Franco-Provençal varieties might also be interpreted as evidence that SCI inversion is located higher than another projection related to main interrogatives, occurring only in main interrogatives, as I have proposed here. The data come from Ronjat (1937: 624). He reports that in certain Franco-Provençal dialects, SCI is separated from the verb by an interrogative morpheme *lo*, which is invariable for all persons:

(53)   a. Ven-lo-li?   Morgeux
          come-interr marker-he
          'Are they coming?'

       b. Ven-lo-lou?
          come-interr marker she?
          'Is she coming?'

It might be plausible at first sight to connect this interrogative marker to the spoken French *ti*, which is used as an interrogative marker (see Roberts 1993c for a detailed analysis of *ti*). However, the French *ti* is not followed by an enclitic, whereas Franco-Provençal is. Because we want to maintain sentence structure as a constant, at least for those dialects that are very similar in all their grammatical components (not only in syntactic terms), it is plausible to locate the Franco-Provençal *lo* in the same projection in which the Fassano *pa* is located, that is, lower than SCI. The comparison with Fassano *pa* is attractive: *lo* may be interpreted as a bound morpheme to which the verb adjoins when it moves to the SCI position, hence as the X° counterpart of *pa*. Therefore, we obtain the order V-lo-SCI, which reflects the layering of the functional projections in the reverse order.

Cases like (53) can also be analyzed in a different manner (cf. Hulk 1993); the interrogative morpheme *lo* occurs in the head of T°, which is marked with the [+wh] feature and then moves higher. By connecting the evidence for the CP structure that we have obtained from the various dialects, we get a complex structure of the CP projections involved in main interrogative sentences:

(54) $[_{C1}$ ch $[_{C2}$ deictic SCL $[_{AgrC3}$ SCI $[_{CP4}$ [$_{SPECC4}$ pa] $[_{C°4}$ ch/lo]]]]]

As illustrated in (54), interrogative sentences can make use of four CP projections. Certain dialects mark only AGRCP with a phonologically overt element and have a structure with a wh-item followed by SCI, as in many Veneto varieties.

Other dialects make only CP4 phonologically visible and have the wh-item followed by a complementizer and no SCI (as the complementizer acts as a barrier to verb movement). This is the case in Portogruarese and Fassano. Fassano has another possibility: it can fill the CP4 projection with a specifier, and in this case we obtain SCI, as there is no restriction to the movement of the inflected verb to the SCI projection. Therefore, Fassano sentences, which show SCI and *pa* overtly, mark two CP projections, AGRCP and CP4.

Other dialects such as certain Piedmontese varieties mark CP1, occupied by a complementizer; CP2, occupied by the deictic clitic *a*; and AGRCP, where SCI occurs. Other dialects, such as Friulian and Emilian, mark CP2 and AGRCP, and we observe a deictic clitic followed by SCI. At this point, one could ask whether we really need this complex structure or if there are other possible explanations for the variation examined here. In this section, I have attempted to show that we need four CPs on the basis of the morphemes that occupy the head positions of the four projections. A complex structure like (54) not only is necessary to account for dialectal variation in interrogative sentences but also can be exploited to capture some interesting interpretative differences (presented in the next section) and different properties of wh-items (discussed in section 3.3.5).

3.3.4   Interpretative Differences

In this section, I present evidence that shows that the activation of different heads is reflected in the interpretation of the interrogative sentence. Let us start from CP4, the lowest projection. This encodes the feature that corresponds to what is defined in pragmatic studies as rhetorical interpretation. This interpretation does not require a true answer but simply expresses the point of view of the speaker; it is often used to convey the meaning of a reproach, an order, or the disappointment of the speaker to an action of the hearer. As we have seen, this projection is occupied by the particle *pa,* which marks different values of the head, depending on the dialect. The Fassano interrogative marker *pa* is used to mark the value of a rhetorical question.[13] The difference between (55a) and (55b) is that in (55b) the speaker knows that the hearer has no intention to go anywhere, and intends to stay where he or she is, or that there is no place to go.[14]

(55) a. Olà vas-to?   Pera di Fassa
          where go-you?
          'Where are you going?'

      b. Olà vas-to pa?
          where go-you pa?
          'Where are you going?'

In Badiotto, the use of *pa* in wh-interrogatives is simply reversed: the presence of *pa* in wh-questions triggers an out-of-the-blue interpretation, hence a true request for information, as in (56), and its absence conveys the rhetorical interpretation. In fact, when *pa* is absent, the wh-item is strongly focalized. Badiotto is thus similar to Fassano in the sense that the occurrence of the particle encodes the rhetorical interpretation, but with the opposite value.

(56) Ulà t'a-i pa ody?   S. Leonardo di Badia
      where you have-they pa seen?
      'Where did they see you?'

(57) ULA' t'a-i ody?
      where you have-they seen?
      'Where did they see you?'

In wh-questions, *pa* is present when the whole sentence has focus, whereas another constituent receives focus when *pa* is absent. If it is the wh-item, the sentence is interpreted as rhetorical.

To give a more precise analysis of this particle, I now consider its distribution in Badiotto. *Pa* does not occur only in interrogative clauses in Badiotto; it also occurs in affirmative and negative sentences, in exclamative and imperative clauses:

(58) a. Al è pa bun!   S. Leonardo di Badia
          SCL is particle good
          'It IS good!'

      b. A n è pa bun!
          SCL not is particle good
          'It ISN'T good!'

      c. Ci bel ca l'e pa!
          how nice that SCL is particle
          'How nice it is!'

      d. Faal pa!
          Do-it particle!
          'Do it!'

Although *pa* comes after the verb in affirmative and negative clauses, it can still be considered CP element because Badiotto is a V2 dialect, as is shown in chapter 4. The same is true for exclamative contexts, which use a higher CP projection than left dislocation (cf. Benincà 1996 and chapter 6). *Pa* also occurs in a low CP in imperative clauses, as it is incompatible with a complementizer in suppletive imperatives (see section 3.2). As for the semantic contribution of this particle to the meaning of the sentence, it is not easy to find a common semantics among the sentences in (58). In (58a)–(58c) it appears that *pa* introduces a presupposition that is confirmed by the use of the particle. However, it is not easy to see the presupposition it introduces in (58d), which is perceived by the speaker as a "strong order." In Poletto and Zanuttini (1998) it has been proposed that *pa* is a focus marker: the presupposition induced in (58a)–(58c) is a side effect of this. Being a focus marker, it can occur in all types of clauses—in affirmative and negative clauses and in exclamatives and imperatives. In wh-questions, it is necessary to get an out-of-the-blue interpretation. If *pa* is not there, the focus conditions change and the wh-item has contrastive stress, triggering the rhetorical interpretation. The contrast between Fassano,[15] on the one hand, and Badiotto and Gardenese, on the other, is interesting because it shows that the way in which the lowest CP projection we have found in main interrogative sentences is marked as visible (or active) is not unique, not even in very similar languages (as Rhaetoromance dialects are).[16] In Badiotto, *pa* is a focus marker, expressing the pattern of an out-of-the-blue interrogative, whereas in Fassano it signals a rhetorical interpretation. In Fassano, *pa* is used when the wh-item is contrastively stressed, and this triggers the rhetorical interpretation.

Rhaetoromance varieties show that there is dialectal variation in the use of the morpheme that realizes the value of the lowest CP, namely, the one we can now call FocusP. In some dialects, this CP is marked by the particle *pa*. In other dialects, *pa* signals that only the wh is focalized, and this conveys the rhetorical interpretation of the interrogative clause, whereas the out-of-the-blue interpretation does not require any special morpheme. However, the fact that different dialects mark the same type of interpretation, activating the same CP projection, is an argument in favor of the idea that each CP projection is connected to a semantic type of question and that what varies is the way in which CP4 is marked in order to get the relevant interpretation.

Other varieties show that the same low CP projection is the position where the rhetorical interpretation is encoded; in varieties like Portogruarese, this CP contains a complementizer and is activated to mark "true" questions, that is, a request for information without involving any presupposition:

(59)   a. Cossa che te fa?   Portogruaro (Veneto-Friulian)
        what that you do?
        'What are you doing?'

       b. COSSA te fa?
        WHAT you do?
        'What on earth are you doing?'

Example (59a) represents an out-of-the-blue interrogative, and (59b) represents a rhetorical question. The speaker utters a question like this when he or she sees the hearer doing something that the hearer already knows he or she should not do, exactly the same context we have described above for Rhaetoromance. From a pragmatic point of view, this is not a true question because it is not a request for information. Instead, it signals the fact that the hearer is doing something prohibited and should stop it.

It is interesting to note that other Veneto dialects use this structural opposition to distinguish rhetorical from out-of-the-blue interrogatives, though exactly in the opposite way:

(60)   a. (Ou) Coss' che ti fa?   Venice
          (Hey!), what that you do?
          'What on earth are you doing?'

       b. Coss ti fa?
          what you do?
          'What are you doing?'

Example (60a) is a rhetorical question (notice the presence of the complementizer), as indicated by the particle at the beginning of the clause, and (60b) is an out-of-the-blue question. The difference between Portogruarese and Venetian is thus the following: in Portogruarese the complementizer is obligatory in an out-of-the-blue question, whereas in other Veneto dialects its presence triggers a rhetorical interpretation. Here, we find the same distinction that has already been noted in Rhaetoromance dialects: in one dialect an overt element marks the rhetorical interpretation, and in another it marks the out-of-the-blue interpretation. It is not clear whether zero has to be interpreted here as a totally empty head or as a zero morpheme located in the C°. As I do not have any evidence to decide whether a null element occupies this C° head when the complementizer does not appear, I leave this question open. From this discussion, it clearly emerges that the lowest CP is the position where the [+/–rhetorical] interpretation is encoded. Moreover, dialects differ in the morpheme that marks the opposition.

Let us now examine the AgrCP projection that contains SCI in the dialects in which it is instantiated:

(61)   Cossa fa-lo?   Cereda
       what does-he
       'What is he doing?'

This structure is generally connected with an out-of-the-blue interpretation and does not encode any particular meaning in the dialects of the sample.[17] In some varieties it may sound old-fashioned or is uttered only by older speakers; younger generations use an alternative structure, though it does not convey any other presuppositional or modal meaning. Hence, AgrCP can be assumed to be the default interrogative interpretation, as it always corresponds to a true request for information. The fact that AgrC is the only projection that is never used to mark any special or additional character to the true request for information is interesting and is discussed in section 3.4.

If SCI is associated with a deictic SCL, as in Friulian, the interpretation is one of surprise. In Friulian, this structure is associated with what has been defined by informants as surprise at the action performed by the hearer. Here, the speaker is asking for more information. Therefore, this is not a rhetorical question, such as the ones examined in Rhaetoromance and Veneto dialects and that do not require an answer; this corresponds to another interpretation. Example (62) illustrates the point:

(62)   a. Mangi-tu un milus?   S. Michele al T. (Friulian)
            eat + you an apple?
            'Are you eating an apple?'

     b. I mangi-tu un milus?
       SCL eat-you an apple?
       'Are you eating an apple!?'

In (62a), the speaker is simply asking whether the hearer would like to have an apple. In (62b), the speaker notes that the hearer is already eating an apple and is asking why he is doing so (as it is already lunchtime, for instance). There is no sense of reproach or disappointment in this case. The contrast that we have already noted between Fassano and Badiotto and between Portogruarese and Venetian can also be found for this type of question.

    In some Emilian varieties, such as in Piacentino, sentences like (63), which correspond directly to (62b), are used in out-of-the-blue questions.[18]

(63)   A mangium-ia l pom?   Piacenza (Emilian)
      SCL eat-we the apple?
      'Are we going to eat the apple?'

In the variety of Guastalla, this structure is used in out-of-the-blue questions both in yes/no questions and in wh-questions:[19]

(64)   a. A gin-v da gnuatar?   Guastalla (Emilian)
       SCL come-you to us?
       'Are you coming to us?'

     b. Parchè a magna-t an pom?
       why SCL eat-you an apple?
       'Why are you eating an apple?'

     c. Indu a va-i?
       where SCL go-they?
       'Where are they going?'

Again, we find that the filling of one and the same projection can give rise to either an out-of-the-blue question, as in some Emilian dialects, or a particular interpretation, namely, a request for additional information, in Friulian dialects. There is another variety in which surprise is expressed in a question with an additional morpheme—Fiorentino:

(65)   a. O 'ndo tu vai?   Florence
       particle where you go?
       'Where are you going'

     b. O che vieni?
       O that come?
       'Are you coming?'

This *o* morpheme is perceived by the speakers as the same as that found in vocatives. Note that there is no SCI in this case, but the Fiorentino dialect spoken in town has lost inversion in all interrogative structures, not only in interrogatives with this particular meaning.[20] The very fact that *o* precedes wh-words located in SpecC indicates that more than one projection is activated by interrogative sentences; this is an interesting fact that, for our theory of the CP field and the way in which wh-features are instantiated and checked in the syntax, presents a problem, which is discussed in section 3.4, with respect to Rizzi's (1991) proposal of the wh-criterion.

The last type of structure that has a distinct interpretation is the "modal" question type. In standard Italian, this type of question is expressed by a future tense:

(66)   a. Cosa avrà fatto, in quella situazione così disperata?
         what will-have done, in that situation so desperate?
         'What could he have done in such a situation?'

       b. Gli avrà parlato?
          to-him will-have spoken?
          'Will he have spoken to him?'

Here the speaker is wondering what somebody will be doing or what somebody might have done on a certain occasion. I define this type of structure as modal because it conveys a modal meaning of possibility and can be translated with a modal verb, as in the example above, or in a better way, as "I am wondering what he might have done." In the eastern dialects this type of interrogative sentence is expressed by a subjunctive verb. This is not possible in standard Italian and in the western dialects examined in this work.

(67)   a. Se ch a l vedi fat?   S. Michele al Tagliamento (Friulian)
          what that SCL SCL have + subjunctive done?
          'What might he have done?'

       b. Cossa che el gabia fato?   Venice
          what that SCL have + subjunctive done?
          'What might he have done?'

What is interesting here is the fact that in Friulian, in which deictic SCLs are realized, the wh-item is followed by a complementizer, which is followed by a deictic SCL:

(68) $[_{C1}$ ch_j+a_i $[_{C2}$ t_{j+i} $[_{AgrC3}$ t_j $[_{CP4}$ $[_{C°4}$ $t_j]]]]]$

In (68), the complementizer moves from the lowest C° position in which it is merged to the position of the deictic SCL and adjoins to it (see the analysis in chapter 2). Then the complex complementizer + deicticSCL moves one step further to the next head, as in the structures we have examined for Piedmontese data.[21] In these examples, the wh-item climbs up to SpecCP1 or even to a higher specifier because the doubly filled Comp filter prohibits the filling of both the specifier and the head of a projection by nonagreeing elements.[22]

We have seen that in some Piedmontese dialects it is possible to activate CP1 with an out-of-the-blue interpretation [cf. (44), section 3.3.3], whereas CP1 is activated in Friulian and Veneto, yielding a modal interpretation. Note, however, that in Piedmontese the verb is inflected in its indicative form, whereas in Friulian and Veneto it is a subjunctive. It is plausible to assume that when the [+modal] value is selected, the verb must agree with it and be inflected in a form that expresses the [+modal] feature as subjunctive or (as in standard Italian), as future, or it can be expressed by a modal verb, as is the case for English.

Therefore, CP1, CP2, and CP4 can be occupied by some phonetically visible elements and mark an "out-of-the-blue" question or give a particular sentence interpretation, whereas AGRCP is used only in out-of-the-blue questions when no other projections are activated.[23] Every projection is thus associated with a different interpretation of the interrogative sentence; the lowest CP conveys the meaning of a rhetorical question, the CP containing a deictic SCL is a request for more information, and CP1 corresponds to a modal interpretation. The fact that each projection corresponds to a different semantic interpretation strengthens our analysis that splits the CP space where interrogative features are checked in four distinct positions.

3.3.5   Different SpecCs for Different Wh-elements

Here, I have proposed the hypothesis that dialectal variation may be accounted for by splitting the interrogative CP into four distinct projections. Each of these projections can have a lexically filled head. We have seen that the lowest CP can also be filled by a specifier, represented in Rhaetoromance varieties by the interrogative marker *pa*. But what can be said about wh-items? They could occupy the specifier position of the highest CP or different Spec positions, depending on the interpretation of the sentence or the dialect. Most of the data we examined in previous sections consistently show the wh-item as the leftmost element of the sentence. This would lead us to the assumption that wh-items always climb at least as high as SpecC1 or even higher, if we assume that the complementizer and wh-items did not undergo a Spec-head agreement process and therefore cannot occupy the head and the specifier of the same projection. A clear case in which the wh-item occupies a lower position (probably lower than CP2 if we assume that the morpheme *o* occurs in CP2) is that of the Fiorentino surprise interrogatives examined in the previous section:

(69)   O 'ndo tu vai?   Florence
        particle where SCL go?
        'Where are you going?'

If the interrogative morpheme *o* that expresses surprise is located in CP2, the wh-item can be located only in SpecAGRCP or SpecCP4. It is not clear exactly which of the two specifiers is occupied by the interrogative morpheme since Florentine has lost SCI and verb raising is not immediately visible. Therefore, we do not have any way of deducing the location of the wh-item (SpecAgrC or SpecC4) from the position of the verb. One could assume that the loss of the inversion morpheme corresponds to the loss of verb movement to AgrC, but there are many well-known cases of verb movement without morphology (cf. Roberts's 1993c analysis of the loss of V to I movement in English in these terms).

Friulian data are more revealing, as they show that the position of wh-items can vary, depending on the type of wh-item and the interpretation. As mentioned earlier, certain Friulian wh-items are compatible with a deictic clitic, and the presence of the clitic influences the interpretation of the sentence (see section 3.3.5).

(70)   a. Dulà a van-u?   S. Michele al Tagliamento (Friulian)
          where SCL go + they?
          'Where are they going?'

       b. Dulà van-u?
          where SCL go + they?
          'Where are they going?'

       c. Coma i a-tu fat il compit?
          how SCL have + you done the task?

       d. Coma a-tu fat il compit?
          how have + you done the task?
          'How did you do the task?'

Other wh-elements are totally incompatible with a deictic clitic, as already noted in section 3.2:

(71)   a. *Do a van-u?   S. Michele al T.
           where SCL go + they?
          'Where are they going?'

       b. *Se a fan-u?
          what SCL do + they?
          'What are they doing?'

       c. *Quant i mangi-tu?
          how much SCL eat + you?
          'How much do you eat?'

   A third class of wh-elements requires the presence of the deictic clitic; otherwise, the sentence is ungrammatical:

(72)   a. Quant *(i) mangi-tu?   S. Michele al T.
          when i eat + you?
          'When are you going to eat?'

       b. Quantis caramelis *(i) a-tu mangiat?
          how many sweets i have + you eaten?
          'How many sweets did you eat?'

All wh-items apart from *do* (the short form for *dulà* 'where') are compatible with a complementizer in another type of interrogative structure with a modal interpretation (cf. section 3.3.4), and the same is true for embedded sentences:

(73)   a. Dulà ch'al vedi mitut chel libri?   S. Michele al T.
          where that he have (subjunctive) put that book?
          'Where could he have put that book?'

       b. Sè ch'al vedi fat?
          what that he have (subjunctive) done?
          'What could he have done?'

    c. Quant ch'al rivi?
       when that he comes (subjunctive)?
       'When could he come?'

(74)   *Do ch'al vedi mitut chel libri?   S. Michele al T.
      where that he have (subjunctive) put that book?
      'Where could he have put that book?'

The distribution of the wh-items in embedded interrogatives is the same as that found in modal interrogatives. (We will return to this interesting fact in section 3.5):

(75)   a. A mi an domandat dulà ch al era sut.   S. Michele al T.
       SCL OBL have asked where that he was gone
       'They asked me where he had gone'.

     b. No sai sè chi la mama a vepi crompaat par sena.
       Not know what that the mum SCL have + subjunctive bought for dinner
       'I do not know what mum has bought for dinner'.

     c. A mi an domandat par'se ch' a nol riveva.
       SCL OCL have asked why that SCL not SCL arrived
       'They asked me why he did not come'.

Hence, we have four classes of wh-items in Friulian:

1. Those that are compatible with deictic clitics and for which the presence versus the absence of the clitic gives rise to different interpretations (an out-of-the-blue versus a surprise interpretation, as described in section 3.3.4)
2. The wh-items that obligatorily co-occur with a deictic clitic
3. The wh-items that do not tolerate deictic clitics in inversion structures but do tolerate them in complementizer + deictic clitic modal interrogatives
4. *Do*, the short form for the wh-item "where," which is always incompatible with a deictic clitic and cannot occur in modal interrogatives, where a complementizer is realized. Friulian embedded interrogatives behave like modal interrogatives: a complementizer is always obligatory and is always clustered with a deictic clitic.

We can thus sum up the four classes of Friulian wh-items in the following schema:

(76)

	Main interrogative + complementizer + deictic SCL	Main interrogative + deictic SCL	Main interrogative V + SCI
Dulà	+	+	+
Sè	+	−	+
Do	−	−	+
Quant	+	+	−

This complex distribution can be accounted for in the following way. Let us first examine the distribution of *do*, the short form for "where," which is never compatible with a complementizer + deictic clitic structure and can occur only in

AgrCP. I propose the hypothesis that it has a different status than all other wh-items. Let us consider the following examples:

(77) a. *Do e quant van-u?   S. Michele al T.
         where and when go-they?
         'Where and when do they go?'

      b. Dulà/*Do?
         where?

      c. Di dulà/*di do al vegna?
         from where SCL come?
         'Where does he come from?'

      d. I so-tu zut dulà? *I sotu zut do?
         SCL are + you gone where?
         'Where have you gone?'

Do cannot be coordinated, it cannot occur in isolation, it cannot be expanded by a preposition, and it cannot occur in a focus position such as the one occupied by wh in situ. Therefore, we can consider *do* as a clitic element that needs to be procliticized to the AgrC° head where the inflected verb occurs. In modal and embedded interrogatives, this head is filled by the trace of the complementizer, which is not an acceptable host for the clitic element.

The second class of wh-items that does not tolerate a deictic clitic can appear only in SpecAgrC in a Spec-head configuration with a head marked as [+wh], which is the inflected verb located in AgrC° or a complementizer in embedded clauses (and modal interrogatives). The need to appear in a Spec-head configuration is probably due to the fact that these types of wh-items are weak elements and not strong forms. Cardinaletti and Starke (1999) explicitly propose this condition of weak elements. If this is correct, both positions where this type of wh-item occurs must be positions where the head can undergo a Spec-head agreement process with its specifier.

In sections 3.2 and 3.3, I have assumed that the inflected verb in AgrC can undergo a process of Spec-head agreement with a wh-item and that this process avoids the prohibition of filling both the head and the specifier of an FP. Here, I am assuming that the same is true for the complementizer, which has a [+wh] feature assigned by the matrix verb in embedded interrogatives.[24] As mentioned in note 8, Friulian dialects are precisely those varieties that possess agreeing complementizers, so the assumption that the complementizer can undergo an agreement process with the complementizer in Friulian is a plausible hypothesis.

Deictic SCLs, which clearly do not have any operator features, never undergo a process of Spec-head agreement with any wh-item. Therefore, deictic SCLs are not compatible with weak forms. The complementizer can enter a Spec-head relation with weak wh-items. However, it is not compatible with other types of specifiers, such as the particle *pa* in Central Rhaetoromance varieties. A plausible assumption to account for the difference between *pa* and weak wh-items is to assume that the Spec-head relation must be "complete" and that the incompatibility between *pa* and the complementizer is probably due to a mismatch of features between the two elements—*pa* is a sort of adverbial, and the complementizer is a nominal element. The Spec-head agreement relation, which is the only way to circumvent the doubly filled Comp filter, must be complete in the sense that all features of the head and specifier must be compatible. This would imply an analysis of all the features of the elements that can undergo the Spec-head agreement process.

Another possible way of dealing with the distribution of weak wh-items and *pa* is to assume that only weak forms can undergo the Spec-head agreement process; strong forms always saturate the projection. This hypothesis has far-reaching consequences on the position of subject and object DPs, which are usually assumed to obtain case through a Spec-head agreement process. To adopt this hypothesis, one would have to show that the Spec-head relation is only accessible to weak pronouns because these elements are the only ones that lack some features identified by the head. As a consequence, DPs should always be located higher in the structure (see chapter 6). For the moment I leave the decision between the two options open, as they both require more research.

The third type of wh-items that are compatible with deictic clitics (and the deictic clitic contributes to the interpretation of the sentence) can occur in SpecAgrC, the specifier of the CP and where SCI occurs, or in SpecC higher than the deictic SCL. If it occurs in SpecAgrC, the sentence is interpreted as an out-of-the-blue interrogative, as we have seen in section 3.3.4. If the wh-item occupies the higher SpecC position, the meaning corresponds to the activation of the CP2 projection that conveys a surprise interpretation. This class of wh-items is probably morphologically ambiguous between a weak form which needs to occur in a SpecAgr position (see Cardinaletti and Starke 1999 for this assumption), such as SpecAgrCP, and a strong form that occurs in a higher position.

The last type of wh-items needs the presence of the deictic clitic, which is located in a higher position than SpecAgrC. This fact can be accounted for in several different ways: we may formulate the hypothesis that these elements are unambiguously strong wh-items that cannot occur in the position of weak elements. We can sum up the proposal about the distribution of wh-items as in (78):

(78) $[_{CP}$wh che $[_{CP}$ wh $[_{CP}$ a $[_{AgrC}$ wh V + SCL]]]]
     dulà   dulà
     /   se
     quant   /
     /   *do

(79) $[_{CP}$ wh $[_{CP}$ wh che $[_{CP}$ t $[_{CP}$ t $[_{CP}$ t]]]]]
     dulà   dulà
                    se
     quant
     *do   *do

Example (78) illustrates the distribution of wh-items in main clauses, whereas (79) illustrates the situation in embedded and modal clauses. On the basis of the previous discussion, we can state that the specifier depends on the type of wh-item; if it is a weak element, it will be attracted by the agreement position inside the CP domain and will be located in SpecAgrC or in the Spec of the complementizer; strong forms are located in a higher position. Wh-items that have an ambiguous form are found both in the SpecAgrC position of weak wh-items and in the SpecC positions with empty heads of strong wh-items.[25]

There are other similar cases in other varieties. The Fassano dialect of Pera di Fassa (the 'brach' variety of Fassano) and the Fassano dialect of Campitello (the 'cazet' variety) also show an interesting distribution of SCI that is triggered or not depending on the wh-item used. One class of wh-items has optional inversion, as we saw in the case of *olà*, 'where,' in the previous sections. Also belonging to this class is *can* 'when'; as illustrated in (80), *can* can occur either with SCI or without. Note that the verb position changes, as already discussed in section 3.2.

(80) a. Can vasto pa?   Pera di Fassa
         when go-you particle?
         'When are you leaving?'

      b. Can pa tu vas?
         when particle SCL go?

Other wh-items (the "weak" ones) require inversion: this is true of *che* 'what' and *co* 'how'.[26]

(81) a. Co l'fasto pa?   Pera di Fassa
         how it do-you particle?
         'How do you do it?'

      b. *Co pa tu l fas?
         how particle you it do?

(82) a. Che compresto pa?
         what buy-you particle?
         'What are you buying?'

      b. *Che pa tu compre?[27]
         what particle you buy?

The wh-items corresponding to 'what' and 'how' need SCI. As mentioned for Friulian, we see that different structures are produced according to the type of wh-item used. In this case, it is not the wh-item that changes its specifier position, as in Friulian; some wh-items require SCI, whereas others do not. As Fassano does not have deictic clitics, the phenomenon noted in Friulian is not visible, but the effect on SCI could also be due to a different position of the wh-item: when SCI is triggered, the wh-item is located in SpecAgrC; when no SCI occurs, the wh-item is located in another specifier.

We could also interpret this case by assuming that certain wh-items require a Spec-head relation with the inflected verb, whereas others do not. If all wh-items are realized in this variety in SpecAgrC, some of them require the head to be filled but others do not. The former could be weak elements such as Friulian *se* 'what'.

Note that the wh-item corresponding to 'what' is a weak element in many varieties. In general, if there are weak elements in a dialect, 'what' (or at least one of the possible forms for 'what') is one of them. Other wh-items that are frequently weak are the forms (or one of the forms) corresponding to 'who', 'where', and 'how'. I have never found cases of weak elements corresponding to wh–complex phrases and the wh-word corresponding to 'why'. Moreover, there is an implication scale in the set of wh-items that becomes weak: if the wh-item corresponding to 'when' is weak (a rare case), even wh-items corresponding to the arguments of the verb have this status. Even in wh-situ varieties, 'what' has a particular status. Munaro (1997) provides a detailed analysis of Lombard and Veneto wh–in situ phenomena. He has noted that wh-phrases can never be left in situ, which is a possible structure only for wh-words in Bellunese (Veneto) (the data are from Munaro 1995):

(83)   a. Che tosat a-tu incontrà?   Tignes d'Alpago (Northern Veneto)
          which boy have-you met?/Which boy did you meet?

       b. *A-tu incotrà che tosat?
          have-you met which boy?/Which boy did you meet?

       e. Qual atu comprà?
          which have-you bought?/Which one did you buy?

       f. A-tu comprà qual?
          have-you met which?/Which one did you buy?

(84)   a. Quanti libri a-tu ledcst?   Tignes d'Alpago
          how many books have-you read?/How many books have you read?

       b. *A-tu ledest quanti libri?
          have-you read how-many books?

       c. Quant ghen a-tu magnà?
          how much of it have-you eaten?/How much did you eat?

       d. Ghen'a-tu magnà quant?
          of it have-you eaten how much?

(85)   a. In che botega a-tu compra sta borsa?   Tignes d'Alpago (Munaro 1997)
          in which shop have-you bought this bag?/In which shop did you buy this bag?

       b. *A-tu comprà sta borsa in che botega?
          have-you bought this bag in which shop?

       c. ??Andè va-lo?
          where goes-he?/Where is he going?

       d. Va-lo andè?
          goes-he where?

Note that if the wh-item is represented by a whole phrase it can occur only in a SpecC position, whereas wh-words have two options: they can either be moved to SpecC or left in situ. Munaro (1997) suggests that the possibility of remaining in situ depends on the nominal head that is internal to the wh-item being uniquely identified for elements that move to SpecC. Therefore, the contrast illustrated above depends on the internal structure of the wh-item. In Bellunese, all wh-words (but not complex wh-phrases) can be left in situ or moved to SpecC. However, the SpecC option is not possible for the wh-item corresponding to 'what', that is, *che*, or for the one corresponding to 'who/m' *chi* (either as a subject or an object):

(86) a. *Che a-tu fat?   Tignes d'Alpago
          what have-you done?/What have you done?

      b. A-tu fat che?
          have-you done what?

(87) a. *Chi laore-lo?   Tignes d'Alpago
          who works-he?/Who is working?

      b. E-lo chi che laora?
          is-he who that works?

Munaro notes that the wh-items corresponding to 'where' and 'how' are preferred in the in situ position, even though the SpecC position is not completely excluded:

(88) a. Va-lo andè?   Tignes d'Alpago (Munaro 1997: 3.62)
          goes-he where?/Where is he going?

      b. ??Andè valo?
          where goes-he?

(89) a. Se ciame-lo comè?   Tignes d'Alpago (Munaro 1997: 3.64)
          himself call-he how? What is his name?

      b. ??Come se ciame-lo?
          how himself calls-he?

This is not the case for quando 'when' and quanto 'how much':

(90) a. parte-tu quando?   Tignes d'Alpago (Munaro 1997: 3.66)
          leave-you when?/When are you leaving?

      b. quando parte-tu?
          when leave-you?

(91) a. quant a ve-o laorà?   Tignes d'Alpago (Munaro 1997: 3.72)
          how-much have-you worked?/How much did you work?

      b. ave-o laorà quant?
          have-you worked how-much?

    The Bellunese wh–in situ phenomenon shows a first split between wh-words (which are left in situ) and wh-phrases (which cannot be left in situ), treated by Munaro as a consequence of the internal structure of wh-phrases and a second split internal to the wh-word class. This second split relates to the possibility of moving to the SpecC position or not. Here, we again find that the elements 'what', 'who', where', and 'how' behave alike, 'what' being the one that strictly needs to be left in situ, whereas this condition can be marginally relaxed for 'where' and 'how'. Elements like 'when' and 'how much' can climb to SpecC and give rise to perfectly grammatical sentences. Moreover, Munaro analyzes the diachronic development of the wh–in situ phenomenon and shows that it began with the item corresponding to 'what' (cf. Munaro 1997: chap. 4).

The same hierarchy is found inside the wh-word class in Friulian and Fassano, even though in all these dialects it manifests itself on the basis of different phenomena, such as the possibility of occupying different SpecC positions, the necessity to enter into a Spec-head relation with the inflected verb, or the possibility of climbing to a SpecC position.

Another variety shows the same internal partition within the class of wh-words. In the case of Monnese, a Lombard variety examined in section 3.2 for its fa-support feature, wh-items may be moved to SpecC, left in situ, or duplicated in SpecC and in situ. The only elements that can use the duplicating structure (with an expletive operator realized as *ch´* or with the duplication of the wh-item itself) are those corresponding to 'what', 'who', 'where', and 'how'.

(92) a. ch e-l chi che maja le patate?   Monno (Eastern Lombard)
         wh is-he who that eats the potatoes?/Who is eating potatoes?

      b. che fe-f fa què ades?
         wh do-you what, now?/What are you doing now?

      c. ngo fet andà ngont?
         where do-you go where?/Where are you going?

This structure is never found with 'when' and 'how much':

(93) a. *quan l'e-t vist quand?   Monno
         when OCL have-you seen when?/When did you see him?

      b. *quata fe-t majan quata?
         how much do you eat-of it how much?/How much did you eat of that?

I do not analyze here why there is an internal split in wh-words. I simply point out that the split reflects the difference between arguments and adjuncts: 'what' and 'who' are always selected by the verb; 'where' is frequently selected, for instance, by movement verbs; and 'how' (which oscillates between the two classes) can be selected by such verbs as 'behave'. A possible line of research that looks promising connects the class of wh-words that tends to become light elements connected to an AgrC projection to the fact that they are arguments of the verb, and thus there could be an agreement position in the CP structure.[28]

The hypothesis presented here needs to be refined and elaborated on the basis of a wider sample of data to see if it is true that the items corresponding to arguments of the verb tend to develop shorter forms that show a particular behavior in several varieties. The purpose of this section is to show that for interrogative sentences, we need not only the head positions of the four projections we have postulated but also the specifier positions to account for the distribution of wh-items.

3.4   THEORETICAL IMPLICATIONS OF SPLIT INTERROGATIVE CP

In this section, I consider some theoretical implications that have not yet been discussed. I show that the previously presented data clearly prove that Rizzi's (1991) proposal of a wh-criterion—according to which both the specifier and the head marked with a [+wh] feature must occur in a specifier-head agreement relation at the relevant level of structure—does not exhaust the scenario of interrogative structures. Rizzi's wh-criterion is formalized in the following way:

(94)   Wh-criterion: Rizzi (1991)

    a. A wh-operator must be in a Spec-head relation with a +wh-head.

    b. A +wh-head must be in a Spec-head relation with a wh-operator.

Rizzi's proposal has the advantage of relating V to C movement to the wh-criterion: because the verb is the head that bears the wh-feature in Italian (as in French and English), V to C movement must occur to satisfy the Spec-head relation with the wh-item.

(95)   Infl is +wh in standard Italian.

The complexity of the situation described in section 3.3 for NIDs clearly emerges from those data, where more than a single projection is activated. For instance, we may ask why we need an interrogative marker such as *pa* located in a lower projection if we already have the Spec-head agreement relation, which satisfies the requirements of both the wh-item and the inflected verb marked with the wh-feature? I have proposed that the presence of elements like *pa* (or a complementizer) have to do with focus conditions imposed on interrogative sentences. Therefore, we have to assume that there are additional conditions imposed on interrogative structures that are not subsumed under the wh-criterion. Given that the wh-criterion does not exhaust the restrictions on interrogative sentences, this approach has a few potential difficulties.

One problem is that verb movement is not necessary in varieties such as Portogruarese, in which the lowest head C°4 contains a complementizer that quite simply blocks verb movement to the CP domain. The complementizer is an independent head and cannot host the inflected verb, as a bound morpheme does (cf. Franco-Provençal dialects, in which a bound morpheme permits verb movement to the higher SCI position). Note, however, that adjunction of the inflected verb to the complementizer should in principle be a possible option, as is, for instance, the adjunction of a clitic to the verbal head. The type of structure in which a complementizer blocks verb movement to the CP domain, as seen in the Portogruarese example, does not represent a real problem for Rizzi's (1991) theory of the wh-criterion. As proposed in Poletto (1993b), in these cases the inflected verb is simply not marked with the [+wh] feature at all. It is the complementizer that hosts this feature and enters the Spec-head relation with the wh-item. The inflected verb remains in the same position as in declarative sentences. All we have to assume is a parametrization of the heads that can be endowed with the wh-feature.

However, there are other problematic cases. As we have seen, verb movement depends on several different factors: SCI is obligatory for some wh-elements but not for others, as illustrated by Fassano data:

(96) a. Can vasto pa?   Pera di Fassa
         when go-you interr.marker?/Where are you going?

      b. Can pa tu vas?
         when interr marker you go?

(97) a. Co l'fasto pa?
         how OCL do-you interr marker? How do you do it?

      b. *Co pa tu l fas?
         how interr marker OCL you do?

(98) a. Che compresto pa?
         what buy-you interr marker?/What do you buy?

      b. *Che pa tu compre?
         what interr marker you buy?

Therefore, we are forced to assume that verb movement depends on the type of wh-item; weak wh-items require it, whereas strong wh-items do not. To explain this difference, I have adopted Cardinaletti and Starke's (1999) theory of weak elements, which are elements that lack the highest internal FP (corresponding to a TopP inside the DP functional projections) and need to move to SpecAgr position so that the features realized in this FP can be recovered from the Spec-head relation with the Agr° head. I have assumed that the SCI position is an AgrC position, where agreement features are realized within the CP domain. Weak elements will thus be attracted to the SpecAgrC position, just as other weak elements (pronouns or adverbs) are attracted to the relevant agreement positions in Cardinaletti and Starke's account of weak elements. Weak wh-items need to be in a Spec-head relation with the head of AgrC, which must be filled by the complex formed by the inflected verb plus the enclitic morpheme. Strong elements do not need this relation [see the Fassano data in (96)]. Within Rizzi's (1991) framework, one would have to postulate that weak elements enter a Spec-head relation with the inflected verb, which must be marked with an operator feature, and strong elements enter the Spec-head relation with the inflected verb or with a phonetically unrealized element in the AgrC° position. Alternatively, one could imagine that strong elements may also occur in another SpecC position, whose C° is phonetically unrealized. One would be forced to postulate that within the same language, two distinct heads can be marked with the operator feature: the inflected verb and a phonetically unrealized C°. This is not implausible, as Rizzi already assumes this case to capture the difference between indicative and subjunctive verbs in embedded interrogatives in standard Italian (see chapter 6 for a discussion on this point). However, it is not clear how the choice of the head is to be related to the type of wh-item.

Among the structures we have examined, the clearest cases that present a problem for Rizzi's theory are those where a complementizer and/or a deictic clitic is followed by SCI inversion, repeated here:

(99) Parchè a magna-t an pom?   Guastalla (Emilian)
      why SCL eat-you an apple? Why are you eating an apple?

Here, we see that the wh-item is immediately followed by a deictic clitic; thus the head that enters the Spec-head relation with the wh-item is not the inflected verb. However, the inflected verb moves to the CP domain all the same, as SCI shows. Again, we are forced to conclude that the reason that the inflected verb moves is not that postulated by Rizzi (1991), to enter the Spec-head relation with the wh-item; there must be another reason that forces verb movement to the CP domain, as we observe SCI without a Spec-head relation with the wh-item. Verb movement in the varieties that present more than one CP head filled by a phonetically realized element must be triggered by another factor. I propose that the mechanism that not only triggers verb movement but also requires more than one $C°$ head to be filled with phonetically realized elements is the same mechanism that requires functional heads to be realized within the IP domain and in V2 contexts— some strong features must be checked. Different types of wh-items can occupy different specifiers, depending on their requirements; weak elements can survive only in a Spec-head environment, whereas strong wh-items require an empty head.

Chomsky (1995) assumes that the functional projections are already present inside the numeration and are then merged inside the structure of the sentence. In some languages, functional projections are not visible, in the sense that they are not occupied by any lexically filled morpheme, and it could also be assumed that they are totally absent from the structure of these languages. In other languages, we see phonetically realized functional heads, such as bound morphemes or independent morphemes (auxiliaries or complementizers). Alternatively, the head is activated through movement of an element moving inside the $F°$ (as the inflected verb does inside the IP layer).

The NIDs show four distinct $F°$s that may be activated to give the interpretation of an interrogative sentence. The complete structure is the following:

(100) $[_{CP1}$ che $[_{CP2}$ a $[_{CP3/AgrCP}$ SCI $[_{CP4}$ $[_{SpecC4}$ pa] $[_{C°4}$ ch/lo]]]]]]

We have seen that it is possible to activate more than one CP in a single sentence and that these are the possible combinations:

1. Only CP4 (yielding the structure wh-complementizer SCL-inflected verb)
2. Only AGRCP, yielding the structure wh-item V + SCI
3. AGRCP and CP4, yielding the structure wh-item V SCI + interrogative specifier (*pa*) or V+interrogative bound morpheme (lo) + SCI
4. CP2 and AGRCP, yielding the structure wh-item-deictic clitic V + SCI or interrogative marker (*o* in Florentine) wh-item + SCL + V
5. CP1, CP2, and AGRCP, yielding the structure wh-item-complementizer-deictic clitic V + SCI

Not all possible combinations are found. It is not clear whether the unattested ones are excluded in principle or if they have not been found because of the limited sample of varieties examined. One interesting fact is that there are no cases of discontinuous projections; for instance, I have not found cases in which CP1 and AGRCP are visible but CP2 is not, or where CP2 and CP4 are visible but

AGRCP is not. If the lack of these combinations is not casual, it tells us something about the way in which the activation of FPs proceeds; in other words we could make the hypothesis that it is possible to activate higher positions only if lower FPs have been activated, at least inside a restricted domain such as the structural encoding of interrogative interpretations. The only exception for the constraint I propose here concerns CP4, which is not visible, even though AGRCP is activated. Note, however, that if AGRCP were occupied by a complementizer, verb movement to AGRCP could not occur, as it would constitute a violation of the head movement constraint. Hence, the head of CP4 must remain empty to permit movement of the inflected verb across it. Thus CP4 is activated, although it does not contain a phonetically realized morpheme, because it contains the trace of the verb that has moved higher.[29]

At the end of the second chapter, when referring to different types of SCLs, I made a similar proposal for the activation of clitic heads inside the agreement field, namely, that there is an implication between the occurrence of lower SCLs with respect to the occurrence of higher SCLs. If higher clitics occur we also find lower clitics, but not vice versa. The same is true within the interrogative CP domain; higher heads are filled only if lower heads are. In chapter 2, I attempted to account for this fact in terms of a condition on feature scattering, according to Giorgi and Pianesi's (1997) theory of the way in which universal features are projected into the syntax of the various languages. The data examined in this chapter confirm the hypothesis put forth in chapter 2.

Turning back to the original problem, we see that verb movement is not triggered by the wh-criterion but by the necessity to check features on a given functional head that are checked and deleted, yielding the correct configuration only if the verb is moved to AgrC°. As we have seen, dialects differ in the activation of interrogative CP projections, and therefore in verb movement, which is necessary in the varieties in which the head of AGRCP is marked with a strong feature that does or does not need to be checked and deleted by the corresponding strong feature of the inflected verb. This fact does not question the core of Rizzi's (1991) proposal concerning the wh-criterion, that is, the need for a Spec-head relation between the wh-item and a head marked with the same [+wh] feature; we simply have to state that the head with the [+wh] feature varies across dialects, as it has been proposed above (and as Rizzi already admits). Thus, the wh-criterion can be maintained even in a split-CP analysis, where verb movement is triggered by a different factor but does not depend on the wh-criterion.

3.5   EMBEDDED CONTEXTS

In main interrogative contexts, we have seen that there are two possible positions in which a complementizer may appear—in the head of CP4 and in the head of CP1. I now analyze embedded interrogative contexts, showing that the complementizer always moves at least as high as deictic SCLs in embedded interrogatives. This could be one way of dealing with Rizzi's (1997) theory of split CP, as he postulates that the complementizer in embedded declaratives in standard Italian is located in the highest C° position. We have seen that a complementizer may be merged very low in the CP structure, lower than the AgrC projection in main interrogatives in some dialects (cf. Portogruarese, Fassano, etc.). It could be hypothesized that the complementizer can also be merged into the structure in the lowest CP in declarative clauses before moving to higher positions, depending on the features it has to check. In embedded declaratives, it has to check features in the highest CP projection, and therefore it moves there. An argument in favor of this hypothesis has already been presented in chapter 2 and regards the interaction of deictic clitics with complementizers. The result of the analysis of main interrogative sentences is that the position of deictic clitics, which are located inside the CP domain, is CP2 and hence higher than AgrC, where the feature of the complex form V + SCL is checked. This immediately explains why deictic clitics interact with typical CP elements such as the complementizer and wh-items. In section 3.3, I have discussed and analyzed the Friulian case mentioned in chapter 2, in which the occurrence of deictic clitics is obligatory, impossible, or optional, depending on the wh-item.

An interesting pattern noted in chapter 2 is that of obligatory clustering with the complementizer; in all dialects in which deictic clitics are realized, the clustering with the complementizer is obligatory:

(101) a. Ara ch'a vegno.   Loreo (Southern Veneto)
          Look that + SCL come "Look, I am coming."

       b. *Ara che a vegno.

This suggests that the deictic clitic and the complementizer are located on the same head, following a process of adjunction. As adjunction to the right is excluded, it cannot be the deictic clitic that right-adjoins to the complementizer. Hence, it must be the complementizer that left-adjoins to the deictic clitic. This means that the complementizer must have moved from a lower head to the position of the deictic SCL. Thus, the idea that the complementizer can be inserted low in the structure and then move to higher CPs, adjoining to the elements it finds on its way (such as deictic SCLs), explains why there is obligatory clustering between the complementizer and deictic clitics. If embedded declarative sentences have the complementizer inserted low and then moved higher, what can be said about embedded interrogatives?[30] In embedded interrogatives there is less variation than in main interrogatives. The structures usually found are the following:[31]

(102) a. Al so ca chi c a laverà i piac.   Livigno (Alpine Lombard)
          SCL-OCL know not who that SCL will-wash the dishes
          'I do not know who is going to wash the dishes'.

       b. Nu so chi segge arrivou.   Chiavari (Ligurian)
          Not know who be-subjunctive arrived
          'I do not know who has arrived'.

In some dialects, a complementizer is found after the wh-item, but in others it is not. Some varieties even show complete optionality for the occurrence of the complementizer, without any interpretative difference (see below for discussion).

Varieties in which SCI is used in embedded interrogatives appear to be very rare, and in these dialects SCI is usually found in declarative contexts, too (as in the Romagnolo dialects examined in section 3.2). This type of inversion has been analyzed in chapter 2.

Therefore, for most varieties, which exclude SCI in embedded interrogatives, we have to assume that the complementizer has to originate in the lowest head position, that is, the one located lower than AgrC. In this way, the verb cannot climb to the SCI position because the complementizer blocks the rising process, being an intervening head.

There are no empirical arguments that lead us to the assumption that the structure used by varieties in which the complementizer is phonetically realized is different from that used by varieties in which the complementizer is not realized. Therefore, I assume that in both cases the C° head is occupied by an element that prevents verb movement. However, in all dialects that have deictic clitics, the order found is complementizer–deictic clitic. This means that in all the varieties in which the movement of the complementizer can be tested on the basis of the coalescence with deictic clitics, the complementizer moves at least up to the interrogative C2 filled by the deictic clitic.

Note that the lack of SCI in embedded sentences in most dialects cannot be explained simply by assuming that the C° head is marked with the [+wh] feature and therefore satisfies the wh-criterion. In section 3.4, I have assumed that the reason for verb movement is not the satisfaction of the wh-criterion but rather the checking of a special feature in the AgrC head. Therefore, the fact that a complementizer follows the wh-item and enters the Spec-head relation with it is not a guarantee of the lack of verb movement. Note that the reason for the asymmetry in verb movement in main and embedded interrogatives can only be captured by the assumption that embedded interrogatives must have a complementizer that originates in the lowest C° position. This blocks the movement of the verb, whereas the situation in main interrogatives is different. In main interrogatives a complementizer can be generated in the lowest C° head, and in this case verb movement is banned, or the complementizer can be generated in a head higher than AgrC, as in the Piedmontese dialect examined in sections 3.2 and 3.3. In other words, the need to realize a complementizer in the lowest C° is why we see the asymmetry between main and embedded sentences. If the complementizer did not originate lower than AgrC°, the verb could move to AgrC° and we would have the complex form V + SCL.

If the complementizer originating in the lowest C° position moves at least to the C° position, where the deictic clitic is located, it means that the wh-item in embedded questions is forced to occupy a position higher than SpecAgrC, whereas in main interrogatives at least one more position (SpecAgrC) is available. This difference could explain some morphological differences noticed between wh-items in main interrogatives and wh-items in embedded interrogatives in a few varieties. In the variety of Monno, examined above, wh-items can have two distinct forms, depending on the main versus embedded character of the sentence where they occur:

(103) a. Chi che maja?   Monno (Eastern Lombard)
          who that eats?/Who is eating?

       b. M'domandio **cu** che sarà 'nda a ca.
           myself ask who that be + future gone to home/I ask myself who will have
             gone home.

(104) a. Che fe-t majà de solit?
           what do-you eat usually?/What do you usually eat?

       b. I ho domandà col che l'ha fat.
           SCL have asked what that SCL has done/I asked him what he did.

The wh-item corresponding to 'who' is *chi* in main interrogatives, as (103a), and
cu in an embedded context, as (103b). The same occurs to the wh-item corresponding to 'what'. The form *che* occurs only in main interrogatives, whereas in embedded contexts the form *col* has to be used. We have seen that wh-items can
occupy different SpecCP positions, depending on their interpretation and on the
type of wh-item, which may be weak or strong as pronouns. Weak wh-items are
attracted by the AgrC projection corresponding to AGRCP, where SCI occurs.
Strong forms may also occur in SpecCP1 or SpecCP2. We have seen that wh-items
can occupy only SpecCP1 or SpecCP2 in embedded interrogatives, as the complementizer moves at least up to the C° position, where the deictic clitic is located,
adjoining to it. If this is so, it may mean that in embedded interrogatives only strong
wh-forms can be used. The distribution of the morphological altenants *chi/cu* and
che/col could just be due to the fact that *chi* and *che* are weak forms located in
SpecAGRCP, available only in main interrogatives, and *cu* and *col* are strong forms
that can occupy SpecCP2 or SpecCP1, the only SpecCP position available in
embedded interrogatives. We can conclude that embedded interrogatives differ
in main interrogatives, as the complementizer is always inserted in the lowest C°
and then moves up to other C° positions.

3.6 CONCLUSION

In this chapter, I show that the CP domain where interrogative wh-elements are
moved does not consist of a single projection. The reasons for such an analysis
are the following: first, we see different X° elements in interrogative contexts
occupying distinct positions. Second, wh-items can occupy different specifier
positions. Third, the position of the wh-item inside a given specifier is relevant
for the interpretation of the interrogative sentence, which can be an out-of-the-
blue, rhetorical, surprise, or modal interrogative. Moreover, we have seen that the
complementizer may occupy different heads within the interrogative CP domain
and can move from one head to another, raising to the highest head position of
the domain.

I also propose an analysis of SCI while seeking to defend the hypothesis that
for the majority of dialects a CP analysis is indeed correct and that the AgrCP

position, where the features of the complex form V + SCL are checked, is located immediately higher than the position in which the complementizer is merged (and then moved higher) in embedded interrogatives. This analysis could also be extended to standard French, as noted earlier.

In chapter 4, I examine a space located higher than interrogatives in the CP domain, the V2 context in Rhaetoromance varieties.

FOUR

Rhaetoromance Verb Second

A Split-CP Perspective

4.1   INTRODUCTION

This chapter focuses on a number of Central Rhaetoromance varieties that have maintained a V2 structure similar to that present in Old Romance texts (cf. Benincà 1995b for a detailed analysis of this phenomenon in Old French and in the medieval stage of northern Italian dialects; see Roberts 1993c for a proposal about Old French). An analysis of these very conservative dialects enables investigation into several interesting properties in the higher part of the CP field. Chapter 3 describes the variation shown by interrogative structures within the northern Italian domain. I propose that the comparative data about interrogative structures can be accounted for only by a split-CP perspective. Only one portion of the structure in Rizzi's (1997) hypothesis of a split CP in a language like standard Italian is examined here, namely the subfield that is activated in interrogative structures. Rhaetoromance verb second will help us to focus on the higher portion of the CP domain.

Current literature on verb second is extremely vast, but the debate has concentrated on three main proposals. The first involves a "classical" analysis (den Besten 1984; Koster 1975), which explains main versus embedded asymmetry in languages like German and Dutch, postulating verb movement to the C° position in main clauses where C° is empty. In embedded clauses, C° is filled by the complementizer and the verb cannot raise. According to this analysis, there is no difference between subject-initial and topic-initial clauses, which all have the verb in C° and the initial XP in SpecC.

A second hypothesis has been proposed for so-called generalized V2 languages, such as Icelandic and Yiddish, which display verb second, both in main and embedded sentences. According to the Santorini (1989) proposal, in these languages the target position for the verb (and initial topic) is not CP but IP. Thus, the difference between a language like German and one like Yiddish concerns the A or A' status of the IP projection. Again, no distinction is made between subject-initial and topic-initial clauses. The third hypothesis (put forth by Zwart 1993 on the basis of Dutch data) assumes that there is a structural difference between topic- and subject-initial clauses, that is, that subject-initial clauses are IPs and topic-initial clauses are CPs.

Because the Central Rhaetoromance dialect examined here is not a language with a generalized verb second like Yiddish or Icelandic (cf. section 4.5, where it is shown that relatives and embedded interrogatives cannot have a V2 structure, although embedded V2 is much more liberal than in German), Santorini's hypothesis is not discussed here (see note 9). The two competing hypotheses that are considered here are (1) the "classical analysis," which always assumes V to C, and (2) the "asymmetric analysis," in which subject-initial sentences are IPs but topic-initial clauses are CPs. I show that neither of the two is suitable for analyzing Rhaetoromance data, although both of them are partially correct. The hypothesis presented here combines several assumptions of both analyses. In fact, there is indeed a difference between subject-initial and topic-initial clauses, as assumed by the asymmetric analysis. However, subject-initial clauses are CPs, as assumed by the classical analysis, and not IPs, although the subject is in a distinct CP projection. Zwart's (1993) leading idea that V2 is not a unitary phenomenon is further developed, by showing that different types of topic elements, such as adverbs or arguments, target different CPs. In this analysis, the V2 constraint is not derived from the fact that only one CP position is available, but it is rather a side effect of a Spec-head obligatory relationship established between the moved XP and the inflected verb.

This chapter is organized in the following way. Section 4.2 shows that Rhaetoromance varieties are indeed V2 by examining the system found in the variety of S. Leonardo di Badia. Section 4.3 discusses an interesting asymmetry between declarative and interrogative contexts, for which an account in terms of split CP is proposed. Sections 4.4 and 4.5 further develop the idea that V2 is not a unitary phenomenon, in the sense that it does not involve a single CP projection but rather an entire set of CP projections. The subject position is located inside this set, and not in IP, as illustrated in section 4.6. Section 4.7 describes several points of comparison with Germanic languages, which do not display the same structure as Rhaetoromance. I do not attempt to make a systematic comparison between Germanic and Rhaetoromance V2 here; this is the subject of a future work (see Poletto and Tomaselli 1998).

4.2 RHAETOROMANCE V2: DATA

It is fairly simple to show that Rhaetoromance obeys the V2 contraint, as two XPs can never precede the verb at any one time. If an XP other than the subject is located in first position, the subject appears immediately after the inflected verb, as illustrated in (1):

(1)   a. **T** vas gonoot a ciasa sua   S. Leonardo
         you go often at home his
         'You often visit him'.

b. Gonoot vas-**t** a ciasa sua
often go-you at home his

c. *Gonoot t vas a ciasa sua
Often you go at home his

In (1a), the adverb *gonoot* is located after the verb and the SCL *t* precedes it. If the adverb is located in first position, the SCL must be enclitic, as shown by the contrast between (1b) and (1c). The adverb and the SCL cannot both be located before the verb. This is generally true, as two preverbal constituents always lead to ungrammaticality (though some examples of left-dislocated elements are discussed below). In the following examples, all possible combinations of two preverbal XPs are considered:[1]

(2) a. *Duman trees l fej-**l**
tomorrow always it does-he
'Tomorrow he is going to do it the whole day long'.

b. *Trees duman l fej-**l**
always tomorrow it does-he

(3) a. *Da trai l liber ti a-**i** de a Giani
sometimes the book to-him have-I given to John
'Sometimes I gave a book to John'.

b. *L liber da trai ti a-**i** de a Giani
the book sometimes have-I given to John

(4) a. *L liber Giani ti a(-**al**) de
the book John to-him has-he given
'He gave the book to John'.

b. *Giani l liber ti a(-**al**) de
John the book to-him has-he given

c. *Giani l liber al ti a de
John the book he to-him has given

In these examples, two adverbials are located in a preverbal position in (2), whereas (3) combines an object and an adverbial and (4) a direct object and the subject. None of these possibilities is grammatical. Hence, it may be concluded that the variety spoken in S. Leonardo displays the V2 property. Rhaetoromance dialects are particularly interesting because they combine V2, which is widely attested in Germanic languages, with other typical features of Romance languages, such as SVO order with raising of the inflected verb inside the IP layer, pro-drop, and so on. The possibility of examining V2 phenomena inside a "Romance structural type" opens up several research perspectives. However, only those concerning the CP layer are considered here, leaving the others for future work. The next section examines the distribution of left-dislocated elements.

4.3   LEFT DISLOCATION:
THE DECLARATIVE-INTERROGATIVE ASYMMETRY

Declarative and interrogative sentences differ in the distribution of left-dislocated items in the variety considered here. In a declarative sentence, it is never possible to left-dislocate an element before the V2 structure (as already noted by Benincà 1985/6). The examples from (5) to (10) show various different combinations of V2 and left-dislocated items. A direct object cannot be left-dislocated in front of a V2 structure, where the V2 element is another object, as in (5); an adverb, as in (6); or the subject, as in (7). Nor can an adverb be found in a left-dislocated position if the V2 element is the subject, as in example (8) (regardless of the presence of enclitic or proclitic SCLs), an object, as in (9); or another adverb, as in (10):

(5)   a. *L liber, a Giani ti(l) a-**i** bel de[2]
         the book to John to him (it) have-I already given
         'I already gave the book to John'.

      b. *L liber, a Giani i til a bel de
         the book to John I to-him-it have already given

      c. *A Giani, l liber ti(l) a-**i** bel de
         to John the book to-him (it) have-I already given

(6)   a. *Giani, duman l vaighes-**t**
         John tomorrow him see-you
         'Tomorrow you are going to see John'.

      b. *Duman, Giani l vaighes-**t**
         tomorrow John him see-you

(7)   a. *L liber, Giani til a(-**al**) de
         the book John to-him-it has-he given
         'He gave the book to John'.

      b. *Giani, l liber til a(-**al**) de
         John the book to-him-it has-he given

      c. *Giani, l liber al til a de
         John the book he to-him-it has given

(8)   a. *Duman, Giani al mangia . . .
         tomorrow John he eats . . .
         'Tomorrow John is going to eat . . .'

      b. *Giani, duman al mangia . . .
         John tomorrow he eats . . .

      c. *Duman, Giani mangia . . .
         tomorrow John eats . . .

      d. *Duman, Giani mange-**l**
         tomorrow John eats-he . . .

     e. *Giani, duman mange-l
       John tomorrow eats-he . . .

(9) a. *Da trai, l liber ti a-**i** de a Giani
       sometimes the book to-him have-I given to John
       'Sometimes I gave him the book'.

     b. *L liber, da trai ti a-**i** de a Giani
       the book sometimes have-I given to John

(10) a. *Duman, trees l fej-**l**
       tomorrow always it does-he
       'Tomorrow he is going to do it the whole day long'.

     b. *Trees, duman l fej-**l**
       always tomorrow it does-he

Note that left-dislocated direct objects have a clitic, which doubles them, whereas adverbs do not (see note 2). Hence, the sentences in which adverbs are left-dislocated are identical to those in which double V2 is tested [cf. (2) and (3)]. However, the intonation is different, implying a pause after the left-dislocated element (represented by a comma) that is not present in double V2 structures.[3] By examining the data in examples (5)–(10), one may conclude that left-dislocated elements are never possible in V2 structures.

    The situation changes radically in interrogative sentences, as it is possible to left-dislocate all XPs in front of a wh-item; this may be a subject, as illustrated in (11); an object, as in (12); or an adverb, as in (13) and (14).

(11) a. Giani, ci o-**l** pa?
       John what wants-he interrogative marker?
       'What does John want?'

     b. *Ci, Giani o-**l** pa?
       what John wants-he interrogative marker?

(12) a. L liber, che l tol pa?
       the book who it takes interrogative marker?
       'Who is going to take the book?'

     b. *Che, l liber l tol pa?
       who the book it takes interrogative marker?

(13) a. Gonot, ula va-**al** pa?
       often where goes-he interrogative marker?
       'Where does he often go?'

     b. *Ula, gonot va-**al** pa?
       where often goes-he interrogative marker?

(14) a. E bun, can l fej-**l** pa ?
       and good when it does-he interrogative marker?
       'When does he do it well?'

   b. *Ula, trees va-**al** pa?
      where always goes-he interrogative marker?
      'Where does he always go?'

   c. Duman, che mangia pa chilò?
      tomorrow who eats interrogative marker here?
      'Tomorrow who is going to eat here?'

Whereas the sequence left dislocation/wh-item is grammatical, the opposite
wh-item/left-dislocation order is totally excluded [as shown in examples (5)–(10b)].

   Left dislocation displays the usual properties of Romance left dislocation:
(1) recursivity [cf. (15)] and (2) free word order of left-dislocated elements [as
shown by the grammaticality of the pairs (15a) and (15b) and (15c) and (15d)]
and (3) the occurrence in embedded contexts, as illustrated in (15e).

(15)   a. Giani, inier, ci a-**al** pa fat?
          John yesterday what has-he interrrogative marker done?
          'What has John done yesterday?'

       b. Inier, Giani, ci a-**al** pa fat?
          yesterday John what has-he interrogative marker done?

       c. Giani, inier, l as-**t** odu?
          John yesterday him has-you seen?

       d. Inier, Giani, l as-**t** odu?
          yesterday John him has-you seen?

       e. Al m a demanee Giani, can c al vagn a ciasa.
          he me has asked John when that he comes at home
          'He asked me when John is coming home'.

The contrast between declaratives and interrogatives is illustrated in (16) by a
minimal pair:

(16)   a. *Giani, duman l vaighes-**t**
          John tomorrow him see-you
          'You will see John tomorrow'.

       b. Giani, duman l vaighes-**t**?
          John tomorrow him see-you
          'Will you see John tomorrow?'

   Rhaetoromance left dislocation is similar to standard Italian left dislocation
(because it is recursive, all orders of left-dislocated elements are possible and
embedding is allowed), although this is a V2 variety. The only difference with
respect to standard Italian is the limited context in which left dislocation may
occur in Rhaetoromance. However, this detail is dealt with in section 4.7, when a
comparison with the Germanic CP structure is made.

   As mentioned in the introductory section, neither the classical CP analysis
nor Zwart's (1993) asymmetric analysis account for the asymmetry illustrated in
(16). An alternative proposal involves Rizzi's (1997) idea that wh-elements are
located quite low in a split-CP structure.

The sharp asymmetry found between declarative V2 clauses and the inter-rogative clauses illustrated in (16) may be expressed in terms of split CP if one makes two preliminary assumptions. First, the V2 constraint depends on a Spec-head relation required by all V2 XPs and by the inflected V that forces verb move-ment to the head position, whose specifier is filled by the V2 constituent. This restriction applies to V2 constituents and wh-items but not to left-dislocated XPs, which do not require the verb to occupy the head position of the projection where they are realized. Hence, even though there are several CPs, it is not possible to fill them all at the same time because each of them requires the inflected verb to occur in its C° position in order to enter a Spec-head relation. As only one in-flected verb may enter one Spec-head relation, only one CP may be filled in each sentence. This assumption implies that V2 does not occur in a single FP located in a precise point of the sentence structure. Rather, it is conceived of as a struc-tural relation between an XP and an F° which must be filled by the inflected verb. In this perspective, V2 turns out to be a case of Spec-head agreement, a syntactic relation already exploited by Rizzi (1991) for his wh-criterion and by Haegeman (1995), who proposes a negative criterion parallel to the wh-criterion.[4]

If one assumes that V2 does not occur in a single FP, it may also be possible to better understand which feature triggers V2. However, determining what kind of feature triggers V2 is not a simple matter; it cannot be topic or focus because both focalized and topicalized elements may undergo V2; and it cannot be case because adverbs and PPs also undergo V2. As has been proposed for Germanic V2 by many authors (see Tomaselli 1990 and references quoted; Vikner 1990), the feature checked by V2 in CP is one of agreement. However, if one considers agreement not as a feature but as a structural relation that is required by a set of different features (checked at different points of the CP structure), an explanation for the fact that all sorts of elements are found in V2 contexts would be that the Spec-head relation is required by wh-items (as assumed by Rizzi 1991), negation (as assumed by Haegeman 1995), focalized XPs, topicalized XPs, subject, scene-setting adverbs, and so on.

In chapter 3, an argument was presented against Rizzi's (1991) hypothesis that in non-V2 Romance languages the inflected verb moves to C° in interroga-tive clauses in order to enter into a Spec-head relation with the wh-item. In NIDs, verb movement is triggered even though there is already another head entering into the Spec-head relation with the wh-item. Nevertheless, these are not argu-ments against the wh-criterion itself but only against the connection between verb movement to C and the structural requirement of the wh-item. In other words, the wh-criterion could in principle be correct; what is actually wrong is the identifi-cation of the [+wh] head with the inflected verb and hence the residual V2 char-acter attributed to non-V2 languages. One may suppose that non-V2 languages do not show any V2 residue and that the difference between V2 and non-V2 lan-guages has to do precisely with the need to move the inflected verb to a C° head when its specifier is occupied by an XP. In V2 languages there is always an XP immediately followed by the inflected verb, whereas in non-V2 languages there may be elements occurring in CP but the inflected verb remains inside the IP layer or at a lower CP level. In other words, the wh, the negative, the focus, the subject, and the topic criteria select the verb in V2 languages and a C° head in non-V2 languages. It is therefore only in V2 languages that the constraint that prohibits a sequence like XP-XP V[5] is active.

The second preliminary assumption that one needs to make is that left dislocation always constitutes a barrier for verb movement, as has been proposed by Rizzi (1997). A verb cannot move any further than the left-dislocated position because the LD° head is not "a suitable host for I movement" (p. 20), and this constraint must be operative in V2 languages, too. Hence, verb movement over the LD position is ultimately excluded by the head movement constraint. The fact that the order in (11a)–(14a) is grammatical indicates that the LDP is higher than the CP where wh-items occur. The left-dislocation position is a barrier for verb movement, but this is not a problem for wh-structures, as the wh-CP is lower than the LD position; the inflected verb can reach the C° head of the projection where the wh is and enter the Spec-head relation:

(17) $[_{CP}$ LD $[_{CP}$WH $[\,_{C°}$V] [IP]]]

The co-occurrence between wh-items and V2 is excluded by the fact that both V2 items and wh-items require a Spec-head relation with the inflected verb. Now, let us suppose that V2 items occupy a CP projection higher than LD, as illustrated in (18):

(18) $[_{CP}$ V2 $[_{CP}$ LD $[_{CP}$WH [IP]]]]

Then the verb has to move higher than left dislocation to the C° position where V2 is realized in order to enter the Spec-head relation with the V2 constituent. However, this instance of verb movement violates the head movement constraint, as it has to cross the LD° position without passing through it.

Hence, if left dislocation prevents the verb from reaching the C° position where it enters the Spec-head relation with the V2 constituent, V2 and LD are not compatible and never occur together in the same sentence.[6] A split CP-perspective may directly explain why left dislocation occurs only in interrogative structures in the variety we are considering. Other facts indicate that the V2 position itself in (18) needs to be split up into several projections. These data are now taken into account.

4.4   DIFFERENT DEGREES OF FOCALIZATION

It has often been noted that not all XPs located in first position in V2 clauses have the same degree of focalization. Subjects and circumstantial adverbs (cf. Cinque 1999 on this class) are not focalized at all:[7]

(19)   a. Magari mang-**el** a ciasa, nco.   **-focus**
            perhaps eats-he at home, today
            'Perhaps he will eat at home today'.

         b. Nco mangiun-**z** a ciasa.   **-focus**
            today eat-we at home
            'Today we are going to eat at home'.

    c. Da trai mang-**el** a ciasa //Giani   **-focus**
        sometimes eats-he at home, John
        'Sometimes John eats at home'.

(20)   Duman n vagn-**l** pa nia.
        tomorrow not goes-he not not
        'Tomorrow he is not coming'.

(21)   Giani va a ciasa, sagn.
        John goes to home, now
        'John is going home now'.

However, this does not mean that they cannot be focalized in first position:

(22)   DUMAN n vagn-**l** pa nia.
        tomorrow not goes-he not not (interpretation not-tomorrow)
        'He is not coming tomorrow'.

    If the adverb is focalized, its scope is reconstructed under negation, whereas this is not the case if the adverb is not focalized. This fact suggests that focalization implies movement from a position located lower than negation (or the position where negation is interpreted), whereas in cases like (20) the adverb has not moved from IP and the sentence can be interpreted as basis generation of the adverb in the SpecC position.[8] Circumstantial adverbs may therefore occur in CP as the result of two different strategies: (1) they move from an IP position lower than NegP when they are focalized, and (2) they are base-generated in CP when they are not focalized.

    Objects are always strongly focalized when they are in first position:

(23)   a. L LIBER ti a-**i** de a Giani.
        the book to-him have-I given to John
        'You gave the book to John'.

    b. AD AL ti pans-**i** trees.
        to him to-him think-I always
        'I always think of him'.

    c. CUN GIANI a-i bel bajè.
        with John have-I already spoken
        'I already spoke to John'.

    The so-called "lower adverbs"[9] exhibit the distribution features described below. Some of them cannot be moved into first position at all, and this is the case for *bel* 'already', *plœ* 'anymore', or the postverbal negative markers *min* and *nia*. All of these adverbs can be found only in first position inside a VP topicalization,[10] but they are never moved to SpecC alone [as illustrated by the contrast between (24a) and (24b)]:

(24)   a. *Bel a-**i** mangè
        already have-I eaten
        'I have already eaten'.

    b. Bel i biscoti a-**i** mangè.
        already the biscuits have-I eaten
        'I have already eaten the biscuits'.

This type of adverb behaves as a weak element because it cannot be focalized (cf. Cardinaletti and Starke 1999). The other lower adverbs are always strongly focalized when they are moved to the first position:

(25) a. TREES mang-**el** a ciasa, Giani.
         always eats-he at home, John
         'He always eats at home'.

      b. MAI n mang-**el** a ciasa, Giani.
         never not eats-he at home, John
         'John never eats at home'.

(26) a. TREES n l fej-**l** pa nia.
         always not it does-he not not (interpretation not always)
         'He does not do it always'.

      b. MAI n l fej-**l**.
         never not it does-he (interpretation negative concord)
         'He never does it'.

The scope interactions between the moved adverb and negation are revealing, as the adverb is reconstructed inside a lower position than that in which negation is interpreted. Moreover, the negative adverb *mai* 'never' does not yield an instance of double negation that occurs with the negative marker; its interpretation is one of negative concord, as is normally the case when the adverb is c-commanded by the negative marker. Therefore, lower adverbs are moved up from a position lower than NegP and are always focalized when moved to SpecC.

Another group of adverbs that is neither circumstantial nor made up of lower adverbs considered by informants to be weakly focalized when occurring in first position:

(27) Gonoot n mang-**el** nia a ciasa, Giani
      often not eat-he not at home, John
      'He does not often eat at home'.

(28) D sigu a-**al** mangè a ciasa, Giani
      for sure has-he eaten at home, John
      'John surely ate at home'.

Because they are interpreted inside a position lower than negation, which suggests that there is a variable operator structure in these contexts, I assume that they behave as lower adverbs and that there is no distinction between that which is perceived by informants as strong or weak focus.

Thus objects, lower adverbs, and higher adverbs have to be analyzed in the same way: they are all moved from the inside of the clause to a SpecC position, where they are focalized. Circumstantial adverbs can also follow this pattern and move from IP to SpecC, where they are focalized. In this case, they reconstruct inside a lower position than NegP. Nonfocalized circumstantial adverbs do not reconstruct inside a position lower than negation; therefore it is plausible to assume that they are base-generated in the SpecC position where they surface. Moreover, the position where nonfocalized circumstantial adverbs are merged could be a different "scene-setting" position from the FocusCP targeted by adverbs and objects when they move from IP.

In the next section, this observation is interpreted as indicating that there are several positions hosting V2 constituents and that the structure given in (18) must be expanded, as the position defined as V2 is not a single projection.

4.5   EMBEDDED V2

To show that V2 is not confined to a single CP, one has to consider the phenomenon of embedded V2 with different verb classes. Badiotto is a language that is somewhat in between the "German type," in which only so-called bridge verbs tolerate embedded V2, and Icelandic and Yiddish, in which even interrogative sentences tolerate V2 (cf. Vikner 1995 for a detailed discussion on the two groups). The V2 structures are possible with all types of verbs in declarative contexts but are ungrammatical in interrogative[11] and relative clauses:[12]

(29)   a. A i m a domanè s al fus bel.
        they-they me have asked if it was nice
        'They asked me whether it was nice'.

    b. *A i m a domanè s fuss-**al** bel.
        they they me have asked if was-it nice

    c. A i m a domanè s al fus pa nia bel.
        they they me asked if it was not not nice
        'They asked me whether it was not nice'.

    d. A i m a dumanè can c la s n e e juda.
        they they me have asked when that she herself has gone
        'They asked me when she had gone'.

(30)   a. L liber c al s a tuut sagn e mii.
        the book that he has taken now is mine
        'The book he took is mine'.

    b. (?)?L liber c sagn s a-**al** tuut e mii
        the book that now has-he taken is mine
        'The book that he has taken just now is mine'.

(31)   La Maria che t vaiges duman . . .
        the Mary that tomorrow see-you
        'Mary, whom you will see tomorrow'
        *La Maria c duman vaiges-**t** . . .
        the Mary that tomorrow see-you
        'Mary, whom you often see . . .'

    Also, V2 is possible in embedded declarative sentences, as illustrated in (32). It should be noted that the V2 structure follows a complementizer, as in Scandinavian languages. This is true with both bridge verbs such as *di* 'say' and nonbridge verbs such as *desplejè* 'to be sorry':

(32) a. Al m a dit c magari mang-**el** a ciasa.   Bridge V
         he me has told that perhaps eats-he at home
         'He told me that perhaps he will eat at home'.

      b. Al s depleej c magari mang-**el** a ciasa.   Nonbridge V
         he is sorry that perhaps eats-he at home
         'He is sorry that perhaps he will eat at home'.

Note that this is a real instance of the phenomenon V2, as the V2 constraint still applies: the sentence is ungrammatical if two constituents are placed in front of the verb, regardless of their respective order:

(33) a. *Al m a dit c sagn l liber cumpr-**el**
         he me has told that now the book buys-he
         'He told me that now he is going to buy the book'.

      b. *Al m a dit c l liber zagn cumpr-**el**
         he me has told that the book now buys-he

Let us first examine the distribution of circumstantial adverbs in embedded declaratives:

(34) a. Al m a dit c DUMAN va-**al** a Venezia.   +**focus**
         he me has told that tomorrow goes-he to Venice
         'He told me that he is going to Venice tomorrow'.

      b. Duman va-**al** a Venezia.   −**focus**
         tomorrow goes-he to Venice
         'Tomorrow he is going to Venice'.

Circumstantial adverbs are perfectly grammatical in embedded V2 sentences, though they are necessarily focalized. Informants perceive a clear contrast between (34a) and (34b) in focalization. Whereas (34b) is perfectly grammatical with flat intonation, (34a) can be uttered only if the adverb located at the first position of the embedded clause is strongly focalized. The reconstruction test under negation illustrates the point:

(35) Al m a dit c DUMAN n vagn-l pa nia.
      he to-me told that tomorrow not comes-he not not
      'He told me that tomorrow he is not coming'.

As is the case for focalized constituents in main clauses, the adverb can only be interpreted within the scope of negations in embedded clauses. Hence, the adverb has been moved from its basic position inside the clause and is not base-generated in a very high position, as in matrix clauses [cf. (22)].[13] Circumstantial adverbs are also strongly focalized if the V2 clause is embedded under a non-bridge verb, as in (36):

(36) a. Al s despleej c SAGN va-**al** a ciasa.   +**focus**
         he is sorry that now goes-he at home
         'He is sorry that now he is going home'.

b. Sagn va-**al** a ciasa.   **–focus**
   now goes-he at home
   'Now he is going home'.

These facts receive a natural interpretation within a split-CP framework by
assuming that the scene-setting position where nonfocalized circumstantial adverbs are merged is not available in embedded contexts. As James Higghinbotham
pointed out to me, this assumption is plausible from a semantic point of view. In
fact, embedded clauses do not need to have a "scene-setting" position because it
is already present in the matrix clause. Therefore, circumstantial adverbs can be
located only in a focus position, which is available in embedded clauses. They
are merged inside the IP and then moved to the CP layer (leaving a variable in the
base position, as reconstruction under negation shows). Thus, there are two V2
CPs: one where focalized adverbs (and objects) are located, which is present in
both main and embedded clauses, and one where scene-setting adverbs are located, which is projected only in main clauses:

(37)   [scene-settingCP nonfocalized circ. advs.[FocusCP   [LD   [WH [IP]]]]]

If this hypothesis is correct, it may be plausible to assume that the scene-setting
position is very high in the CP structure and that it is never selected; in embedded
V2, only lower CPs are selected. It should be noted that in all embedded V2 clauses,
a complementizer in front of the V2 item is still obligatory; hence there must be
an additional position higher than the embedded V2 structure and lower than the
scene-setting position (which occurs only in main clauses).

The following contrast suggests that the CP structure has to be split even
further:

(38)   a. Al m a dit c L GIAT a-**al** odù.
          he me has told that the cat has-he seen
          'He told that he has seen the cat'.

       b. *Al s despleej c L GIAT a-**al** odù
          he is sorry that the cat has-he seen
          'He is sorry that he has seen the cat'.

The V2 clauses embedded under bridge verbs differ from the V2 clauses embedded under nonbridge verbs when an object is located in the first position. An
embedded V2 clause where the first position is occupied by an object is grammatical only when the verb that selects the V2 structure is a bridge verb and not
otherwise. The fact that bridge verbs admit more cases of embedded V2s has already been reported in the literature. Bridge verbs also permit embedded V2 in
languages like German and mainland Scandinavian, in which embedded V2 is
generally excluded. What is surprising here is not the contrast between bridge and
nonbridge verbs but the fact that this difference only surfaces for some V2 constituents and not for V2 in general. The contrast between the two verbal classes is
only found with objects and lower adverbs, which are all strongly focalized when
moved to first position, as illustrated by the following examples:

(39)   a. ?Al m a dit c CIAMO' a-**al** mangè.
           he me has told that already has-he eaten
           'He told me that he has already eaten'.

        b. *Al m despleej c CIAMO' a-**al** mangè
           he is sorry that already has-he eaten
           'He is sorry that he has already eaten'.

Circumstantial adverbs are not sensitive to the class of the selecting verb, as the grammaticality of both (35) and (36) shows. This means that there is a split inside the V2 phenomenon and that the V2 structure illustrated in (38) and (39) is not identical to the one illustrated in (35) and (36). There is an interesting way to capture this fact: if one maintains the split-CP perspective adopted so far, the contrast in (38) and (39) could be interpreted as indicating a structural difference in the V2 clauses, depending on the selecting verb; if this is a bridge verb, a wider structure is selected and the position where focalized objects and lower adverbs occur is available. If the selecting verb is not a bridge verb, the position where objects and focalized adverbs occur is not available, and hence the ungrammaticality of (38b) and (39b).

The difference between the two structures selected by different types of verbs is the following:

(40)   [$_{\text{mainscene settingCP}}$ [$_{\text{emb CP}}$XP + foc [$_{\text{embCP}}$ XP + foc.circ.foc [$_{\text{LDCP}}$ [$_{\text{WHCP}}$ [$_{\text{IP}}$]]]]]]

The scene-setting position is excluded from all embedded structures. In other words, embedded V2s always lack a scene-setting position, which can never be selected in embedded contexts (most likely for semantic reasons).[14]

The CP projection where focalized adverbs and objects occur is selected only by bridge verbs. It is possible to move an object or a focalized adverb to the first position of the embedded clause only when the main verb belongs to this class. The position that contains focalized circumstantial adverbs (which can also be used as scene-setting adverbs in main clauses) is selected by both verb classes, and thus focalized circumstantial adverbs can occur in all types of embedded V2.

To sum up the situation, there are three V2 projections in the variety considered here. The highest is the scene-setting position, which is possible only in main clauses and hosts circumstantial adverbs when they are not focalized. An intermediate position hosts focalized adverbs and objects and is selected both in main contexts and in embedded clauses only if the selecting verb is a bridge verb. The third position is selected by both main and embedded contexts with all types of selecting verbs and hosts circumstantial adverbs when they are focalized.

A potential problem in this respect arises from the fact that in all embedded contexts a complementizer appears in front of the V2 structure. Hence, there is always a head position that is higher than the embedded V2 structure with all classes of selecting verbs. This raises the following question: does the complementizer occupy a single position or can it occur in more than one C° head at different levels of the CP layer? If we assume that the complementizer can occupy only the highest position among those selected in embedded contexts, in accordance with

Rizzi (1997), we maintain that the embedded structures always select the same CP projection, namely, the highest one, which contains the complementizer. This contrasts directly with the proposal that different verbal classes may select different CPs. Nevertheless, if we follow Rizzi's assumption that the inflected complementizer is always in the higher C° head, the data in (38) and (39) receive no explanation. One would have to postulate a mechanism that enables the selecting features to percolate through the CP projections, activating some of them and leaving some of them inert (whatever this might mean). This surely would make our analysis less elegant and direct, although it remains an alternative to the approach presented here.

Some independent evidence against the assumption that the inflected complementizer always occurs in the highest C° head has already been presented in chapter 3. It has been shown that the complementizer can occupy very low positions in the CP layer[15] in interrogative clauses. Therefore, the analysis discussed above, according to which differing verbal classes select different CP projections that are used as a landing site for different V2 elements, is maintained. It has been suggested that selecting verbs actually "cut" the CP layer at different points, so bridge verbs select a larger set of CP projections and nonbridge verbs select a smaller structure.[16] This provides a more flexible system than that of verbal selection, which might be used in other contexts also, and shows that V2 is a complex phenomenon that does not occur in a single projection but can be conceived of as a Spec-head relation that exploits different CP projections, as assumed in section 3.

4.6   SUBJECT POSITIONS

As mentioned in the introductory section, the issue concerning the subject position has been widely discussed for Germanic languages. The traditional analysis hypothesizes that the subject is itself in SpecCP when it moves to the first position. However, Zwart (1993) suggests that subject-initial sentences can be better analyzed as AgrSPs, with the subject in the SpecAgrS position and the verb in Agr°. Not all the arguments that Zwart presents for Dutch are considered here, but we look at Romance V2 in order to determine whether this hypothesis may be applied to Rhaetoromance as well. Rhaetoromance V2 syntax offers a clear test for deciding whether the subject is located in CP or in IP, that is, the order with respect to left-dislocated elements.

If the subject occupies the SpecAgrS position, it should occur after left-dislocated elements, in parallel with wh-items (which are located lower than left dislocation). A relevant example follows:

(41)   *L gelato Giani (l) a bel mangè
        The ice cream, John (it) has already eaten
        'John has already eaten the the ice cream'.

(42)   ??L gelato// i (l) a bel mangè
        the ice cream I (it) have already eaten
        'I have already eaten the ice cream'.

As example (41) shows, it is impossible to have a left-dislocated element preceding the preverbal subject. However, there is a small contrast between (41) and (42), in which the subject is expressed by a subject clitic. This appears to indicate that subject clitics can marginally remain lower than subject DPs, most likely in a position within the agreement field analyzed in chapter 2. Subject DPs must always move to the CP layer when they occur in preverbal position; they can never remain lower, as the test with left-dislocation shows.

There is another test for determining the position of the subject inside the CP projections. As seen earlier, embedded V2 does not select the whole CP layer; for instance, the scene-setting position occurs only in main clauses. Bridge verbs select a focus position where objects and focalized adverbs can move and also have focalized circumstantial adverbs as V2 items; nonbridge verbs select only the lower position, where circumstantial adverbs move when they are focalized, but not the higher position, where lower adverbs and objects occur. And what can be said about the subject? If the position of the subject inside the CP field were higher than the one occupied by focalized lower adverbs and objects, a preverbal subject in CP would be impossible in embedded sentences selected by a nonbridge verb. Let us test this prediction:

(43)   a. Al m a dit c Giani va a ciasa.
            he me has told that John goes at home
            'He told me that John goes home'.

       b. Al m despleej c Giani va a ciasa.
            I am sorry that John goes at home
            'I am sorry that John goes home'.

There is no difference between (43a), where the selecting verb is a bridge verb, and (43b), where the selecting verb is a nonbridge verb.[17] Moreover, as preverbal subjects are grammatical, regardless of the class of the selecting verb, we have to assume that the subject position inside the CP field must be lower than the CP where focalized objects and adverbs occur.

There are two possible positions for the subject, higher than left-dislocation and lower than the projection where focalized lower adverbs and objects occur:

(44)   a. scene-setting   [$_{emb\ CP}$XP + foc obj/adv[$_{embCP}$ XPcirc.foc   **SubjP**   LD   WH]]

       b. scene-setting   [$_{emb\ CP}$XP + foc obj/adv[$_{embCP}$ **SubjP**   XPcirc.foc   LD   WH]]

Whereas in (44a) the subject occurs lower than the position where focalized circumstantial adverbs occur, in (44b) it is higher than this position. I have not been able to find any test to distinguish between these two possibilities. Hence, I simply state that the subject position inside the CP field is higher than left dislocation and lower than focalized lower adverbs and objects.[18]

Another interesting observation that could help us to comprehend the connections between V2 and nominative case assignment concerns subject inversion, namely, the possibility of occurring immediately after the inflected verb has moved to C°. As already mentioned, inversion is always possible with subject clitics, which always appear in enclisis after the verb has moved to C°. However, Germanic V2

languages also show DP subjects in the position immediately following the inflected verb in C°. This is valid for Germanic and Old Romance V2 languages.
Within the Central Rhaetoromance domain, there is variation in this feature; in
the S. Leonardo variety considered so far, there is a contrast between subject clitics
and full DPs:

(45) a. *Sagn mangia Giani n pom   S. Leonardo
         now eats John an apple
         'Now John is eating an apple'.

      b. Sagn mang-**el** n pom.
         now eats-he an apple
         'Now he is eating an apple'.

      c. Sagn mang-**el** n pom, Giani.
         now eats-he an apple, John

As illustrated in example (45), only subject clitics can occur immediately after
the inflected verb in C°; full DPs cannot. In a V2 structure like that of (45), the
only possible position for the subject is a right-dislocated one.[19] This is not true in
other Rhaetoromance varieties, such as the one spoken in S. Vigilio:

(46) a. Sagn maia Giani n meil.   S. Vigilio di Marebbe
         now eats John an apple
         'Now John is eating an apple'.

      b. Sagn maie-**l** n meil
         now eats-he an apple
         'Now he is eating an apple'.

The S. Leonardo variety displays the same restriction found in chapter 3 for interrogative sentences in non-V2 dialects because only subject clitics can occur immediately after the verb in C°. Subject clitic inversion is also found in interrogative Rhaetoromance sentences, as the following examples show:

(47) a. l vaighes-**t**?
         him see-you?
         'Do you seen him?'

      b. ci fej-**l**?
         what does-he?
         'What is he doing?'

As seen earlier, the CP projection where wh-elements are checked is very low
in the CP field. Because enclitic subject clitics can occur even in these contexts,
enclitics are located at least as low as the interrogative CP. The same contrast found
between S. Leonardo and S. Vigilio declarative clauses—where a subject DP can
occur only after the inflected verb in C° in S.Vigilio but not in S. Leonardo—is
duplicated in interrogative sentences. In S. Leonardo, only enclitics can occur
immediately after the inflected verb, whereas in S. Vigilio this position is also
accessible to full subject DPs:

(48)   *Ci a-**al** pa Giani fat?   S. Leonardo
       what has-(he) john done?
       'What has John done?'

(49)   Ci a-**al** pa Giani fat?   S. Vigilio

The difference between the two varieties could be accounted for in the following way: in the dialect of S. Leonardo, where only enclitics can be found to
the right of an inflected verb in C°, the SpecAgr position is never occupied by a
subject DP. Hence, the auxiliary DP subject/past participle sequence is ungrammatical. There are three positions in which a DP subject can occur in main interrogatives: a left-dislocated position to the left of the wh-item; lower down, to the
right of the past participle in the postverbal subject position; or a right-dislocated
position in declarative and interrogative clauses. In the S. Vigilio variety, the
SpecAgr position is available to full DPs, which can fill this position when the
inflected verb has moved to C° and an adverb or object enters the Spec-head agreement relation with the inflected verb.[20] As in the S. Leonardo dialect, they can
also occur in a postverbal position after the past participle and in a right-dislocated
position in declarative and interrogative sentences or in a left-dislocated position
in interrogative sentences. The difference between the S. Leonardo and S. Vigilio
dialects is the accessibility of the SpecAgrS position: in the S. Vigilio dialect, this
position can be filled by a subject DP, whereas in the S. Leonardo dialect this is
not admitted. However, this hypothesis is too restrictive. A closer look at the
S. Leonardo data shows that the SpecAgrS position can be occupied in sentences
like the following:

(50)   A i m a domanè can c Maria s n e juda.
       SCL SCL to-me have asked when that Maria herself is gone
       'They asked me when Mary had gone'.

An embedded interrogative clause, where the wh-element (obligatorily followed
by a complementizer) occupies a low CP (recall that left-dislocation can precede
it), can have a subject DP in preverbal position. As this subject cannot be in the high
CP position illustrated in (44), it is most likely located in the SpecAgrS position.
This example shows that SpecAgrS is indeed available for a subject DP in the S.
Leonardo variety, though only if the inflected verb has not moved to the CP domain, presumably for case reasons. Vikner (1995) assumes that in V2 languages it
is always the C° head that assigns case under government to the subject. He further
speculates that this could be the most salient property of V2 and that V2 is triggered
when the inflected verb in C° is able to assign case under government to the subject
DP in SpecAgrS.[21] The parameter that distinguishes V2 from non-V2 languages
would thus be reduced to a case parameter, attributing the possibility of assigning
the nominative case to C°. Vikner discusses this possibility and concludes that "nominative being assigned from C° is not necessarily the reason for V2, however. It is
perfectly possible that there is another reason and that these conditions on nominative assignment are only 'side effects' of the 'real' V2 reason." The S. Leonardo
dialect shows that V2 survives even when no nominative case is assigned through

government from the inflected verb in C° to the SpecAgrS position. This raises the issue of finding an alternative way in which the subject clitic may acquire case in V2 contexts, or whether case is needed at all in these structures because an enclitic subject clitic appears to be incorporated into the verb (see Roberts's 1993c discussion on case and incorporation in Romance languages). If the enclitic SCL is not a true subject but the head of an AgrC projection, as hypothesized in chapter 3, the contrast between (45a) and (45b) is accounted for.

The question of case assignment in V2 languages is far more complex than has been outlined here. This issue constitutes the subject of a future work.

4.7   A BRIEF COMPARISON WITH GERMANIC V2

A discussion on Rhaetoromance V2 cannot exclude a brief comparison with Germanic V2. As already mentioned, Rhaetoromance V2 can be accounted for in a split-CP perspective, where left dislocation is located above the interrogative CP projection but lower than the V2 projections. Furthermore, it has been shown that nonfocalized circumstantial adverbs are located very high in the structure of CP, as they only occur in main contexts. Focalized adverbs and objects are located higher than focalized circumstantial adverbs and subjects, which are in turn higher than left dislocation and interrogative CPs. The structure of the Rhaetoromance CP layer, as outlined previously, is this:

(51)   scene-setting $[_{emb\ CP}$XP + foc $[_{embCP}$?SubjP   XP + →-foc   SubjP? LD   WH]]^{22}

A question that comes to mind about the structure in (51) is whether it may be possible to draw a parallel with Germanic languages. In particular, we may ask whether they have the same structure as the one found in Romance; or is the CP domain different, and in what ways? It is not possible to give a detailed comparison of all Germanic languages with the structure in (51) because the literature about Germanic V2 is extremely vast, and a discussion of all phenomena found in these languages would lead away from the empirical domain being considered here. However, a number of major differences between the two language groups deserves mention.

Left dislocation of the Romance type is not found in languages like German. There are cases of left dislocation in German also, such as the following examples:

(52)   a. Den Hans, den habe ich gesehen.
           the Hans, rel. pronoun have I seen
           'Hans I already saw him'.

         b. Den Hans, wer hat ihn gesehen?
           the Hans, who has him seen?
           'Hans, who saw him?'

(53)   *Die Gretel, den Hans, die wird den schon noch überzeugen   (Altmann 1981: 6–7)^{23}

            the Gretel, the Hans, she will him surely convince
            'Gretel, Hans, she will surely convince him'.

However, German left dislocation is not recursive, as indicated by the ungrammaticality of (53), and does not distinguish between declarative and interrogative contexts, as the grammaticality of (52b) shows. Moreover, it cannot be found in embedded sentences, as illustrated in (54):

(54)   *Ich glaube dass den Hans, den habe ich gesehen
        I think that the John, him have I seen
        'I think that I have seen John'.

It is not clear whether Romance left dislocation is entirely comparable with German left dislocation, and in particular whether or not they occupy the same position. One could attempt to derive the differences from the type of relation instantiated by the left-dislocated item with the pronoun in the clause; in German, left dislocation requires a d-pronoun in the SpecC position, whereas Romance languages use clitic heads or pro. Alternatively, one could make the hypothesis that German left dislocation is located higher up in the structure than Romance left dislocation, as it cannot be embedded (whereas this is possible in Romance languages). Moreover, German left dislocation appears to precede V2 structures, whereas Romance left dislocation follows it (at least in Central Rhaetoromance).

If one also considers the fact that in Germanic languages such as Icelandic or Yiddish, which display generalized embedded V2 and V2 in embedded interrogatives,[24] the order of the V2 element and wh-item is as follows:

(55)   a. Ikh veys nit far vos in tsimer iz di ku geshtanen.   [Vikner 1995: 74 (25)]
           I know not why in the room has the cow stood
           'I do not know why the caw was standing in the room'.

        b. Ikh veys nit [OP tsi ot dos bukh er geleyent   [Diesing 1990: 66 (40)]
           I know not whether PRT the book has he read
           'I do not know whether he read the book'.

        c. Ikh freg zikh vos es hot emitser gekoyft.   [Diesing 1990: 68 (43a)]
           I ask myself what there someone bought
           'I wonder what someone bought'.

Because the wh-item always precedes the V2 element in all these examples, it must be assumed that in these Germanic languages wh-items occupy a position higher than the SpecC occupied by V2 elements. This is exactly the opposite of what has been postulated for Rhaetoromance V2 on the basis of the asymmetry in left dislocation. This opens up the possibility of a parametrization concerning the position of wh-items.

From a first comparison between Rhaetoromance and Germanic V2, two major differences emerge: left dislocation is probably not in the same position, Romance left dislocation being lower than German left dislocation; and wh-items are also located in different positions, that is, lower than V2 in Rhaetoromance but higher than V2 in Yiddish. Hence, it is likely that the structure of the CP field is the same in both language groups, although the same projections are used for different elements. We may conclude this brief discussion by pointing out the fact that the structure found in Rhaetoromance does not have an immediate correspondence within the Germanic domain and that more detailed research is needed to compare the two language groups.

FIVE

Subjunctive Clauses

The Modal Field

5.1   INTRODUCTION

In this chapter, I consider several cases of complementizer deletion in subjunctive selected and nonselected clauses. I show that the inflected V raises higher in subjunctive than in indicative clauses. Moreover, the position of the verb varies, depending on the modal feature that the verb has to check: in optative and counterfactual clauses, the verb moves higher than in suppletive imperatives. The syntactic space-encoding modal distinction is higher than TP and (the set of projections corresponding to) AgrS. Cinque (1999) provides arguments for five distinct modal FPs, each encoding a distinct modal feature and hosting a different type of adverb in its specifier position. The structure he proposes for the modal FPs is the following (see section 5.4.3.2 for discussion):

(1)   [speech act mood frankly [evaluative mood fortunately [evidential mood allegedly [epistemic mood probably [TP past once [TP future then . . .]]]]]]

Cinque (1999) does not debate the question of whether this set of modal FPs is located in IP or in the CP layer. However, some effects observed on the complementizer distribution when the verb is found in a modal F° suggests that the syntactic layer of the modal field is CP. For now, I concentrate on the tests that show verb movement, such as SCI, the complementary distribution between the complementizer and the inflected verb, and adverb positions in modal contexts. Cases of complementizer deletion, referring to languages like English and standard Italian, are well known in the literature. Benincà (1994a) distinguishes four types of complementizer deletion:

1. Old Italian complementizer deletion, which is extended to a wide range of embedded clauses, including relative clauses
2. Modern English complementizer deletion, where the complementizer may be omitted in restrictive relative clauses on the object but not in appositive relative clauses and in restrictive relative clauses on the subject

3. Modern Tuscan deletion, which occurs in appositive relative clauses
4. Modern Italian complementizer deletion in subjunctive clauses selected by bridge verbs

Perhaps not all of these cases are to be interpreted as V to C movement, which blocks the insertion of a complementizer. Some might be better accounted for by a theory that assumes null complementizers or IP selection instead of CP selection. I examine only those cases of complementizer deletion in modern standard Italian and in NIDs, in both selected and unselected contexts, which can be best analyzed in terms of V to C movement.

In the framework outlined here, there are two dimensions along which we find linguistic variation within the CP domain:

1. An intralinguistic dimension: that is, within the same language, the position of the complementizer inside the CP layer can vary in the features marked as strong in a given structure (declarative, interrogative, optative, etc.). Hence, declarative complementizers are located in the highest C° (as Rizzi 1997 assumes), whereas interrogative complementizers are located in a lower C.
2. An interlinguistic dimension: the features of a given structure (interrogative, exclamation, etc.) can be either strong or weak, depending on the language. Hence, some dialects like Portogruarese overtly realize an interrogative complementizer in main and embedded clauses, whereas other dialects like Milanese do not show any overt head in the CP layer in main interrogatives.

If the features in CP are strong, they may be realized in one of two ways:

- There can be movement of the complementizer or the verb from the lowest C° to the position endowed with strong features.
- There can be a combination of two or more lexically realized elements (a complementizer plus the verb plus a type of SCL or, if Zanuttini 1997 is right, even a negative marker), and each element is directly merged into the syntactic position corresponding to the strong feature it checks.

We can also have a mixed situation in which certain elements check more than one strong feature by moving and other elements are merged directly into the position of the strong feature.[1] I exploit these possibilities to account for dialectal variation inside the following empirical domains. Disjunctive clauses are discussed in section 5.2, where it is shown that the complementary distribution between complementizer and inflected verb + SCI constitutes a strong argument in favor of a V to C analysis. Section 5.3 extends the analysis of counterfactual and optative clauses proposed for English to NID data. Another case that may be interpreted as an instance of V to C movement in standard Italian is complementizer deletion in subjunctive clauses selected by a bridge verb (this is examined in section 5.4) . This type of structure is not grammatical in NIDs, even though some sporadic cases of complementizer deletion in cleft sentences and subjunctive clauses selected by the verb *bisogna* 'be necessary' are found.

The last case examined is that of suppletive imperatives with a subjunctive verb like the following:

(2)   a. Che nessuno si muova!
          that nobody himself moves
          'That nobody moves!'

       b. Entri pure, signor Antonio.
          come adverb mister Antonio
          'Come in, Mister A.'

Example (2a) represents a case of nondeictic suppletive imperatives, (2b) a case of deictic suppletive imperatives. For these cases, the empirical argument in favor of a V to C analysis is based on a number of cross-linguistic implications about the occurrence of a complementizer. Here, I do not attempt to extend the analysis to other languages that show similar phenomena, such as English, as the properties of verb movement are quite different from those outlined in NIDs.

5.2 DISJUNCTIVE CLAUSES

In this section, I consider disjunctive clauses, which usually show a subjunctive form of the verb in both standard Italian and in most northern Italian varieties. Standard Italian shows an optional complementizer in these cases, as illustrated in (3):

(3)   a. Che piova o che non piova, noi facciamo una passeggiata.
          that rains or that not rains, we make a walk
          'Whether it rains or not, we are going for a walk'.

       b. Che venga o che non venga, noi facciamo una passeggiata.
          that comes or that not comes, we make a walk
          'Whether he comes or not, we are going for a walk'.

       c. Piova o non piova, noi facciamo una passeggiata.
          rains or not rains, we make a walk

       d. Venga o non venga, noi facciamo una passeggiata.
          comes or not comes, we make a walk

I compare two alternative analyses that account for the lack of a complementizer. The first accounts for sentences like (3c) and (3d) as instances of a phonetically null complementizer, the other as verb movement to the complementizer position. I do not consider an analysis of (3c) and (3d) in terms of IP, as the choice between CP [(3a) and (3b)] and IP would be entirely optional and provide no explanation for the complementizer distribution I intend to present during this discussion.

Within the northern Italian domain, the most widespread structure is the one represented in (3a) and (3b), in which the complementizer is realized in both conjuncts. In some varieties, this is the only acceptable possibility, as in the Vicentino of Cereda or in the Friulian variety of Palmanova.

(4) a. Che piove o che no piove, noialtri ndemo fora.　　　　Cereda (Vicentino)
　　　　that rains or that not rains, we-other go out
　　　　'Whether it rains or not, we are going out'.

　　　b. *Che piove o no piove . . .
　　　　that rains or not rains

　　　c. *Piove o non piove
　　　　rains or not rains

　　　d. C a l plovi o c a nol plovi . . .　　　　Palmanova
　　　　that + SCL SCL rains or that + SCL not + SCL rains . . .

　　　e. *Al plovi o nol plovi . . .
　　　　SCL rains or not + SCL rains

　　　f. ??Cal plovi o (a) nol plovi . . .
　　　　that + SCL rains or (SCL) not + SCL rains

Note that this type of dialect may be analyzed by using both the V to C analysis and the null complementizer analysis. When adopting the first hypothesis, we have to assume that the verb cannot move to the CP layer in these cases. According to the second analysis, we simply state that these varieties do not have null complementizers in their lexicon.

Other varieties also show the possibility of deleting both complementizers, as in the example below. This type of structure is quite rare and has been found in only 6 out of 100 dialects: those spoken in Brione s. M. (in Switzerland, though typologically a northern Lombard dialect), Vaprio d'Adda (Lombard), Cles (Trentino), Forni Avoltri (Friulian), Remanzacco (Friulian), and Pramaggiore (Veneto).

(5) a. Vegni o no vegni . . .　　　　Remanzacco
　　　　comes o not comes
　　　　'Whether he comes or it does not . . .'

　　　b. Plovi o no plovi . . .　　　　Forni Avoltri
　　　　rains or not rains
　　　　'Whether it rains or it does not . . .'

On a par with the data in (4), this type of structure does not help us to discriminate between an analysis in terms of verb movement and one that postulates the existence of phonetically null complementizers. According to the V to C analysis, in these dialects V to C is possible, whereas according to the null complementizer analysis, these dialects can check the disjunctive feature in C° through a null complementizer.

The structure that helps us to discriminate between the two analyses is found in many Friulian, Lombard, and Trentino varieties:

(6) a. Piov-el o non piov-el . . .　　　　Castello (TN)
　　　　rains-SCL or not rains-SCL
　　　　'Whether it rains or it does not . . .'

　　　b. Plov-el o non plov-el . . .　　　　Forni Avoltri (Friulian)

   c. Pio-el o pio-el mia . . .   Malonno (BS)
      rains-SCl or rains-SCL not

The existence of SCI and the fact that it never cooccurs with a complementizer[2] shows that these varieties have V to C movement of the verb in these structures (cf. chapter 3 for a detailed discussion of SCI and for arguments in favor of the hypothesis that it has to be analyzed as V to C).

As the verb moves to a position higher than its usual position in indicative clauses, and this movement is the result of feature checking, one may ask, What is the feature inside the CP layer that must be checked by verb movement? Higginbotham (1991) proposes that disjunctive clauses have a null operator in CP. Hence, the structure of sentences like those in (6) would be very similar to the structure of main interrogative sentences, in the sense that an operator is located in a specifier position of the CP layer. As for interrogatives, we have seen in chapter 3 that the wh-item is not always located in the SpecAgrC position; it may also be located in higher specifiers. Because the disjunctive operator is not a visible one, it is not simple to determine which SpecC position it would occupy. I leave this matter open for the moment, simply pointing out that the presence of an operator in these structures could explain the SCI phenomenon found in the varieties mentioned above. If we apply the analysis of SCI proposed in chapter 3, we obtain a structure like the following:

(7) $[_{AgrCP}$ Op? $[_{AgrC°}$ V + encl.SCL] $[_{CP} [_C$ t] $[_{IP}]]]$

In the varieties that have SCI, the verb reaches the AgrC° position, thus preventing the insertion of a complementizer and showing the enclitic morpheme. Let us sum up all the possible structures found in the sample.

1. In those varieties in which the only possible structure is that shown in (1a) and (1b), where the complementizer is realized in both conjuncts, the strong disjunctive feature in C° is checked by the complementizer, which is, in fact, obligatory in both conjuncts. While examining interrogative clauses in chapter 3, I proposed that the complementizer is merged in the lowest C° position and then moves to higher C° positions, as shown by the clustering of the complementizer with vocalic clitics (see section 2.2.3). As in all dialects that have vocalic clitics, the complementizer also appears to the left of the vocalic clitic in disjunctive clauses [cf. (4d)]; it is plausible to assume that these structures are similar to interrogatives since the complementizer moves at least as high as the vocalic clitic. The structure of sentences like those in (4d) would thus be as follows:

    (8) $[[_{CP} [_{C°}$ ch + SCL $[_{AgrCP} [_{AgrC°}$ t] $[_{CP} [_C$ t] $[_{IP}]]]]]]$

    In this case, if we assume that a null operator is present in these structures, it might be located in the highest SpecC represented in (8) or even higher.
2. The varieties like those in (6) clearly favor a V to C analysis for complementizer deletion cases in disjunctive clauses, as SCI shows.
3. The most dubious cases are those varieties in which no complementizer is present and no SCI is triggered, as in the examples in (5), and we do not

have any direct evidence of verb movement. As mentioned, we have two alternative hypotheses for these dialects: we could assume that these dialects (and standard Italian) have a zero complementizer, which is used in these contexts and is restricted to this usage because it is marked with a strong disjunctive feature that can only be checked in these structures. The second possibility is to admit verb movement to the CP layer, even in those varieties where no SCI is visible.

As noted, the very existence of structures in which V to the CP layer is morphologically visible favors the analysis of V to C movement for the varieties such as those exemplified in (6). The fact that in certain dialects we have a clear indication that the verb moves to C° also favors the same analysis for all varieties in which no complementizer is present, hence even for cases like (5). In fact, if we assume that in some dialects the lack of a complementizer is due to V to C movement, whereas in other dialects the same phenomenon is due to the presence of a null complementizer, we introduce a redundancy in the theory. Therefore, I pursue the hypothesis that complementizer deletion in disjunctive clauses is always due to V to C movement in order to check a strong disjunctive feature. Let us suppose that we follow this hypothesis; a problem emerges immediately concerning why SCI is not always found. Some varieties never show SCI, not even in interrogative clauses, and one might suppose that in these dialects the movement of the verb stops lower than AgrC, probably in the lowest position C°, where the complementizer is inserted, or reaches AgrC°, although no overt morpheme is visible. This is true for dialects such as many Ligurian and Lombard varieties, which have lost SCI altogether at approximately the beginning of this century. However, in Friulian dialects, although SCI is maintained in interrogatives, nevertheless the examples in (5) do not show SCI.

Note, however, that in the varieties in which SCI is grammatical in disjunctive structures, the verbal form used is never the subjunctive but the indicative (or in some cases, the indicative form is indistinguishable from the subjunctive when SCI is added):

(9) a. Plo-el o plo-el miga . . .   Monno
        rains-SCl or rains-SCL not
        'Whether it rains or it does not . . .'

     b. Che l ploes o che l ploes miga . . .
        that SCL rains or that SCL rains not

In the variety of Monno (Eastern Lombard) , SCI occurs only with the indicative. If the subjunctive mood is used, a complementizer is realized.

In the variety of Malonno, inversion occurs with the indicative form:

(10) a. Egn-el o egn-el mia . . .   Malonno (Eastern Lombard)
         comes indicative-SCL or comes indicative-SCL not
         'Whether he comes or he does not . . .'

      b. Pio-el o pio-el mia . . .
         rains indicative-SCL or rains indicative-SCL not
         'Whether it rains or it does not . . .'

In the variety of Bagnolo S. Vito (Emilian), only inversion is possible, and the form is ambiguous between an indicative and a subjunctive verb:

(11)   Vegna-l o vegna-l mia . . . .   Bagnolo S. Vito (Emilian)
       Come-SCL or comes-SCL not
       'Whether he comes or he does not . . .'

In the variety of Villa Lagarina (Trentino), inversion occurs only when the form is ambiguous between indicative and subjunctive, whereas no inversion and no complementizer appear when the form is unambiguously subjunctive. The same is true in the Friulian dialect of Forni Avoltri:

(12)   a. Piov-el o non piov-el . . .   Villa Lagarina
          rains-SCL or not rains-SCL
          'Whether it rains or it does not . . .'

       b. Vegna o nol vegna . . .
          Come or not SCL comes
          'Whether he comes or he does not . . .'

       c. Plovi o no plovi no i fazin uno chiaminada.   Forni Avoltri
          rains subjunctive or not rains subjunctive, we make a walk
          'Whether it rains or it does not, we are going for a walk'.

       d. Plov-el o no plov-el . . .
          rains indicative-SCl or not rains indicative-SCL
          'Whether it rains or it does not . . .'

From these data, we can conclude that SCI is possible only when the verb is inflected in its indicative form. We can reformulate this observation with the following descriptive generalization:

(13)   The present subjunctive does not tolerate SCI in NIDs.

This statement may be interpreted in two ways: we can assume that the present subjunctive can also move to the C domain as the indicative form, though this movement is not visibly encoded by SCI, or alternatively we could hypothesize that the lack of morphology corresponds to a lack of movement and that the present subjunctive lacks SCI because it does not move to the CP domain. In other words, there are two possible reasons that SCI is incompatible with the present subjunctive, even though the present subjunctive moves to AgrC°: (1) a morphological reason or (2) a strictly syntactic reason. As we have assumed that SCI is the morphological instantiation of verb movement to the AgrC position, one could assume that this morphological reflex of verb movement is not found in present subjunctive forms for purely morphological reasons (it is a fact that the subjunctive in most varieties shows less agreement morphology than the corresponding indicative form) and that V movement to AgrC occurs all the same. However, the imperfect subjunctive also shows less agreement morphology than its corresponding indicative form and SCI with the imperfect subjunctive is still found in many contexts and in many dialects (see section 5.3). Therefore, the fact that SCI and the present subjunctive are incompatible cannot be due to the poor agreement morphology of the present subjunctive. There might be another reason for the incompatibility, or one could assume that the present subjunctive does not have an SCI because this form never reaches AgrC; it remains lower down in the structure, even though it reaches the lowest C° position, thus entering the CP layer. One might assume that in dialects like Monnese in (9b), repeated here as (14a), the subjunctive remains inside IP and a complementizer is realized; in varieties like that of Forni Avoltri [example (14b)] it raises to the lowest C position, thus preventing the occurrence of the complementizer:

(14)   a. Che l ploes o che l ploes miga . . .   Monno
            that SCL rains + subjunctive or that SCL rains not
            'Whether it rains or it does not . . .'

       b. Plovi o no plovi no i fazin uno chiaminada   Forni Avoltri
            rains + subjunctive or not rains + subjunctive, we make a walk
            'Whether it rains or it does not, we are going for a walk'.

The sample of 100 dialects examined for this work does not contain a single variety that admits SCI with the present subjunctive form in any of the contexts in which SCI is triggered. This is clearly a fact that needs to be explained, though for the moment I leave the matter open, as it requires a very subtle analysis of verb movement of all verbal forms in each of the varieties considered.

If it is true that SCI is possible only for the indicative form (whatever the reason might be) and that the present subjunctive never shows inversion even though it moves to the CP layer, we can treat those dialects that show no SCI and no complementizer [cf. (5)] as involving V to C movement also, at least to the lowest C° position, even though this movement is not morphologically visible. This analysis of complementizer deletion in disjunctive clauses of NIDs as V to C movement could also be extended to standard Italian. As I do not have strong arguments to support this extension, I leave the question open for further research.

5.3   OPTATIVE AND COUNTERFACTUAL CLAUSES

Another type of sentence in which complementizer deletion is found is represented by optative and counterfactual clauses, which in standard Italian show the same complementizer occurring in embedded yes/no questions, namely, *se*:

(15)   a. Fosse arrivato in tempo!
            were arrived in time
            'Had he arrived in time!'

       b. Se fosse arrivato in tempo!
            if were arrived in time
            'If he had arrived in time!'

(16)   a. Se fosse stato più attento non sarebbe a questo punto.
            if were been more careful, not be + subjunctive at this point
            'If he had been more careful, he would not be in such a situation'.

       b. Fosse stato più attento, non sarebbe a questo punto.
            were been more careful, not be + subjunctive at this point

(17)   a. Se andasse anche Giorgio, saremmo felici.
           if go + subjunctive also Giorgio, (we) were + subjunctive lucky
           'If Giorgio went there too, we would be happy'.

        b. Andasse anche Giorgio, saremmo felici.
           go + subjunctive also Giorgio, (we) were + subjunctive lucky

Standard Italian admits both possibilities, although the one without the complementizer is more stylistically marked.[3] These cases have already been noted by Rizzi (1982) and are well known in the literature for triggering subject inversion in English, as the glosses show. Inversion is also possible in standard Italian, and this is an argument for analyzing the Italian phenomenon as V to C movement in comparison with the English case:

(18)   Avesse Giorgio comunicato la variazione al direttore, tutto sarebbe a posto,
        adesso.
           had G. communicated the change to the director, everything be-subjunctive OK
           now
           'Had Giorgio told the director about the change, everything would be OK by
           now'.

In English, this structure is possible only with auxiliaries, whereas in Italian, it is also grammatical with lexical verbs, although it has an optative meaning in addition to a counterfactual one.[4]

(19)   a. Lavorasse anche Gianni, finiremmo prima.
           worked + subjunctive also Giorgio, (we) finish earlier
           'If John worked too, we would finish earlier'.

        b. Se lavorasse anche Gianni, finiremmo prima.
           if worked + subjunctive also Giorgio, (we) finish earlier

(20)   a. Li lavasse anche Giorgio, finiremmo prima.
           them washed also Giorgio, finish earlier
           'If John washed them, too, we would finish earlier'.

        b. Se li lavasse anche Giorgio, finiremmo prima.
           if them washed also Giorgio, finish earlier

The NIDs show that this is a context of subject inversion and may therefore be analyzed as V to C. In fact, many varieties show SCI exactly when no complementizer appears:

(21)   a. Fuse-lo lugà par temp!   Cencenighe Agordino (northern Veneto)
           were-SCL arrived for time
           'Had he arrived in time!'

        b. Fos-el rivat in timp!   Forni Avoltri (Friulian)

        c. Fossi-al rivat in timp!   Sutrio (Friulian)

        d. Fose-lo ruè a temp!   Laste (Rhaetoromance)

        e. Fusse-lo riva in tempo!   Padua (Central Veneto)

    f. Fuss-al arivè a d'ore!   Cesena (Emilian)

    g. Fossel arivè in temp!   Bologna (Emilian)

Also, SCI is possible in counterfactual clauses:

(22) Gavesse-lo fato presto, nol gavaria perso el treno.
      had-SCL done hurry, not-SCL had missed the train
      'Had he not been late, he would not have missed the train'.

Thus the presence of SCI shows that a V to C analysis, already proposed for the English case, is also correct for Romance varieties, most probably even for standard Italian, even though the evidence from subject inversion in standard Italian is limited to auxiliary structures. A case comparable to standard Italian is found in many varieties that do not show SCI even when the complementizer is not realized; the SCL remains in preverbal position:

(23) a. El fus arivà en temp!   Cles (Trentino)
         SCL were arrived in time!
         'Had he arrived in time!'

      b. El fudes rivà in temp!   Milano (Lombard)

      c. A fussa rivà an temp!   Turin (Piedmontese)

      d. Al fos riat en temp!   Malonno (eastern Lombard)

Here, there is no evidence of movement of the verb to the CP layer. Some of these varieties have lost SCI in all contexts (like Milanese, for instance) and are identical to standard Italian, in the sense that these languages do not morphologically encode verb movement to the CP layer. We can only suppose that movement has occurred for two reasons: (1) internal evidence—the complementizer is missing; and (2) cross-linguistic evidence—in other varieties we see that SCI is obligatory when the complementizer is missing.

A more complex case is that of dialects like Cles or Malonno, in which SCI is still possible in other contexts. In the Cles variety, SCI occurs in main interrogative clauses:

(24) Cant parti-o po?
      when go-SCL interrogative marker?
      'When are you leaving?'

In the Malonno variety, SCI is obligatory in main interrogative clauses (with do-support) and in disjunctive clauses (without do-support) (see Benincà and Poletto 1998 about this difference and the do-support phenomenon in general):

(25) a. Fa-i nda ndoe?
         do-SCL go where?
         'Where do they go?'

      b. Pioe-l o pioe-l mia . . .
         rains-SCL or rains-SCL not . . .
         'Whether it rains or it does not . . .'

Thus in these varieties the inflected verb has not moved to the SCI position in optative and counterfactual clauses, even though the complementizer is missing,

One could see this as an argument for an analysis of these cases as instances of null complementizers. However, verb movement would still have to be postulated, as SCI actually does occur in some dialects. Therefore, I try to reduce all cases of complementizer deletion in these contexts to cases of verb movement, though the verb does not move up to the SCI (AgrCP) position but only to a lower CP projection.

As seen in chapter 3, the AgrCP projection that hosts SCI is not the lowest CP projection, the position where the complementizer is merged in the lowest C°, located immediately below AgrCP. The complementary distribution between the complementizer and the verb does not imply movement to the SCI position, which can occur at a lower level. Even though the complementizer moves to higher C° positions to check its features, it cannot occur if its basic position is already occupied by the inflected verb.

Another interesting phenomenon that can shed some light on this discussion is found across the northern Italian domain. Many varieties use the declarative complementizer *che* instead of the complementizer *se* for optative and counterfactual clauses:

(26)   C al fossi rivat in timp!   Cesarolo (Friulian)
       that SCL were arrived in time!
       'Had he arrived in time!'

In a split-CP perspective the specialization of different complementizers for different C° positions is just what we expect to find. Languages can have a single complementizer that has neutralized all morphological differences corresponding to different strong syntactic features and that moves to different C° heads, depending on the features it is endowed with; or we can find languages in which different C positions require morphologically different complementizers. The declarative complementizer is morphologically different from the interrogative complementizer, located lower in the interrogative subpart of the CP layer. In these varieties, the complementizer used in optative and counterfactual clauses is the declarative and not the interrogative one. In section 5.5, I consider varieties that have a special complementizer for suppletive imperative clauses.

5.4   COMPLEMENTIZER DELETION AND VERB MOVEMENT IN ITALIAN

5.4.1   Introduction

In this section, I examine a well-known phenomenon in standard Italian (cf. Rizzi 1982) , complementizer deletion (CD). As I have proposed in sections 5.2 and 5.3, this is interpreted as the result of verb movement to a low C° position, probably the lowest C° position of the CP layer.

In this work, I have assumed a split-CP perspective. Cinque (1999) adopts a similar approach in the IP domain, providing evidence for a very fine-grained functional structure on the basis of the relative positions of the verb (past participle and inflected verb) and adverbs. Combining the two proposals, we obtain a very rich sentence structure that I use to explain the phenomenon of CD. As in the previous sections, the first empirical observation to be explained is the possibility of omitting the complementizer in certain embedded structures. I show that an analysis in terms of verb movement to the C position, where the complementizer originates, is plausible for the three following reasons: (1) the class of verbs selecting CD complements is exactly the same as the Germanic selected V2 contexts; (2) when the complementizer is deleted, the verb cannot occur to the right of higher adverbs, whereas this is possible when the complementizer is realized; and (3) the occurrence of a preverbal subject appears to be quite restricted, as in main interrogatives, for which we admit V to C movement.

5.4.2. Complementizer Deletion as V to C

5.4.2.1 *The Data*

Complementizer deletion is possible in standard Italian under certain particular conditions. Example (27) illustrates this case:

(27) a. Credo che abbia già parlato con te.
       think that have + subj already spoken with you
       'I think that he has already spoken to you'.

      b. Credo abbia già parlato con te.
       think have + subj already spoken with you

The CD is optional and stylistically marked: the sentence in (27b) is slightly more formal than in (27a). The CD is possible only if the embedded verb is inflected for the subjunctive [as in (27)], future indicative, or conditional, as in (28) and (29), respectively[5,6]:

(28) Credo sara' interessante ascoltarlo.
      think it be + fut interesting to listen to him
      'I think that listening to him will be interesting'.

(29) Credo funzionerebbe meglio, se lo riparassi.
      think work + cond better if (you) repaired it
      'I think that it worked, if you repaired it'.

Moreover, CD is possible only if the embedded sentence occupies the basic complement position, as in (30), and not if it is a left-dislocated clause, as in (31a), or a subject (31b) (cf. Cinque 1999):

(30) a. Tutti credono che sia una spia.
       all think that be + subj a spy
       'Everybody thinks that he is a spy'.

      b. Tutti credono sia una spia.

(31)   a. *(Che) sia una spia, lo credono tutti
       that (he) be + subj a spy, everybody believes it
       'Everybody thinks that he is a spy'.

      b. *Sia una spia è risaputo
       that (he) be + subj a spy, is well known

On the basis of these examples, we may conclude that CD has at least two requirements, one for the position of the embedded clause and one for the kind of inflection on the embedded verb. Only the subjunctive, future indicative, and conditional permit CD, and only when the embedded sentence occupies a complement position.

The third restriction on CD concerns the selecting verb, which needs to be of a particular class:[7]

(32)   a. *Mi dispiace lo faccia
       me sorry it do + subjunctive
       'I am sorry that he does it'.

      b. Credo lo faccia.
       think it do + subjunctive
       'I think that he does it'.

It is interesting to note that CD is also possible when the selecting element is an adjective or, at a higher stylistic level, a noun:

(33)   a. Sono certo tu lo possa fare.
       am certain you it can do
       'I am sure that you can do it'.

      b. La probabilità si tratti di uno scambio di persona è molto remota.
       The probability is a case of mistaken identity is very remote
       'The probability that it is a case of mistaken identity is very remote'.

Thus, CD applies when three distinct conditions are satisfied:

1. The embedded clause has to be in the complement position of a verb, a noun, or an adjective.[8]
2. The embedded verb has to be a subjunctive, a conditional, or a future indicative.
3. The selecting element has to belong to a special class.

5.4.2.2   Analysis

The CD phenomenon was originally reported by Rizzi (1982), who connects it to structures of Aux to C without explicitly arguing that it is a case of verb movement to the C° position. Scorretti (1981) analyzed CD as a case similar to raising contexts, in which the CP projection is not projected and the structure embedded under the lexical verb is simply an IP. Italian verbs like *credere* 'believe' are similar to raising verbs, in the sense that they can select an IP instead of a CP as their complement. It may be noted that the CP versus IP selection possibility would be completely optional.

This view, though appealing, is not the one I take here. As I already mentioned in the introduction, it is fairly difficult to deal with optionality in a minimalist framework. Moreover, bridge verbs in standard Italian would be completely different from bridge verbs in the Germanic languages because they are assumed in the former standard to select a recursive CP, a larger structure with respect to other verbs and not a smaller structure such as IP, as proposed by Scorretti for Italian bridge verbs. Moreover, a split-CP approach enables us to account for different selection restrictions of matrix verbs in syntactic terms, if we make the hypothesis that different verbal classes select different CPs. This hypothesis has already been put forth while analyzing data of Rhaetoromance V2 dialects, which show different V2 restrictions depending on the selecting verb. I capitalize on the observation that the class of Italian verbs that permits CD is the same class that permits V2 in embedded contexts in V2 languages like German, in which V2 is restricted to matrix clauses. It may be interesting to establish a connection between Italian bridge verbs and Germanic bridge verbs that permit embedded V2.[9]

Therefore, I hypothesize that the selection properties of bridge verbs are different from those displayed by other verbal classes, although they are the same in Italian and Germanic languages. I draw a comparison between the following two sentences:

(34)   a. Credo sia già partito.
        think is already gone
        'I think he has already gone'.

       b. Ich glaube er ist schon weg.
        'I think he is already away'.

The classical analysis of V2 in Germanic languages such as German, Dutch and mainland Scandinavian is well known and has already been outlined in chapter 4: it deals with V2 as a case of V to C° movement and the movement of an XP into the SpecC position. The fact that in these languages V2 is a matrix phenomenon is immediately captured by the fact that in embedded sentences a complementizer occupies the C° position, preventing V to C° movement. However, cases of embedded V2 selected by a special class of verbs (usually referred to as bridge verbs) in German and mainland Scandinavian (but not in Dutch) appear to establish a counterexample to the claim that the complementizer and the verb can occupy the same position. It is interesting to note that in German the complementizer alternates with the moved verb, whereas in mainland Scandinavian the complementizer and the moved verb co-occur.

Most proposals in the literature concerning the solution to this problem refer to the selection properties of bridge verbs, which are seen in a certain sense as "special" verbs: it has been proposed that bridge verbs are capable of selecting a "double CP" where CP recursion occurs, and this is the solution that we are forced to adopt for languages like MLSC since both the complementizer and the verb are found at the left periphery of the sentence. Another approach considers bridge verbs as having no selection properties at all so the CP projection of their complement is free from selection features and may host V2 exactly as matrix contexts. Note that the hypothesis of a double CP also accounts for the Scandinavian facts, whereas the second hypothesis does not leave enough room for both the complementizer and the verb.

I discuss a possible analysis of this problem later. Let us assume for the moment that embedded V2 is a case of V to C, at least in the subset of Germanic languages we are considering here. Hence, we can maintain the hypothesis that all instances of V2 are cases of V to C movement. This is true even in embedded contexts, where the complementizer is not realized because the inflected verb occupies its position, as in (34b), in German or when a higher complementizer is realized in mainland Scandinavian.

If we want to adopt this analysis for the Italian CD phenomenon as well, we can formalize our proposal as in (35):

(35)   a. [$_{CP}$ [$_C$ che] [$_{AgrP}$ [$_{Agr°}$ abbia] [$_{TP}$]]]

      b. [$_{CP}$ [$_C$ abbia] [$_{AgrP}$ [$_{Agr°}$ t] [$_{TP}$]]]

When the complementizer is not realized, as in (35b), the inflected verb has moved to C° and fills this position, exactly as in German V2 contexts. Before applying this hypothesis to Italian CD, we need to solve at least two questions: (1) why is standard Italian not a V2 language in all matrix clauses? (2) Why do we find only half of the V2 phenomenon, that is, V to C° movement, but we do not see an XP in the SpecC position in CD contexts, as in the case of Germanic languages?

As for the first problem, many proposals in the literature (see, among others, Tomaselli 1990, and Vikner 1990) consider V2 to be a movement phenomenon triggered by a morphological feature in C°, which must attract the verb in order to be satisfied. Standard Italian is not a V2 language, so no morphological feature is realized in C° in the normal case. Nevertheless, I propose that there is a feature in C° that can attract the verb to C in standard Italian only in the CD context and in other restricted cases, such as interrogatives. We look at what kind of feature this can be later. For the moment, let us call it feature F and note that it must clearly be selected by the lexical verb. Hence, I do not propose anything new with respect to the analyses that consider embedded V2 under bridge verbs to be a consequence of special selection properties of these verbs.

The same has to be admitted in V2 Rhaetoromance varieties discussed in chapter 4, where we have seen that only certain types of adverbs can be moved to a SpecC position, triggering V2 if the selecting verb is a nonbridge verb. However, if the selecting verb is a bridge verb, all types of adverbs can be moved into a SpecC position. This contrast has been treated in terms of split CP by saying that bridge verbs select one CP projection more than other verb classes and that precisely this projection is the landing site for certain types of adverbs when they are moved to the CP layer. Hence, even in a split-CP framework, bridge verbs have the special property of selecting one CP more than other verbs, although this property is defined as the selection of a different (higher) projection, not as "CP recursion."

Hence, generally speaking, the fact that standard Italian is not a V2 language does not imply that the V2 strategy is excluded from all contexts. In certain special structures such as CD contexts or interrogative sentences, the V2 phenomenon can be found even in standard Italian.

The second problem we mentioned involves the second half of the V2 phenomenon, the movement of the XP to the SpecC position. This is indeed possible in Italian, at least for some speakers, as the following example shows:

(36) a. Credo LA MELA abbia mangiato.
      think the apple has eaten
      'I think that he has already eaten the apple'.

  b. Ich glaube den Apfel hat er gegessen.
     I think the apple has he eaten

The example is grammatical only with a strong focus on the preposed object *la mela* 'the apple'. However, in standard Italian it is not obligatory to fill the SpecC position in CD structures. The verb can be the first element of the embedded clause, as the above examples show [cf. (34)].[10]

Therefore, I provisionally assume that CD can be treated as a case of V to C movement, though it partially differs from the Germanic embedded V2 because it does not require the movement of an XP to the SpecC position. In the next section, I provide three arguments in favor of this hypothesis.

5.4.3 Arguments for V to C

5.4.3.1 *Comparison with German Bridge Verbs*

The first piece of evidence for treating CD as a case of verb movement to C°, as already mentioned in the previous section, is the similarity between CD and embedded V2 in V2 languages like standard German. The class of elements (verbs, adjectives, or nouns) that permits CD in Italian is the same class that permits embedded V2 in German (see Cinque 1989 for adjectives and adverbs):

(37) a. Ich glaube du hast es getan.
      I think you have it done
      'I think that you have done it'.

  b. Credo tu l'abbia fatto.
     (I) think you it have + subj done

(38) a. Es ist gefährlich, dass du es tuest.
      it is dangerous that you it do
      'It is dangerous for you to do it'.

  b. *Es ist gefährlich du tuest es
     it is dangerous you do it

  c. E' pericoloso *(che) tu reagisca cosi'
     is dangerous (that) you react so
     'It is dangerous that you react in this way'.

(39) a. Die Hoffnung, er wird es schaffen, nimmt ständig zu.
      the hope, he will it do, is increasing
      'The hope that he will succeed is increasing'.

b. La speranza si tratti di un errore non è ancora svanita.
the hope is an error is not yet faded
'The hope that it is an error has not faded yet'.

Moreover, elements that do not select embedded V2 clauses in German as factive verbs do not permit CD in Italian:

(40)   a. *Johann bereut, er konnte nicht kommen
John regrets he could not come
'John regrets that he could not come'.

b. *Mi rammarico non possa venire
I regret cannot come
'I regret that he cannot come'.

It is interesting to note that V to C is a slightly stylistically marked phenomenon in both Italian and in German embedded contexts. This makes the two constructions even more similar than they would appear to be at first sight.

5.4.3.2   Movement Around Adverbs

The second piece of evidence for assuming that CD is an instance of verb movement to C° is provided by adverb positions. As already mentioned in the introduction, I accept Cinque's (1999) analysis of the number and type of FPs that correspond to IP in more traditional terms. I do not sum up all the arguments Cinque gives for proposing such a complex structure but limit myself to outlining the higher portion of the FPs contained in IP that is relevant to our analysis.

The structure of the higher portion of IP, as proposed by Cinque (1999), is the one illustrated in (41):

(41)   [$_{\text{speech act mood}}$ frankly [$_{\text{evaluative mood}}$ fortunately [$_{\text{evidential mood}}$ allegedly [$_{\text{epistemic mood}}$ probably [$_{\text{TP past}}$ once [$_{\text{TP future}}$ then [$_{\text{irrealis mood}}$ perhaps [$_{\text{alethic mood}}$ necessarily]]]]]]]]

Structure (41) shows the order of the FPs and the adverbs located in the specifier position of each FP.[11] Hence, we have a fairly complex syntactic realization of tense, mood, and modality: the highest position is the one occupied by speech-act adverbs like *frankly*, located in the specifier of a speech-act mood head; the next is an evaluative MoodP that hosts adverbs like *luckily*, followed by evidential mood and then followed by an epistemic modality projection that hosts epistemic adverbs. The series of mood projections is broken up by the two tense projections (past and future) that are higher than the irrealis mood and the modal FPs (only the highest is represented here by AlethicModP). If this complex structure is contained in the IP layer and if we accept Cinque's approach in which adverbs cannot be moved from where they appear (apart from wh-movement and topicalization, which are easily detectable), the position of adverbs with respect to the inflected verb provides a good test for establishing where the verb is located. As each of these projections has a head position, in principle the verb could appear in any of the possible positions provided by the adverbs or only in some, perhaps depending on the verb's inflectional features and on the language examined.[12]

Let us restrict our attention to subjunctive, conditional, and future indicative tenses under bridge verbs, that is, the contexts in which CD can apply. If CD does not apply, a lexical verb can appear lower or higher than epistemic adverbs:

(42) a. Credo che sicuramente lo faccia.
          think that surely do + subj. it
          'I think that he will surely do it'.

      b. Credo che lo faccia sicuramente.[13]
          think that do + subj. it surely

Following Cinque's (1999) proposal, we would have to postulate that the verb can move to the EvalMod° head, crossing the position of the epistemic adverb, or remain below, perhaps in the epistemic head or even lower down in the structure. Lexical verbs cannot move to the left of evaluative adverbs, as (43) shows:

(43) a. Dicono che fortunatamente abbia lasciato la città.
          say that luckily left the town
          'They say that luckily he let the town'.

      b. *Dicono che abbia fortunatamente lasciato la città
          say that left luckily the town

Following the structure presented in (41), we can interpret the contrast in (43) as showing that the verb cannot move higher than the evaluative modal head.[14] Let us now examine the same examples following CD:

(44) a. *Credo sicuramente lo faccia
          think surely do + subj. it
          'I think that surely he will do it'.

      b. Credo lo faccia sicuramente.
          think does it surely

      c. *Credo fortunatamente verrà entro domani
          think luckily come + fut. within tomorrow
          'I think that luckily he will come tomorrow'.

      d. Credo verrà fortunatamente entro domani.
          think come + fut luckily within tomorrow

      e. *Dicono evidentemente abbia lasciato la città
          say allegedly has left the town
          'People say that allegedly he left the town'.

      f. Dicono abbia evidentemente lasciato la città.
          say has allegedly left the town

Note that if the complementizer is deleted, the verb has to cross the epistemic adverb and reach a higher position, whereas this movement is not obligatory at all in non-CD contexts. The relevant contrast is therefore illustrated in the following examples:

(45) a. Credo che sicuramente lo faccia.
          think that surely do + subj. it
          'I think that he will surely do it'.

b. *Credo sicuramente lo faccia
   think surely he do + subj. it.

This fact has a clear explanation if we adopt the hypothesis I am proposing here, namely, that CD is an instance of V to C movement. As the verb has to move to C°, it must occur in a higher position than epistemic adverbs. Hence, it must move up not only to the EvalMod head but even higher, to the C° position. This is not true for the non-CD context, where the verb can move to EvalMod, though it may also remain in a lower head position.

If our claim that the verb moves to C° in CD contexts is correct, we may expect the same type of judgment to be found for higher adverbs, like evaluatives; these must be found to the right of the verb that has been raised to C° and cannot occur on its left, as is the case in non-CD contexts:[15]

(46)   a. *Credo fortunatamente riesca a farcela
           think luckily succeeds to do it
           'I think that luckily he will succeed'.

        b. Credo riesca fortunatamente a farcela.
           think succeeds luckily to do it

Example (46a) is out, whereas (46b) is grammatical. This confirms our hypothesis that the verb has to rise higher than the evaluative modal head in CD contexts but does not need to do so when the complementizer is overtly realized. The other relevant contrast for our hypothesis is the one between (43a) and (46a), repeated here as (47):

(47)   a. Credo che fortunatamente lo faccia sempre.
           think that luckily does it always
           'I think that luckily he always does it'.

        b. *Credo fortunatamente lo faccia sempre
           think luckily it does always

Example (47) shows that in non-CD contexts the verb cannot move higher than the evaluative modal head; (46a) shows that in CD contexts the verb has to move higher than the evaluative modal head. This contrast is directly accounted for by our hypothesis that the verb is moved to C° when the complementizer is not there. In (46), the verb has to move to C°, and therefore it occurs higher than the adverb, whereas in (47), the C° position is occupied by the complementizer and the verb has to stay below the adverb.

5.4.3.3 *The Modal Feature*

So far, it has been assumed that CD is analogous to the verb second phenomenon in the sense that it is an instance of V to C movement. As mentioned, German and mainland Scandinavian languages exhibit the embedded verb second under bridge verbs. We have seen that in German no complementizer appears when the verb moves to C° in this context. However, it is a well-known fact that this is not true for all the Germanic languages we are considering: mainland Scandinavian languages show embedded V2 and a complementizer that appears above the CP where the verb is moved:

(48) a. Ich glaube du hast es getan.   German
         I think you have it done
         'I think you have done it'.

      b. Hun sagde at vi skulle ikke kobe denne bog.   Danish
         'She said that we should not buy this book'.

In (48b) the verb is in C°, as it has climbed above the position of the negative marker *ikke*. Vikner (1990), commenting on his example (103) [reported here as (48b)], suggests that there are two C positions in these structures. He considers the phenomenon of embedded V2 as a case of CP recursion. We do not need to postulate CP recursion, however, as the split CP analysis we adopt here already provides the tools for analyzing cases like (48b).

The claim that there exists more than one C position in the Germanic domain has been put forth in a number of recent works. Hoekstra (1992) shows that in Dutch dialects three distinct C positions are available because three complementizers can co-occur, as illustrated in (49) [which corresponds to Hoekstra's (1b)]:

(49) Dat is niet zo gek als of dat hij gedacht had.
      that is not as crazy C1 C2 C3 he thought had
      'This is not as crazy as he had thought'.

Hoekstra reports that it is possible to coordinate sentences at the level of the first, second, or third complementizer, as in (50) [Hoekstra's (4)]:

(50) a. Als of dat hij koning is en dat zij koningin is . . .
         C1 C2 C3 he king is and C3 she queen is
         'As he is the king and she is the queen . . .'

      b. Als of dat hij koning is en of dat zij koningin is . . .
         C1 C2 C3 he king is and C2 C3 she queen is

He points out that these examples show that the three complementizers occupy different head positions and force us to assume that the structure of the sentence above AgrP is much more complex than is normally believed.[16]

In the Romance domain, we have found evidence to assume several CP positions. The interrogative subdomain contains four projections, which can host different heads (the inflected verb + SCI, a complementizer, a vocalic subject clitic, etc.) and whose specifiers are open to wh-elements that are interpreted in different ways, depending on the specifier they occupy.

In chapter 4, some Rhaetoromance dialects were examined, and again a split-CP analysis was proposed, with four positions located higher than the interrogative subdomain: one position for the subject, one for focalized adverbs, and focalized arguments, one for focalized circumstantial adverbs, and a scene-setting position that contains scene-setting circumstantial adverbs.

Now, we face two distinct problems for the analysis of standard Italian CD. The first is the existence of all these CP projections in standard Italian. The existence of these FPs has been postulated on a cross-linguistic basis by examining data collected from different NIDs. However, as already mentioned in chapter 1, NIDs have very similar grammars, and it appears plausible to assume that the functional projections activated are the same in all dialects and that what varies is the verb or complementizer movement range. There is no straightforward proof of this for standard Italian, as we do not have evidence for the existence of the FPs we postulated for NIDs; standard Italian is not a generalized V2 language and does not show any clear morphological device that corresponds to syntactic V to C movement. The second problem concerns the CP structure we have discussed so far and the position of the C° that the verb moves into, thus raising the following question: is it the lowest CP position already postulated for the interrogative domain, or is it a lower or a higher position than the interrogative domain?

Because standard Italian never shows SCI, we have no morphological signal that helps us to distinguish between a very low position inside the CP domain and a high position corresponding to one of the V2 positions of Rhaetoromance or to the highest C° of the interrogative domain. We may capture the CD phenomenon by saying that the inflected verb has access to the CP layer, as the complementizer is usually merged in the lowest C° position. Hence, CD itself does not give us any clues about which C position is reached by the moved verb. Nevertheless, there is a test for verb movement inside the CP layer in standard Italian, too. As mentioned, CD is subject to three distinct restrictions (see section 5.2):

1. The embedded clause has to be in a complement position.
2. The embedded verb has to be a subjunctive, a conditional, or a future indicative.
3. The selecting element has to be of a special class.

Note that CD is possible only if the embedded verb is a subjunctive, a future, or a conditional form. All these forms have a modal quality, in the sense that they all express a possibility and not a reality. Hence, they all express a [-realis] feature. Moreover, the class of selecting elements (verbs, adjectives, and nouns) expresses an opinion. Therefore, the feature it selects can be plausibly assumed to be a [-realis] feature realized on the head of the complement and attracting the verb into the CP domain.[17] As mentioned in section 5.3, where we examine counterfactual, hypothetical, and optative clauses, we may follow Rizzi's (1997) observation that in some languages modal features are realized very low in the CP layer. It may be assumed that this is also true for standard Italian. If standard Italian has a low CP projection, encoding a modal feature, we can hypothesize that a [-realis] feature occurs on the C° head located lower than the interrogative subdomain in CD contexts. This feature must be realized by some overt element: a complementizer or the inflected verb (if it is compatible, i.e., if it can express the [-realis] feature as subjunctive, future, or conditional). Thus, the strong feature of the lowest CP can be realized by the complementizer or by the verb, which is forced to move to the lowest C° position. According to this hypothesis, it must be assumed that the complementizer can occupy the head of this low position in the context we are considering. Instead, Rizzi assumes that finite complementizers in standard Italian are realized only on the highest head, namely, Force°. As mentioned in chapter 3, the interpretation made here and that proposed by Rizzi could be reconciled by assuming that the complementizer is merged in the lowest C° position and then moved, depending on the strong features it may have in a given sentence.

There is one piece of evidence that indicates that the movement of the verb in this context does not cross the left-dislocation position, unlike that which occurs in Rhaetoromance V2 varieties:

(51) Credo, il tuo libro che loro lo apprezzerebbero molto.
      I believe, your book, that they would appreciate it a lot
      'I think that they would appreciate your book a lot'.

In this sentence there is a topic element (*il tuo libro* 'your book'), which precedes the complementizer. As Rizzi judges this sentence to be ungrammatical, he concludes that a complementizer such as *che* can occupy only a head position located higher than TopP, namely, the head of ForceP. However, the sentence in (34) is judged by many speakers to be well formed or at most marginal. One could therefore conclude exactly the opposite, that the complementizer may be realized in a position lower than TopP, or at least this may be so in contexts such as the one we are examining. It may be that for some speakers the complementizer has to move to the highest C position, whereas for others it can remain lower. Given the contradictory judgments that we have from Italian speakers, the data need to be investigated in greater depth. I leave this factual problem open. Let us sum up the proposal made in this section: verbs (adjectives and nouns) that express an opinion select a [-realis] feature located in a low C head inside the CP domain. This feature has to be realized by the complementizer or by the verb that moves into this C°.[18]

5.4.3.4   *A Third Argument: The Subject Position*

In this section, I discuss part of an issue that has not yet been mentioned—the subject position. The analysis of the subject position(s) in CD contexts is presented in the next chapter. Here, I show only that the prediction the analysis of CD as V to C for preverbal subjects is correct. If CD is a case of V to C, there should be some visible effects on the subject, and notably these effects should be similar to those found with other V to C cases, such as main interrogatives. The data for the subject position are rather delicate, as speakers give differing judgments. Giorgi and Pianesi (1997) show that speakers split into two classes: those who admit only a pro subject (class I speakers) and those who admit a lexical subject (class II speakers). For class II speakers who admit a lexical subject, this may appear only to the left of the inflected verb:

(52)   a. Credo Gianni arrivi stasera.
          think John arrive + subj tonight
          'I think that John will arrive tonight'.

       b. Credevo nessuno arrivasse in tempo.
          thought nobody arrive-subj in time
          'I thought that nobody would arrive in time'.

No one accepts sentences in which the subject has inverted, as in Germanic V2 contexts, exactly as in interrogative sentences:

(53)   *Credevo fosse Gianni arrivato
          thought had John arrived
          'I thought that John had arrived'.
          *E' Gianni arrivato?
          'Has John come?'

We discuss this problem in the next chapter, showing that sentences like those in (53) are impossible because there is no position available for the subject after the inflected verb; the usual preverbal position is higher in the CP layer and not in SpecAgrS, as is currently assumed.

Let us concentrate for the moment on class I speakers, who admit only a pro subject.[19] This situation is identical to main interrogative contexts, where no subject can intervene between the wh-element and the inflected verb. Moreover, there is no postverbal position for the subject, as in (54):

(54)   a. *Cosa Gianni ha fatto?
             what John has done?
             'What has John done?'

        b. *Cosa ha Gianni fatto?
             what has John done?

Hence, it appears that this class of speakers treats the subject in interrogative and CD contexts in exactly the same way—only pro-drop subjects are admitted. This fact is immediately captured by our hypothesis that CD is a case of V movement into the CP domain, whereas it would remain unexplained if we assumed an analysis in terms of CP deletion or of empty complementizers. One problem remains— the second class of speakers, who admit a lexical subject in CD contexts. This problem is dealt with in the next chapter, where the position of the subject in declaratives, interrogatives, and CD contexts is taken into account on the basis of the split-CP and split-AgrS analysis.

5.4.4   Conclusion

The CD phenomenon found in standard Italian can be treated as a case of V to C movement triggered by a [-realis] modal feature located in a low C° position on the basis of three arguments. The first is the analogy found with German embedded V2 contexts, where V to C is selected by the same class of verbs that selects CD in standard Italian. The second argument is based on Cinque's (1997) hypothesis for adverb positions; it is shown that the verb must occur to the left of evaluative adverbs in CD contexts, whereas it must occur lower when the complementizer is realized. This suggests that the verb must move higher than the adverbs only when the complementizer is deleted. The third argument concerns the subject position; for a class of speakers, CD shows exactly the same obligatory pro-drop phenomenon found in main interrogatives in which V to C applies.

In the next section, I examine cases of CD in northern Italian dialects.

5.5 COMPLEMENTIZER DELETION IN
THE NORTHERN VARIETIES

The northern Italian domain does not show cases of CD comparable to those found in standard Italian (analyzed in the previous section), apart from Tuscan varieties. In Tuscan dialects, CD appears to be quite widespread in the CD context and is also possible in appositive relatives (see Benincà 1994a):

(55) a. Si credeva (he) fosse tardi   Colle Val D'Elsa
          one believed (that) was late
          'We thought that it was late'.

      b. Sembra (he) abbia gridato qualcuno
          seems (that) have cried somebody
          'It seems that somebody cried'.

      c. Spero sia arrivato in tempo.
          hope be + subjunctive arrived in time
          'I hope he has arrived in time'.

(56) a. Bisogna tu te ne vada subito.   Florence
          is-necessary you yourself from-here go now
          'You have to go away right now'.

      b. Ho l'impressione sia arrivato Mario.
          have the impression be + subjunctive arrived Mario
          'I have the impression that Mario has arrived'.

      c. Mi pare siano molto comode queste sedie.
          me seems be + subjunctive very comfortable these chairs
          'These chairs seem very comfortable to me'.

      d. L'ho detto a Mario, l'ho visto ieri.   Florence (Benincà 1994: 4)
          it said to Mario, him saw yesterday
          'I said this to Mario, whom I saw yesterday'.

Both the CD context and relative appositive complementizer deletion is not found in the sample of dialects examined outside the Tuscan domain. There must be a reason that the CD context does not trigger complementizer deletion in NIDs because other cases of complementizer deletion are indeed possible, as we have seen for optative, counterfactual, and disjunctive clauses.[20] Since all CD contexts appear to be connected to some modal [-realis] feature, one could assume that the difference between Tuscan and standard Italian, on the one hand, and NIDs, on the other, is due to the fact that NIDs can realize the modal feature in the low $C°$ only through the complementizer, whereas Tuscan and standard Italian can realize it through the complementizer or through the rising of the inflected verb.

However, this is not an explanation, just a simple description of the facts. If we want to understand why NIDs do not show CD in [-realis] embedded clauses, we have to look for some other factor connected to the difference between Tuscan and standard Italian on one side, and NIDs on the other. One possibility that comes to mind and is worthwhile exploring is a structural difference between the standard Italian and the NID CP layer. In NIDs, higher positions such as CP2 are activated even in CD contexts, as the presence of deictic clitics that occur in that position shows. This feature could block the percolation of the modal feature down the structural tree from the selecting verb to the low modal C° head.[21] This would not be the case in standard Italian. However, there might be a problem for an analysis cast in structural terms because Tuscan dialects behave like standard Italian and not like NIDs, though they seem to have a CP structure with vocalic clitics and, in more conservative varieties, SCI similar to NIDs.

Another solution to the problem could be based on a difference in the selection properties of the matrix verb. In optative, counterfactual, and disjunctive clauses, there is no selection by a main verb that imposes the modal feature to the embedded CP, as in the standard Italian CD context. The difference might be connected to this fact. Thus NIDs do not have V to C in selected contexts, and this could be ultimately a property of the selecting verb, which does not impose a modal feature in NIDs. This solution is not very appealing because it reduces the ultimate difference between Tuscan, (and standard Italian) and NIDs to a lexical difference in the class of bridge verbs. Moreover, it is more interesting to maintain the selection properties of verb classes constant across languages, as they ultimately derive from their semantics. Hence, bridge verbs probably select a [-realis] complement also in NIDs, as they do in Tuscan, standard Italian, and Germanic languages.

A number of cases of complementizer deletion in embedded contexts in northern Italian varieties can indeed be found. One may be the Romagnolo clauses embedded under a verb like *bisogna* 'to be necessary' (see Benincà and Poletto 1994 for a detailed analysis of the particular structure of a verb like *bisogna*).

(57)   a. Bisogn t vegna anca te.   Forlì
           is necessary SCL come also you
           'You have to come, too'.

        b. E bsogna t vegia vi sobat.   Forlì
           SCL is-necessary SCL go + subjunctive away now
           'You have to go away immediately'.

This apparently suggests that complementizer deletion is indeed connected to a lexical property of the selecting verb and that *bisogna* has the property of marking its embedded clause with a modal feature, whereas other verbs do not. However, it is not by chance that the only verb under which complementizer deletion is admitted in NIDs is *bisogna* because this verb has been analyzed (in Benincà and Poletto) as lacking a thematic grid and being a purely functional element inserted under a modal head but projecting no VP. The selection of a modal feature by a true selecting verb that projects a VP, including a complement clause, appears to be excluded in NIDs.

Romagnolo and Emilian varieties also show complementizer deletion in cleft structures:

(58)   a. T i te t as n vu brisa capir.   Bologna
           SCL is you SCL not want not understand
           'It is you who does not want to understand'.

b. T i te t la comper sempar.
SCL is you SCL it buy always
'It is you who always buys it'.

(59)   Ci te t avrè chicosa da racuntem.   Forlì
is you SCL will-have something to tell-me
'It is you who will have something to tell me'.

These cases do not appear to be similar to those discussed so far, and they could probably be best treated as reanalysis toward a monoclausal structure, not as V to C. What remains to be understood is why selected V to C is not found in NIDs (apart from Tuscan). Therefore, I leave this matter open, as it needs more detailed empirical research on the structural differences encoded in the CP layer in Tuscan and in NIDs.[22]

5.6   SUPPLETIVE IMPERATIVES

The analysis in this section is a very tentative one and has been included to complete the view of complementizer deletion contexts in NIDs and mostly to present the data that could be useful for future research. Therefore, I give a possible extension of the V to C analysis to these CD contexts in a highly speculative manner.

Suppletive imperatives of the third person show a subjunctive verb in standard Italian and in NIDs. The following sentences show some examples of the third person with a quantifier or DP subject in preverbal and postverbal positions.[23] The data are in standard Italian.

(60)   a. (Che) nessuno si muova!
'(That) nobody moves!'

b. (Che) qualcuno mi aiuti!
'(That) somebody helps me!'

c. (Che) non entri nessuno!
(that) not come-in nobody
'That nobody comes in!'

d. (Che) Mario si presenti subito dal direttore!
(That) Mario himself present immediately to the director
'Mario has to go immediately and see the director!'

e. (Che) entri pure anche il vostro amico!
(that) come-in also your friend
'Your friend may come in, too!'

Non-deictic suppletive imperatives have an optional complementizer in standard Italian. This is not the case for the following deictic suppletive imperatives, where the verb is still in its subjunctive form:

(61)   a. (*Che) entri pure, signor Antonio
(that) come-in, Mister Antonio
'You may come in, Mister Antonio'.

b. (*Che) parli pure, signor Antonio
   (that) speak, Mister A.
   'You may speak, Mister Antonio'.

Standard Italian does not admit a complementizer in sentences like those in (61). The distribution of CD in suppletive imperatives in standard Italian is the following: CD is optional in nondeictic imperatives and obligatory in deictic imperatives. The situation in NIDs is partially different. A lot of varieties show a complementizer (obligatory in some cases, optional in others) even in deictic suppletive imperatives; the sentence corresponding to (60d) contains a complementizer:

(62) a. Ch al vegni dentri, sior Toni.   Remanzacco (Friulian)
         that SCL come in mister T.
         'You may come in, Mister Antonio'

      b. Ch l vegna vanti, sior Antoni.   Bellinzona (Northern Lombard)
         that SCL come ahead, Mister Antonio
         'You may come in, Mister Antonio'.

Some varieties of the Ligurian area show a special complementizer, used only with deictic suppletive imperatives. This complementizer cannot be used in other contexts, not even with nondeictic suppletive imperatives:

(63) a. Scia parle pure, su Antoniu   Savona
         complementizer speak Mister A.
         'You may speak, Mister Antonio'.

      b. Scia intre su Antoniu   Savona
         complementizer come in, Mister A.
         'You may come in, Mister Antonio'.

      c. scia l'intre S. Antonio   Chiavari
         complementizer come in, Mister A.
         'You may come in, Mister Antonio'.

The fact that standard Italian makes a difference between deictic and non-deictic suppletive imperatives, and that certain Ligurian dialects have a special complementizer used only with deictic suppletive imperatives, leads us to postulate that the complementizer that appears in the nondeictic suppletive imperative and the complementizer that appears in the deictic suppletive imperatives are different and probably located in two different positions. The cross-linguistic data show that there is a one-way implication between the two complementizers, which can be formulated in the form of the following descriptive generalization:

(64) A given dialect has a complementizer with deictic suppletive imperatives only if
      it always has a complementizer for nondeictic suppletive imperatives.

All dialects confirm this generalization; I have not found a variety that shows an overt complementizer with deictic suppletive imperatives and no complementizer with nondeictic suppletive imperatives. The only dialects found can have

1. A complementizer with nondeictic suppletive imperatives and no complementizer with deictic suppletive imperatives.

2. A complementizer with both deictic and nondeictic suppletive imperatives (the form of the complementizer may differ)

Still following the idea that complementizer deletion corresponds to V to C movement, we see that it is plausible to apply the analysis even to suppletive imperatives. No dialect shows SCI in suppletive imperatives, though this is not surprising since suppletive imperatives have a present subjunctive form, which never shows SCI even in other structures in which SCI is possible with other verbal forms (see the discussion on disjunctive clauses in section 5.2). Nevertheless, if we accept the idea of V to C in these structures also, the implication mentioned above can be immediately accounted for by a split-CP analysis.

Let us suppose, as we did above, that the complementizer of deictic suppletive imperatives occupies a different C° position than the complementizer of nondeictic structures. If the nondeictic complementizer occupies a higher C position and the deictic complementizer occupies a lower position, we may expect that verb movement to the higher position implies verb movement to the lower position:

(65) $[_{\text{-deictic CP}} [_{\text{C}°} \text{ che } / \text{V} [_{\text{+ deictic CP}} [_{\text{C}°} \text{ che/V}]]]]$

The possibilities predicted by (65) are these:

1. Obligatory movement of the verb to both C°s. In this case no complementizer is realized in any suppletive imperative.
2. Optional movement to the higher C° and obligatory raising to the lower C°. In these cases the complementizer is optional in nondeictic imperatives and impossible in deictic imperatives (cf. standard Italian).
3. Optional movement to both C°s, which gives as a result an optional complementizer in both deictic and nondeictic imperatives.
4. Optional movement to the lower C° and impossible movement to the higher C°. This case triggers the occurrence of an obligatory complementizer in nondeictic imperatives and of an optional complementizer in deictic imperatives (cf. Western Lombard and Emilian).
5. No verb movement to any C°. In this case a complementizer is obligatory in deictic and nondeictic imperatives (Northern Lombard).

Hence, if it is possible to omit the complementizer in -deictic structures, this means that the verb has moved up to the higher C° and it can reach the +deictic lower C° position, too. As a result, this will give a type of language in which the complementizer is never obligatory, neither in + deictic nor in –deictic suppletive imperatives. If a language has obligatory movement of the verb to the lower +deictic C° position, the complementizer will never appear in these contexts, as it does in standard Italian.

This approach predicts the nonexistence of a language with the opposite value, that is, a language in which the complementizer is obligatorily omitted in nondeictic suppletive imperatives, though it may be realized in deictic structures. This is precisely what the descriptive generalization in (64) states; a language like this would have to force verb movement to a higher C° position but not to a lower C°, having a complementizer in the lower C° while adopting verb movement for the higher one. A language like this has not been found in the sample of dialects I have examined, and if it turned out not to exist, this would establish a strong argument in favor of a split CP plus V to C analysis. The one-way implication noted above is also immediately accounted for by this approach; if verb movement to the deictic lower C° is blocked and a complementizer fills the position, verb movement to the nondeictic higher C° will also be blocked and a complementizer will be obligatory in this case, too. A language that does not permit verb movement to the lower C° position will not permit movement to the higher C° position, and a complementizer will be necessary in both cases. Several Friulian varieties display this system. Although there is no direct evidence for supposing verb movement in the case of suppletive imperatives, it would be very difficult to imagine an explanation of the implication discussed above in terms of null complementizers; one would have to limit oneself to stating that null complementizers in nondeictic suppletive imperatives imply null complementizers in deictic suppletive imperatives.

A possible problem for analysis in terms of split CP plus V to C movement may be given by nondeictic structures, in which a preverbal subject is realized:

(66)   Nessuno si muova!   Standard Italian
        'Nobody moves!'

If the verb has moved to C, does this mean that the subject has moved to some SpecC position? There is an interesting piece of data, discussed at length in the following chapter, which seems to indicate that the subject can indeed move to SpecC in these structures. Many Piedmontese, Ligurian, and some Northern Lombard dialects show structures such as the one in (67):

(67)   a. Gnun ch' a s bogia!   Turin (Piedmontese)
           nobody that SCL moves!
           'Nobody moves!'

       b. Mario ch a s presenta . . .
           M. that SCL presents himself . . .
           'Mario has to go immediately . . .'

       c. Caidun ch a m giuta!   Riva di Chieri (Piedmontese)
           Somebody that SCL me helps!
           'Somebody help me!'

       d. Nissugn ch 'i s movi!   Cevia Valle Maggia (Northern Lombard)
           nobody that SCL moves!
           'Nobody moves!'

       e. Qualchedun ch um ma giuta!   Borghetto di Varo (Ligurian)
           somebody that SCL me helps!
           'Somebody help me!'

       f. Mario ch u s presenti . . .   Carcare (Ligurian)
           M. that SCL presents . . .
           'Mario has to go immediately . . .'

Here, the subject appears to the left of the complementizer. As QPs are included, this cannot be analyzed as a left-dislocated position; this can only be a SpecC position. I analyze this structure in the next chapter. For the moment let us state that the existence of these examples lends support to an analysis that places the subject in a SpecC position in these structures.

Other interesting data about the interaction between the subject and the complementizer are the following. In nondeictic suppletive imperatives, in which a subject is realized, the presence of a complementizer appears to be connected to the type and position of the subject. If the subject is a preverbal DP, the complementizer is realized in the varieties examined.[24] If the subject is a postverbal DP, most dialects will show a complementizer, although there are dialects in which the complementizer is not realized (again, the phenomenon does not have a typological distribution, as these examples have been found in a few Veneto, Eastern Lombard and Trentino varieties):

(68) a. E vegna dentro anca el vostro amigo.   Altavilla Vicentina (Veneto)
        And comes in also the your friend
        'Your friend may come in, too'.

      b. Al vegna pur anca el vost amis.   Vaprio d'Adda (Lombard)
        SCL comes in also the your friend

      c. El vegna pur anca el vos amico.   Trento (Trentino)
        SCL comes in also the your friend

If the subject is a QP, the complementizer is obligatory when the QP is realized in postverbal position, whereas it becomes optional when the QP is realized in preverbal position (again, the only exceptions are Colle Val d'Elsa and Franco-Provençal).[25]

These data are analyzed in the next chapter, when considering the possible subject positions and case assignments. Anticipating the discussion in chapter 6, I assume that these differences between DP and QP subjects lead us to assume that DPs and QPs do not occupy the same subject positions, whether they occur preverbally or postverbally. Moreover, the fact that the complementizer is sensitive to the subject position may be interpreted as indicating that it has a role in nominative case assignment. In this perspective, NIDs will thus be similar to V2 languages, for which nominative case assignment from the $C°$ position has been proposed, a hypothesis that needs to be refined (see Poletto and Tomaselli 1998).

5.7   CONCLUSION

In this chapter, I have examined several cases of complementizer deletion and proposed a V to C analysis for them. This has already been proposed for Germanic languages (see the literature mentioned above). Although many cases of complementizer deletion cannot be analyzed as V to C, I have tried to show that at least in some cases this is a viable hypothesis. A split-CP analysis, combined with V to C movement, enables us to account for many interesting facts, in both standard

Italian and NIDs. I have not discussed any extension to other languages with a similar pattern, such as English. But the plausibility of a hypothesis in the terms proposed here must first be evaluated on the basis of each single language. A problem that remains open is how to integrate the CP subdomains examined in chapters 3, 4, and 5. The question is whether the interrogative subdomain is the lowest or whether the subjunctive (or modal) subdomain is located at the border with the IP layer. It could also be that they might even coincide or partially overlap. This problem is given a partial solution in the final chapter, though a lot of work still has to be done.

SIX

Subject Positions

6.1 INTRODUCTION

In the course of this work, I have examined the AgrS and CP syntactic spaces, analyzing how many projections build up these structural portions and which elements occupy which positions in NIDs. In this chapter, I discuss the problem of the preverbal subject position(s), leaving aside postparticipial subjects, as I am concentrating on the higher portion of the sentence structure.[1] In chapter 2, I propose the idea that what is called the AgrS position in languages like standard Italian corresponds to at least two SCL positions inside IP (the postnegative ones) and that one more position (the one realizing the [+/–speaker] value) is occupied by the inflected verb. Two more types of SCLs are merged inside the CP layer and located higher than the position in which the complementizer is merged.

I now discuss the problem of the preverbal subject position in the light of the structural hypothesis I have made concerning the agreement field, which has been shown to be a discontinuous set of SCL positions, some of which are realized in IP, others in CP. The structure assumed for the agreement field is the following:

(1) $[_{LDP}$ inv SCL_i $[_{CP}$ deic SCL $[_{whP}$ t_i $[_{IP}$ $[_{NegP}$ $[_{NumbP}$ SCL $[_{HearerP}$ SCL $[_{SpeakerP}$ inflV $[TP]]]]]]]]]$

The leading idea of this chapter is that the SpecAgrS (or SpecT) position is not the final landing site of a DP, nor that of a QP subject in NIDs (and most probably in standard Italian, too), and that the only preverbal position that can be filled by a full subject is located inside the CP field. Moreover, I distinguish between the position of a DP subject and the position of a QP subject. Although the subject position for DPs is probably a "topiclike" position, I do not assume that DP subjects are always left-dislocated because left-dislocated elements occur in front of the subject, and hence in a higher position inside the CP domain.

In section 6.2, I distinguish between preverbal QP or DP subjects; I propose to interpret the dialectal variation found for subject clitic doubling in NIDs as an argument in favor of the idea that DPs and QPs check their case in a different way. Moreover, I provide arguments to show that the subject position is located inside the CP structure and not inside the IP layer, as is currently assumed for all Romance languages. Section 6.3 examines the position of the DP and QP subjects with respect to the verb in main and embedded interrogatives and other constructions, such as exclamative and relative clauses, Aux to C, and absolute participial constructions.

6.2   SUBJECT POSITIONS AND CASE CHECKING

6.2.1   Subject Clitic Doubling in NIDs

The first argument in favor of the idea that QP and DP subjects have different properties comes from the descriptive generalizations of clitic doubling that can be formulated on the basis of the set of dialects investigated here. At first sight, the phenomenon of subject clitic doubling in NIDs appears to be a very complex area of inquiry, as there is a lot of variation inside the sample of dialects considered (for data and discussion, see Poletto 1993). In this section, I give a systematic description of the doubling phenomenon with respect to agreement SCLs, whereas in section 6.2.2.2, I consider cases of SCL doubling with respect to invariable and deictic SCLs. The dialectal variation pattern may be described by a number of generalizations already observed for object clitic doubling in other Romance varieties. These can be expressed in the form of one-way implications, so that if a given type of subject in dialect X is obligatorily doubled, other types of subjects in the same dialect are always doubled too. In Poletto (1993), I discussed two of the three implications reported here:

(2)   a. If DPs are doubled in a given dialect, tonic pronouns are also doubled.

   b. If QPs are doubled, both DPs and tonic pronouns are doubled.

   c. If variables in wh-contexts such as relative, interrogative, and cleft structures are doubled, doubling is always obligatory with all other types of subjects.

The implications in (2) are valid in general for both the preverbal and postparticipial subject positions, which are disjunct, in the sense that there may be doubling with the preverbal position but not with the postparticipial position or vice versa.

   The situation may be summed up in the following table, with dialects corresponding to each stage represented in (3):[2]

(3)		Tonic Pronoun	DPs	QPs	Variables
	a.	+	−	−	−
	b.	+	+	−	−
	c.	+	+	+	−
	d.	+	+	+	+

I illustrate the table with examples, considering only preverbal subjects. The first stage of clitic doubling in (3a) is represented by many Central Veneto dialects. In this type of dialect, the only obligatory doubling occurs with tonic pronouns:[3]

(4) a. TI te magni sempre.   Venice
        YOU SCL eat always

     b. *TI magni sempre
        YOU eat always

Thus, DPs occur only optionally with SCLs. As left-dislocation is usually optional, sentences like (5a) could be considered as left-dislocation structures, in which the subject clitic is similar to the object clitic doubling left-dislocated constituents in many Romance languages. I discuss this hypothesis further in section 6.2.2. Note that in this type of dialect it is not possible to have doubling with QP subjects, which cannot be left-dislocated (cf. Cinque 1990):

(5) a. Nane (el) magna   Venice
        John (SCL) eats

     b. Nisun (*el) magna
        nobody (SCL) eats

The second type of dialect is represented by Trentino and a few Lombard varieties, in which a preverbal definite DP subject is obligatorily doubled, whereas a QP does not tolerate doubling. This is true for lexical verbs; auxiliaries have a different syntax for SCL doubling, as I have shown in Poletto (1993b; see also Roberts 1993c for an analysis of auxiliary SCLs):

(6) a. Nissun (*el) me capis   Montesover (Trentino)
        nobody (SCL) me understands
        'Nobody understands me'.

     b. El popo *(el) magna el pom   Montesover
        'The child SCL eats the apple'

     c. Nisogn (*el) me capess   Lecco (Northern Lombard)
        nobody me understands
        'Nobody understands me'.

     d. El bagai *(el) mangia el pom   Lecco
        'The child SCL eats the apple'

One could assume that Trentino and Northern Lombard dialects have left-dislocated DP subjects, too. However, the phenomenon of doubling is obligatory, not optional, as left-dislocation generally is. Moreover, we have to find a theory that accounts for the difference between Trentino and Northern Lombard, on the one hand, and Venetian, on the other. In both cases, QPs cannot be doubled. However, doubling is obligatory with Trentino and Lombard DPs, whereas in Venetian it is not. One would have to explain why left dislocation is optional in Veneto and obligatory in Trentino and Northern Lombard, and this cannot be enforced simply by a constraint that imposes that the left-dislocation position has to be filled in each sentence. All pro-drop contexts immediately falsify such a constraint. Therefore, the difference between Veneto and Trentino and Northern Lombard is not a simple matter to analyze. I make the hypothesis that subject clitic doubling in Trentino and Northern Lombard is different from left dislocation of the subject, which is the structure assumed for Veneto in doubling sentences.

The third case, illustrated by (3c), is represented by a variety like Milanese and Eastern Lombard dialects, like the variety of Monno. They show doubling with DPs and QPs but not with variables:

(7)   a. El fio el mangia l pom.   Milan
         'The boy SCL eats the apple'

      b. Un quidun el riverà in ritart.
         a somebody SCL will-arrive in late
         'Somebody will arrive late'.

      c. I don che 0 neten i scal in andà via.
         'The women who clean the stairs have gone away'.

      d. L pi l maja l pom.   Monno
         'The boy SCL eats the apple'

      e. Vargu i ruarà tarde.
         'Somebody SCL will arrive late'

      f. Le fomne che netaja le scale e ndade.
         'The women who clean the stairs have gone'

The last case, (3d), is represented by dialects that have spread subject clitic doubling to all types of subjects; the SCL is always present even when the subject is represented by a variable left by wh-movement. This is the case of Friulian,[4] most Piedmontese dialects, and some Ligurian and Lombard varieties:

(8)   a. Al pi al mangia al pom.   Malonno (Eastern Lombard)
         'The boy SCL eats the apple'

      b. Vargu al rierà n ritardo.
         'Somebody SCL will arrive late'

      c. Le fomne che le neta le scale e e ndade via.
         'The women who SCL clean the stairs SCL have gone away'
         Nisun al mi capiss.   S. Michele al T. (Friulian)
         'Nobody SCL me understands'

      d. Qualchidun al telefonarà al profesuor.   Forni Avoltri (Friulian)
         'Somebody SCL will phone the professor'

      e. Gnun a m capiss.   Turin
         nobody SCL me understands
         'Nobody understands me'.

      f. Niscun u me capissce.   Alassio
         nobody SCL me understands

We can conclude that SCL doubling is not a unitary phenomenon in NIDs because it is sensitive to the type of subject being doubled and because the type of subjects that may double vary from one dialect to another. Therefore, the proposal made by Rizzi (1986b), who assumes that SCLs are agreement markers, needs to be refined to account for the differences described above.

As a possible explanation to the implications represented in (3), one could assume that it is the position of SCLs that influences their behavior, determining the possibility of co-occurrence or not with a DP or QP subject. However, the results of a systematic inquiry on the basis of the tests used in chapter 2 that discriminate among different SCL positions have not been able to distinguish between, for instance, Veneto and Trentino third-person SCLs, even though they behave differently in their co-occurrence with DP subjects. Hence, I discard the hypothesis that clitic doubling variation is connected to the different positions of SCLs.

Another possible hypothesis to account for the pattern in (3) concerns the movement of the DP or QP subject from its argumental position inside VP to the preverbal position: one may capture the clitic-doubling phenomenon by assuming that in certain dialects DP/QP move directly to the preverbal position, leaving the specifier of the SCL positions in IP empty, whereas in other dialects the DP/QP subject passes through the SpecSCL positions in IP on its way toward the higher subject position, leaving a trace in each specifier position. The two alternatives are illustrated in (9):

(9)   a. $[_{SubjecP}$ QP/DPSubject$_i$ $[_{NegP}$ $[_{NumbP}$ t$_i$ $[_{HearerP}$ t$_i$ $[_{SpeakerP}$ inflV.[TP]]]]]]
      b. $[_{SubjecP}$ QP/DPSubject $[_{NegP}$ $[_{NumbP}$ $[_{HearerP}$ $[_{SpeakerP}$ inflV.[TP]]]]]]

At this point, two hypotheses may be made for clitic doubling. In the first, the SCL that occurs in the head of NumP or HearerP could be seen as the overt realization of the feature of the subject passed through its specifier; in this case (9a) would correspond to a structure like (10a), where the clitic doubles the subject moved through its specifier, whereas (9b), where the subject has not moved through the specifiers of the SCLs, would be the structure without doubling. Alternatively, we could make the opposite hypothesis: when the subject has passed through the specifier position, and the head is already indexed with the subject features, the SCL does not need to (and therefore cannot) be realized on the Num° or Hearer° head. In this case, (9a) corresponds to (10b), where there is no clitic doubling, and clitic doubling to (10c), where the subject has not passed through the SpecSCL position:

(10) a. $[_{DP}$ DPSubject$_i$ $[_{NegP}$ $[_{NumbP}$ t$_i$ $[$ Num° SCL]$[_{HearerP}$ t$_i$ $[_{Hearer°}$ SCL] $[_{SpeakerP}$ inflV [TP]]]]]]

      b. $[_{DP}$ DPSubject$_i$ $[_{NegP}$ $[_{NumbP}$ t$_i$ $[$ Num°]$[_{HearerP}$ t$_i$ $[_{Hearer°}]$ $[_{SpeakerP}$ inflV [TP]]]]]]

      c. $[_{DP}$ DPSubject$_i$ $[_{NegP}$ $[_{NumbP}$ $[$ Num° SCL]$[_{HearerP}$ $[_{Hearer°}$ SCL] $[_{SpeakerP}$ inflV [TP]]]]]]

Both (10a) and (10b) are plausible hypotheses. Structure (10a) states that the SCL is the morphological realization of a Spec-head agreement process with the DP/QP subject, whereas (10b) considers the SCL as expressing the features of a projection, which would otherwise remain totally empty. The SCL and DP can both check the strong feature present in NumP and HearerP, though they cannot both be present at the same time, presumably because of an economy principle. The crucial point is the following: do we consider SCLs to be the result of an agreement process or independent heads that check the features of their projection? Whatever answer is given to this question, it may be noted that both analyses present the same disadvantage, as neither of them captures the implications represented in (3). We therefore need an additional mechanism that accounts for the fact that doubling of a wh-trace implies doubling with QPs, which implies doubling of DP and which, in turn, implies doubling of tonic pronouns.

In Poletto (1993b), I presented an analysis of only part of the variation found in the sample dialects because it was based on the empirical investigation of a narrower set of dialects, though the basic idea of this analysis could still be correct. My hypothesis is based on Rizzi's (1986b) intuition that SCLs are a nominal substitute for verbal inflection; moreover, it distinguishes several properties that verbal inflection may possess. Verbal inflection can licence and identify pro and assign case to all types of subjects: DPs, QPs, and variables. If we split these properties and state that SCLs can substitute the inflected verb for only some of these properties, we obtain a more flexible system, which is what we need to account for (3). In other words, the different distribution of SCLs that occupy the same position in different dialects can be captured on the basis of the different functions that these SCLs have in the licensing of a DP or QP subject. Hence, they may be considered as differences in the "strength" of the inflected verb, which needs an additional element, the clitic, to license pro and assign case to a DP subject, a QP subject, or a variable.

The differences among dialects described in (3) are thus ultimately due to differences in the realization of the properties of a strong inflectional projection. These properties are licensing and identification of a null subject and case assignment. Let us suppose that the process of nominative case assignment to the subject is performed in Romance through the structural configuration of a Spec-head agreement (as currently assumed in the minimalist framework), in which the matching of the features of the subject with those of the head occurs. Then, the subject would have to pass through the specifier of the case-assigning head. In standard Italian, the inflected verb is strong enough to be a pro-drop language, a language in which pro is licensed and identified by the $Agr°$ where the inflected verb is realized, and all types of subjects are assigned case by its head. Non-pro-drop languages like English occupy the other extreme of a spectrum, where the syntactic properties of strong Agr are weak.

The NIDs are located in between these two extremes and have lost some but not all of the properties of pro-drop languages. The first property lost by Agr is the possibility of recovering subject features, pro identification in Rizzi's (1986a) terms. Some modern Veneto dialects and many older varieties can be shown to have lost only the property of pro identification because the only case in which a SCL is obligatory is that of a referential null subject, the only one that needs identification. Nonreferential null subjects and phonetically realized subjects do not need the clitic.[5]

In other varieties, Agr can be shown to have lost the null subject-licensing property, as an SCL always occurs when no other phonetically realized subject occurs, even with quasi-argumental and expletive subjects (see Poletto 1996 for a detailed discussion, with examples, of this topic). The difference between standard Italian and Veneto dialects lies in the way pro is identified or licensed (depending on the variety considered).

Moreover, if case assignment is performed through the morphological matching of subject features, we may assume that clitic doubling is a phenomenon due to the weakening of a strong inflection. Its effect is that the properties attributed to the inflected verb are taken up by the clitic. The properties lost by the strong inflected verb are those connected with case assignment to different types of subjects. Many authors who have studied the phenomenon of clitic doubling have connected it to case assignment (cf., among others, Cordin 1993 and Jaeggli 1986). I also propose that clitic doubling is a way to assign case and that different types of subjects require different types of morphological matching to check case features. I assume the following requirement for case assignment:

(11) Each subject needs checking of all the features it is specified for, with the head realizing the same feature(s).

Tonic pronouns, which are those specified for person (hence, both speaker and hearer), number, and gender, require matching for those features through Spec-head agreement with the relevant heads (Speaker°, Hearer°, and Number°). The DPs, which are specified for number and gender (but not for person), require matching of the number features. The QPs, which are not specified for gender, in some dialects are specified for number; however, in some others they are not but have only a [+/–human] feature, which requires matching of this feature.[6] Variables, which are empty, do not require the matching of any feature (but probably only the structural relation of Spec-head agreement with an agreement head).

If this is so, NIDs do not differ in the movement of the subject through the SpecSCL positions, as illustrated in (9) and (10), because in all NIDs all types of subject must move to the same SpecSCL position. Tonic pronouns always have to move through all Spec-speaker, Spec-hearer, and Spec-number specifiers, in all dialects. The DPs always have to move through Spec-number, whereas QPs have to move through Spec-number in those dialects in which quantifiers are morphologically specified for singular and plural and through a position where the [+/–human] feature is checked in all dialects. The restriction in (11) appears to be a plausible instantiation, within the hypothesis of an agreement field of the minimalist idea, that case checking occurs through Spec-head agreement, automatically excluding dialects that have a structure like (9b) or (10c) because case checking requires all nominal elements to enter a Spec-head relation with a head that realizes the same features. In standard Italian, the inflected verb is specified for all these number, gender, person, and human features, and therefore it can check all the features of all types of subjects, as illustrated in (12a).[7] In NIDs, there is variation in the position to which the inflected verb can move: in some dialects, the verb moves to positions where the features that need checking are realized [as in (12a), where the checking process of a DP subject is represented], whereas in others the verb does not move and the SCL that corresponds to the feature is realized in the relevant head [as in (12b].

(12)   a. [$_{SubjectP}$ Subject DP$_i$ [$_{NegP}$ [$_{NumbP}$ t$_i$ [$_{Num°}$inflV$_J$][$_{HearerP}$ t$_i$ [$_{Hearer°}$ t$_j$] [$_{SpeakerP}$ t$_j$
[TP]]]]]]]

b. [$_{SubjectP}$ Subject DP$_i$ [$_{NegP}$ [$_{NumbP}$ t$_i$ [$_{Num°}$SCL][$_{HearerP}$ [$_{Hearer°}$] [$_{SpeakerP}$ inflV
[TP]]]]]]]

Let us now examine each single case, one by one:

1. Tonic pronouns need the highest amount of feature checking because they morphologically encode more features themselves; therefore, all the heads—Number°, Hearer°, and Speaker°—must be filled by the verb or by a SCL. Most dialects have SCL doubling in this context (but see note 3); The first case is illustrated by the Venetian examples in (4) and (5); here obligatory doubling occurs only with pronouns but not with DPs or QPs. Furthermore, DPs may be left-dislocated, and when they are, they are doubled by a SCL; QPs cannot be left-dislocated and therefore cannot be doubled by a SCL.
2. The DPs have number and gender features; therefore, the head of NumberP must be filled. In some dialects, the verb can reach this position, although in others the checking head is a SCL, yelding clitic doubling (as in Trentino and Lombard dialects).
3. The QPs have number features in some dialects and only human features in others. The Number° position must be filled in the dialects in which QPs realize number in their morphology; in the dialects in which QPs do not show any number distinction, the only position that must be filled is that where [+/–human] features are located. Again, either the verb or SCL may occupy these positions in different varieties.[8]
4. Variables do not require any feature checking, and in fact they are doubled in few dialects. The question remains open of whether they need any feature to be checked at all or if they simply require a structural Spec-head relation with some agreement head, no matter which.

The restriction formulated in (11) accounts for the fact that the implications in clitic doubling correspond to the morphological implication scale along which nominal elements visibly encode more features because tonic pronouns have more morphological specifications and are more frequently doubled than DPs, which have more morphological specifications and are more frequently doubled than quantifiers, which in turn have more morphological specifications and are more frequently doubled than variables.

It is not a simple matter to translate this correspondence between the rich morphology of the subject and the frequency of clitic doubling in structural terms. One could also imagine the following structural implementation of the implications discussed above: the subjects more frequently doubled are those that must check the highest features in the agreement field. In this case, the verb has to move to the highest position to check the features of the subject, and verb movement to the highest position is the first movement that may be substituted by a SCL. Subjects that have to check lower features are less frequently doubled because the head positions where the checking process is fulfilled are lower and thus more easily accessible to the inflected verb.

Unfortunately, this solution is not viable because the structure of the agreement field that has been proposed in chapter 2 realizes the number feature higher than hearer and speaker. Tonic pronouns have speaker, hearer, and number (and probably gender and human) features to check; hence, the whole path of features must be checked by a head. The DPs have only number (and gender) features, which are higher than speaker and hearer. Therefore, a solution in terms of economy of verb movement, which relates the frequency of SCL doubling to the highest structural agreement positions, is inadequate. There is another way to link the implications in (3) to the structure of the agreement field proposed here. The fact that tonic pronouns are the most frequently doubled type of subject might be related to the number of features that have to be checked. Let us suppose that the inflected verb can support only a limited number of strong agreement features; we may hypothesize that after having been charged with a given number of features, the inflected verb is saturated, in the sense that it cannot assume any additional features. At this point, an SCL is inserted to check the remaining features.

In this system, we obtain exactly the implicational scale described in (3): the types of subjects more frequently doubled are precisely those that have more features to check through a Spec-head relation with an agreement head. An SCL is a sort of substitute for a verb, as auxiliaries substitute for the main verb. In Poletto (1993a), I suggested that auxiliaries do not have their own VP; they are inserted in a functional head when the main verb cannot support a given feature. The same idea is adopted in Cinque (1999), who gives a detailed analysis of the past participle movement in Romance languages. At present, I have no theory that determines the number of strong features that a given element (i.e. a main verb, an auxiliary, a SCL) can check, but it is sure that the number of strong features that can be checked by a given head varies from language to language. Cinque shows that the Spanish past participle moves higher than the Italian one, which moves higher than the past participle in French. The same assumption is proposed here: the implicational scale in (3) has to be derived on the basis of the "number of strong features" the verb can check in each dialect.

Note, however, that (11) cannot be stated as a general principle valid in all languages, as it would imply that nominal and verbal inflection go hand in hand, and this is clearly not always the case. If the inflected verb does not possess enough features to check the case of a tonic pronoun, a clitic will serve the purpose by realizing the features needed for case checking. Hence, the clitic-doubling phenomenon shifts the case-checking head, which is not the inflected verb but the clitic itself. It is not clear whether this is the correct way to capture clitic doubling, which is found in many Romance languages not only with subjects but also with direct and indirect objects. This analysis has to be tested on the basis of other languages and doubling of other arguments of the verb. However, I leave the testing of this hypothesis for direct and indirect object doubling for future research.

6.2.2 Preverbal Subjects in CP

In the preceding section, I examine the mechanism of case assignment of different types of preverbal subjects. I propose the hypothesis that each type of subject
must move through the specifier positions that correspond to the features that it
shows overtly. In this section, I examine the target position of different types of
subjects. I show that all types of preverbal subjects move to the CP layer on the
basis of two arguments—the position with respect to the complementizer and the
position with respect to invariable and deictic SCLs. In addition, I consider a
number of arguments in favor of a hypothesis that splits the position of DPs from
the position of QPs in NIDs.

6.2.2.1 *Preverbal Subjects and Complementizers*

The first and most striking argument I intend to present in favor of the hypothesis
that preverbal subjects target a SpecC position concerns the position of preverbal
subjects with respect to the complementizer. The hypothesis that subject positions
are located inside the CP domain has an obvious consequence for complementizer
placement. More precisely, this hypothesis predicts that the subject can occur to
the left of the complementizer. In fact, this is actually the case in certain varieties.
An interesting piece of data that reveals the fact that there are several complementizer positions is a number of cases of complementizer reduplication in
Provençal and NIDs, as shown in (13a).

Note that in embedded contexts, one complementizer appears to the right of
the subject, the other to the left. Moreover, in the dialect of Arrens and in general
in Gascon dialects, a complementizer is always obligatory in main clauses:

(13)   a. quan credou que la mourt que tustabe au pourtau   (Ronjat 1937)
            when believed that death that knocked at the door
            'When he thought that death was knocking at the door'.

       b. You que parli.   (Ronjat 1937)
            I that speak
            'I speak'.

       c. *You parli
            I speak.

As the complementizer occurs to the right of the subject, it appears plausible to assume that it is the lower one of the two that occur in embedded clauses. In main
clauses, the higher complementizer is not realized, because it probably encodes some
argumental features, since the sentence is the argument of a verb that selects it.

Another variety in which two complementizers are visible is Piedmontese.
As mentioned in chapter 3, a number of speakers of the dialects of Turin produce
sentences in which it is possible to observe the same complementizer + subject +
complementizer sequence found in Occitan:

(14)   a. A venta che gnun ch'a fasa bordel.   Turin (Piedmontese)
            it needs that nobody that + cl do + subjunctive noise
            'It is necessary that nobody make noise'.

   b. A venta che Majo ch'a mangia pi' tant.
      SCL need that Majo that cl eat more
      'Majo has to eat more'.

As (14) shows, the subject realized to the left of the complementizer can be a QP or a DP, so this cannot be a left-dislocated position because quantifiers cannot be left dislocated.[9]

   In Piedmontese, there is another structure, which has been mentioned in chapter 5, where the subject occurs to the left of the complementizer. This is more widespread than the case in (14):

(15)   a. Gnun ch'a s'bogia!
          nobody that + a cl move-subj!
          'Nobody moves!'

       b. Mario ch'a s presenta subit . . .
          Mario that + a cl go-subj immediately
          'Mario has to go immediately . . .'

Example (15a) shows that it is not possible to analyze these cases as instances of left dislocation since a QP can also be found in such structures. Similar cases have also been recorded in the Ligurian dialect of Borghetto di Vara, where informants give sentences like this:

(16)   Sperem che Gianni ch'u lese questu libru.   Borghetto di Vara (Ligurian)
       hope that G. that SCL reads this book
       'We hope that John reads this book'.

This clearly shows that the subject position in embedded clauses is higher than one complementizer position yet lower than another one. The structure of the above examples is the following:

(17)   [$_{CP}$ che [$_{CP}$ subject [$_{CP}$ che [$_{IP}$ [$_{NegP}$ [$_{NumbP}$ SCL [$_{HearerP}$ SCL [$_{SpeakerP}$ inflV [TP]]]]]]]]]

The lower complementizer may be merged in a projection located lower than the subject or in the head of the projection where the subject occurs. In this case there has to be agreement between the subject and the complementizer since I proposed (in chapter 3) that the head and the specifier of a given FP cannot be both filled unless they undergo an agreement process. As there is no visible agreement between the subject and the complementizer, I leave the matter open.

   Gascon reduplication of the complementizer (and in general enunciative particles) has been analyzed by Campos (1986) in a different way; he assumes that the second complementizer is an Infl element, occupying the highest projection in the IP layer and corresponding to a position where the sentence type is expressed. He provides three arguments in favor of his analysis. I revise each one of them in turn to show that they are all compatible with a split CP account.

   1. Campos notes that the complementizer occurs after the subject, and therefore it must be an Infl element. He assumes that CP is a single projection, whereas IP can be split. Therefore, the only position open to the lower

complementizer is an IP head where the sentence type is marked. In a split-CP account such as the one adopted here, the complementizer may occupy a lower C°, and there is no need to assume that it has become an Infl element. Moreover, Campos's claim can be reversed by saying that the subject is in CP because it occurs higher than the complementizer.

2. He notes that enunciative *que* is sensitive to the finiteness of Infl and therefore concludes that it is an Infl element. It may be noted, however, that although the complementizer of standard Italian is also sensitive to the finiteness of the verb, nevertheless it is assumed to occur in C°. The fact that in many languages the complementizer is sensitive to tense restrictions does not show that it is an Infl element. On the contrary, it shows that CP is sensitive to tense (as already proposed by Rizzi 1997).

3. The enunciative complementizer occurs in both conjuncts of a coordinated structure and therefore must occur in Infl. In 5.2, I have considered cases of coordinated structures with a complementizer, and I have considered examples in which the complementizer needs to be repeated in both conjuncts, even though there is no reason to believe that it is located in Infl in those varieties. It remains to be explained what restrictions govern the selection of the structures that can undergo coordination and why in some cases only CPs can be coordinated. However, this is a general problem and applies also to other structures where a complementizer occurs.

Therefore, I consider the lower complementizer that occurs in Gascon and northern Italian dialects to be a CP element. This might also be true for other NIDs, although the lower complementizer is not visible. The difference between the varieties in which two complementizers are found and those in which a single complementizer is realized can be captured in terms of strong versus weak features in the lower C position: in varieties in which two complementizers are found, the lower C position possesses strong features, whereas it does not have them in varieties in which only the higher complementizer occurs.

Alternatively, the difference between languages with one and languages with two complementizers can be accounted for in terms of move versus merge in a minimalist perspective. All the languages in question have the same set of strong features in the CP layer, though some languages realize two complementizers because they merge a second complementizer to realize the strong features on the higher C°. Other languages move the complementizer from the lower to the higher C° to check both the lower and higher strong features with a single lexical item.

In this hypothesis, the differences between languages are attributed to the number of strong features that the same head can check, as discussed in section 6.2.1.

At this point, one might ask whether there are independent facts that suggest that the hypothesis illustrated in (17) should be generalized for all NIDs. In the next section, I discuss some facts that support this conclusion.

6.2.2.2 *Invariable and Deictic SCL Doubling*

As noted, subject clitic doubling is a complex matter. Dialects differ in doubling according to the type of subject. In section 6.2.1, I examined only cases of SCL doubling with agreement SCLs. As for invariable and deictic clitics located in the CP layer, the situation is the following: deictic SCLs always require doubling, as shown in (18):

(18)   a. Mario a nol ven   Friulano (S. Michele al Tagliamento)
           Mario SCL notSCL comes
           'Mario is not coming'.

       b. Nisun a ven.
           nobody SCL comes
           'Nobody is coming'.

In dialects that have deictic SCLs, all types of subjects are doubled by the SCL, and there is no distinction between the types of subject that we have seen for agreement SCLs in section 6.2.1. It is most likely that this type of doubling is not connected to case-feature checking of the subject but rather to certain independent features that need to be realized in the dialects in question.

For invariable SCLs, certain dialects (such as the Paduan variety analyzed in Benincà) do not tolerate any focalized element (including wh-items) or left-dislocated XP in front of the SCL. They do not tolerate a preverbal subject either:

(19)   a. *GIORGIO a ze bravo, no Toni   Benincà (1983: 20)
           GIORGIO, SCL is good, not Toni
           'Giorgio is good, not Toni'.

       b. *Giorgio a vien
           Giorgio SCL comes
           'Giorgio is coming'.

True, invariable SCLs never co-occur with a preverbal subject, only with postverbal subjects.[10] However, the subject position in main declarative clauses is always higher than deictic SCLs. Because deictic SCLs occupy the head of a CP projection, we are forced to assume that preverbal subjects are located inside the CP layer in main declarative clauses, or at least in those dialects that exhibit the co-occurrence of a full subject with a deictic SCL.

(20)   [subject [$_{CP}$ deictic SCL [SCI [$_{CP°}$ch [$_{IP}$ number SCL [$_{IP}$ person SCL]]]]]]

Sentences like (18) show only that the subject must be located inside the CP and higher than deictic SCLs and does not give any evidence of the precise position of the subject, that is, whether it is in the specifier position of the CP, where deictic SCLs occur, or in a higher position.[11]

In section 6.3, I consider the problem of the exact position of preverbal subjects in CP when I examine interrogative clauses. For now, I limit myself to defining the syntactic space where the subject occurs, which is higher than deictic SCLs, SCI, and interrogative complementizers. Hence, dialects that possess deictic

SCLs show the interesting property of having preverbal subjects inside the CP layer.[12]

As for dialects that do not have deictic clitics, there is no way of deciding where full subjects are located, whether they are also in CP or lower down in IP. If the lack of vocalic clitics means that the CP layer is not activated in dialects without deictic SCLs, the subject position of, for instance, Venetian (which does not have deictic SCLs) and Friulian (which has deictic SCLs) will differ, as it will be some SpecC position in Friulian and some SpecI in Venetian. In contrast, if both languages activate CP, the Venetian subject occupies the SpecC position. In section 6.3, I consider an argument based on data from interrogative clauses that suggests that in varieties like Venetian and standard Italian preverbal subjects are located inside CP and not in IP, at least in indicative clauses.

The existence of cases like (18) encourages us to consider all pro-drop languages as those in which the existence of a strong inflection (or of SCLs) that licenses pro blocks the subject positions inside IP, so that the subject has to appear in a higher position within the CP domain. The idea that pro-drop languages are "obligatorily" pro drop—in the sense that their strong inflection or, better, strong Agr° has to licence pro in its specifier, and therefore that the position of a subject is never SpecAgr but always a higher one—has been put forth by various authors (see, among others, Barbosa 1997, Benincà & Cinque 1985, Giupponi 1988, Moro 1997, Ordonez 1997, and Poletto 1992).

I cannot adopt this analysis here because I have assumed that Spec-head agreement with agreement heads is necessary for nominative case assignment (see also Cardinaletti 1997 for arguments against this approach); hence different types of subjects must move through the agreement specifiers in order to get case. These specifiers must therefore be empty and not be obligatorily occupied by a pro subject.

Many authors identify the position of preverbal DP subjects with a left-dislocated position (cf., among others, Barbosa 1997 and Ordonez 1997). I do not believe that this hypothesis is correct: as mentioned, the preverbal subject position is a topiclike position, not the one used by other XPs when they are left-dislocated. I cannot assume that the preverbal position of subject DPs and left dislocation coincide because of the existence of variation patterns, as those described in section 6.2.1. Certain dialects such as Friulian and Trentino always show clitic doubling with preverbal DP subjects, and this may be treated as left dislocation, though other dialects (like Central Veneto varieties) do not have obligatory clitic doubling, as shown in (5a) and repeated here as (21a) and (21b):

(21)   a. Nane magna.   Venetian
           'John eats'.

        b. Nane el magna.
           'John SCL eats'

Following the idea that the optionality illustrated by (21) is only apparent, we can hypothesize that (21b) is a case of left dislocation and that the SCL is obligatorily realized, whereas (21a) is a non-left-dislocated subject, in which the SCL is impossible. We can distinguish between the two structures in the following way: when a left-dislocated object is found between the subject and the verb, we may be sure that the subject is itself in a left-dislocated position. In this case the absence of the subject clitic yields ungrammaticality:

(22) a. Nane el gelato el lo ga za magnà.   Venetian
         John, the ice cream, SCL it has already eaten
         'John has already eaten the ice cream'.

      b. *Nane, el gelato, lo ga za magnà
         John, the ice cream it has already eaten

If (21) were a simple case of an optional SCL, we should not expect the ungrammaticality of (22b). Therefore, we have to distinguish between left-dislocated subjects (which have obligatory clitic doubling in all the dialects examined) and preverbal subjects (which in some dialects do not have clitic doubling).

To assume that the preverbal subject position is a topiclike position implies that nontopic preverbal subjects occupy a different position. This is the case for preverbal QP subjects, which probably occupy an A´ position. In the dialect of Rodoretto di Prali, a Provençal variety, preverbal subject QPs are usually translated with a cleft structure whose focus position is occupied by the QP:

(23) L'ha pa gnun ke m a vit.
      it has not nobody that me has seen
      'Nobody saw me'.

The use of a focusing structure, such as the cleft sentence, leads us to hypothesize that preverbal QPs are always focalized, whereas the usual position for subject QPs is the postverbal one. Alternatively, the preverbal QP position could be an A´ position that corresponds to the semantic interpretation of the quantifier, as proposed by Beghelli (1995), who shows that the QP position varies according to the interpretation of the quantifier itself. I assume that Beghelli's hypothesis is right and that the position of a preverbal subject depends on its interpretation.

6.3 SUBJECT POSITIONS IN NONDECLARATIVE CONTEXTS

Once we have seen that there are arguments for thinking that preverbal subjects are located inside the CP layer, we can exploit this hypothesis to account for a number of facts noted in main and interrogative sentences, as well as in Aux to C constructions.

The position of the subject in interrogative sentences in standard Italian has been discussed by many authors (cf. Antinucci & Cinque 1977, Poletto 1993b, Rizzi 1991, and Roberts 1993c, among others). They noticed that in standard Italian, as in many Romance varieties, it is not possible to have a subject in the preverbal position, either in main or in embedded interrogatives:

(24) a. *Cosa Gianni ha fatto?
         what John has done?
         'What has John done?'

b. ??Mi chiedo cosa Gianni ha fatto
    me ask what John has done
    'I wonder what John has done'.

According to Rizzi, this is due to verb movement to C as a consequence of the wh-criterion (cf. chapter 3.4 for a detailed discussion of the wh-criterion):

(25)   Wh-criterion (Rizzi 1991)

    a. A wh-operator must be in a Spec-head relation with a +wh-head.

    b. A +wh-head must be in a Spec-head relation with a wh-operator.

(26)   Infl is +wh in standard Italian.

In a language in which (26) is chosen, the inflected verb, which is assigned the feature [+wh], must move to C to satisfy the wh-criterion that requires a Spec-head relation between the wh-operator and the wh-head. Rizzi assumes that in standard Italian, (26) is valid in both main and embedded interrogatives, and consequently the inflected verb with the [+wh] feature must move to C° in both cases. As the verb moves to C and the wh-element occupies the SpecC position, the subject cannot occur between the wh in SpecC and the inflected verb in C because there is no structural space for it. In Rizzi's analysis, in both main and embedded interrogatives, the verb has moved to C; therefore, the effect is found in both contexts.

It has also been frequently noted that movement from V to C in main and embedded sentences should give rise to subject inversion in standard Italian, as in English and other Germanic languages. However, subject inversion is sharply ungrammatical in both main and embedded interrogatives, as the following example shows:

(27)   a. *Cosa ha Gianni fatto?
       what has John done?

      b. *Mi chiedo cosa ha Gianni fatto
        me ask what has John done
        'I wonder what John has done'.

This also requires explanation. In literature, two proposals have been made to account for the ungrammaticality of (27); the first has been put forth by Rizzi and Roberts (1989), Rizzi (1991), and Roberts (1993c). They assume that nominative case assignment in standard Italian requires Spec-head agreement, not a government relation. In (27), the Spec-head agreement between the inflected verb and the subject has been broken by verb movement to C. Hence, the subject receives no nominative case and the sentence is out. The difference in English and other Germanic languages (and certain Romance varieties, as some Central Rhaeto-romance varieties) that admit sentences corresponding to (27a) is found in the nominative case assignment parameter; in English, it is possible to assign nominative case through agreement or government, whereas in Italian and French case can be assigned only through agreement. The other possibility is to consider the inflected verb in Italian as a form that corresponds to the French or northern Italian forms that incorporate an enclitic subject clitic. When the inflected verb moves to C, it licenses a pro subject in SpecAgrSP, which cannot be occupied by any other subject. This view has been taken by Benincà (1997).

Before considering this question, I went to discuss some more Italian and dialectal data. It is interesting to note that the effect on the postauxiliary subject is not uniform in all nondeclarative structures. In exclamative clauses we observe the following pattern:

(28) *Quanto furbo è Gianni stato!
       how clever has John been!
       'How clever John has been!'

(29) Quanto furbo Gianni è stato!
       How clever John has been!

In exclamative clauses, it is possible to realize a subject only before the inflected verb. These data indicate that there is no V to C movement in exclamatives (see Benincà 1996 for a detailed discussion on this point). A similar effect is also detectable in relative clauses. On a par with exclamatives, relative clauses do not have V to C movement and the subject cannot occur immediately after the auxiliary:

(30) a. *La torta che ha Gianni mangiato . . .
          the cake that has John eaten . . .
          'The cake that John has eaten . . .'

      b. La torta che Gianni ha mangiato . . .

The lack of V to C movement is clearly visible in NIDs, where there are no attested cases of SCI in any variety. Many speakers accept a preverbal subject in relative clauses, even though in some cases the postparticipial position is preferred:

(31) La torta che ha mangiato Gianni . . .
      the cake that has eaten John . . .
      'The cake that John has eaten . . .'

If we consider Aux to C structures, the picture changes radically. It may be noted that in this case the auxiliary has moved to C (cf. Rizzi 1991); nevertheless, the subject can occur after the auxiliary and before the past participle:[13]

(32) a. Avesse Gianni parlato con te . . .
          had-subj John spoken with you . . .
          'Had John spoken to you . . .'

      b. Avendo Gianni parlato con te . . .
          having John spoken with you
          'As John has spoken to you . . .'

      c. Per aver Gianni parlato con te . . .
          for have + inf. John spoken with you
          'As John spoke to you . . .'

Note that the subject cannot occur preverbally, at least in standard Italian, whereas this structure is grammatical in other Romance languages like French:

(33)   *Gianni avesse parlato con te
       John had + cond. spoken with you
       'Had John spoken to you . . .'

Absolute past participle constructions with ergative verbs, which have been analyzed by Kayne (1989b) and Belletti (1990) as V to C, behave as Aux to C:

(34)   a. Arrivata Maria, siamo partiti
          come-agr Mary, (we) have left
          'As Mary had come'

       b. *Maria arrivata, siamo partiti
          Mary come-agr, (we) have left

Let us now sum up all the cases we have reviewed in a table:

(35)   Preverbal Subject   Postverbal Subject
    a. Aux to C   –   +
    b. Participial clauses   –   +
    c. Main interrogatives   –   –
    d. Exclamative contexts   +   –
    e. Embedded interrogatives   –   –
    f. Relative clauses   +   –

The fact that Aux to C and absolute participial clauses admit postauxiliary
subjects, whereas interrogative clauses do not, is a problem for the theory that
standard Italian does not assign case through government but only by Spec-head
agreement. Roberts (1993c) discusses Aux to Comp structures and assumes that
in these cases we have T to Comp, not AgrS to Comp. The second hypothesis,
which postulates that a pro is obligatorily licensed in subject position when the
verb moves to C, can also account for Aux to C and absolute participial clauses
by assuming that these verbal forms are not strong enough to licence a pro in the
SpecAgrS position.

The situation is more complex than this. It is not only Aux to C and absolute
participial that accept a postauxiliary subject. Even interrogative sentences admit
subject inversion when a particular interpretation of the question is selected. In
general, this interpretation involves modal verbs, as in (36b), a conditional or a
future tense (36a):

(36)   a. ?Cosa mai avra' Gianni fatto in quel frangente?
          what ever have-fut John done in that occasion?
          'What might John have done on that occasion?'

       b. Cosa mai avrebbe Gianni potuto fare in quel frangente?
          what ever have-cond. John could do on that occasion?

The problem we face here may be formulated in the following terms: how does a
sentence like (36) differ from (28)? Is this difference to be interpreted as a consequence of verb movement or not? Neither of these hypotheses accounts for modal
interrogatives. Rizzi and Roberts' (1989) idea that there is no case assignment

through government cannot account for the grammaticality of (36). This is also true of Benincà's (1997) hypothesis that pro drop is obligatory in V to C contexts, as here the inflected verb has moved to C, although it does not licence pro.

To provide an analysis of (36), we have to take into account the data about embedded interrogatives. Rizzi (1991) notes that it is not possible to realize a preverbal subject in embedded interrogative clauses when the verb is inflected in its indicative form:

(37)   ??Mi domando cosa Gianni ha fatto
       me ask what John has done
       'I wonder what John has done'.

He attributes this fact to V to C movement in embedded clauses. As the verb moves to the C head, whose specifier position is occupied by the wh-element, there is no structural space for the preverbal subject in embedded contexts. He reports that subjunctive clauses tolerate preverbal subjects more easily:

(38)   a. ?Mi chiedo cosa Gianni faccia adesso
         me ask what John do-subj now
         'I wonder what John is doing now'.

       b. Mi chiedo cosa Gianni avrebbe fatto in quel frangente.
         me ask what John do-conditional now
         'I wonder what John would have done on that occasion'.

       c. ?Mi chiedo cosa Gianni fara' in quel frangente.
         me ask what John do-future now
         'I wonder what John will do on that occasion'.

In this analysis, the subjunctive mood has a weaker inflection than the indicative, and the [+wh] feature can also be assigned to C° but not to I°. Therefore, the subjunctive verb does not need to move to C°, as it does not have the [+wh] feature, which is realized on C°. The same must be assumed for the conditional and future indicative, which form a natural class with the subjunctive, as already shown in chapter 5 on the basis of complementizer deletion. Note that the future indicative behaves in (38) like the subjunctive and conditional, even though it has a strong agreement morphology entirely analogous to that shown by the present indicative. Therefore, the difference between present (and imperfect) indicative, on the one hand, and subjunctive, conditional, and future on the other, cannot be formulated on the basis of strong versus weak agreement morphology that does or does not "attract" the wh-feature. The fact that the verbal forms that tolerate a preverbal subject are precisely those already examined in chapter 5, in the case of standard Italian complementizer deletion, seems to suggest that it is the modal property possessed by these forms (cf. chapter 5.3) that is somehow involved in the possibility of realizing a preverbal subject, not strong or weak agreement morphology, which attracts the wh-feature on I and triggers verb movement to C.

It is interesting to note that if we assume the hypothesis that the possibility of having a preverbal subject is related to the modal property of certain verbs, we should be able to include yes/no embedded interrogatives into the set of interrogative clauses that have a modal value. Because they introduce a doubt about the truth of the sentence, it is to be expected that yes/no embedded questions work as do the modal tenses and therefore tolerate a preverbal subject. Moreover, this should not depend on the verbal form, as the character of the question already provides the modal property of these sentences. Therefore, yes/no questions are predicted to permit a preverbal subject with both indicative and subjunctive verbs. This expectation is fulfilled:

(39)   a. Non so se Mario l'abbia già fatto.
          not know if Mario it has + subjunctive already done
          'I do not know whether Mario has already done it'.

        b. Non so se Mario l'ha già fatto.
          not know if Mario it has already done

Example (39a) has a subjunctive verb and tolerates a preverbal subject just like the corresponding wh-interrogative. Note that (39b) also tolerates a preverbal subject and that here the verb is inflected for the present indicative, in contrast with the parallel wh-interrogative. Hence, modal contexts, like embedded wh-interrogatives, in which subjunctive, conditional, or future are used, or embedded yes/no questions tolerate a preverbal subject. It therefore appears that a modal property possessed by the verb (cf. Cinque 1999 and references quoted there) has influence on the subject position.

In the discussion that follows, this modal property is related to a similar fact—the possibility of finding subject inversion in main interrogatives with a future indicative or a conditional, as already noted above [cf. (36)]:

(40)   a. ?Cosa mai avra' Gianni fatto in quel frangente?
          what ever have-fut John done on that occasion?
          'What will John have done on that occasion?'

        b. Cosa mai avrebbe Gianni potuto fare in quel frangente?
          what ever have-cond. John could do on that occasion?
          'What would John have done on that occasion?'

Before discussing the formalization that I propose for the presence of a preverbal subject in "modal interrogative" constructions, I present some data that show that the effect on the subject is not connected to verb movement at all. Consider the following NID examples:

(41)   ??Me domando cossa che Nane ga fato casa   Padua
        me ask what that John has done at home
        'I wonder what John has done at home'.

(42)   a. ?Me domandavo cossa che Nane fasesse casa   Padua
          me asked what that John do-subj at home
          'I wondered what John was doing at home'.

        b. Me domando cossa che Nane gavaria fato casa.
          me asked what John do-conditional now
          ' I wondered what John would have done at home'.

c. ?Me domando cossa che Nane farà casa
   me asked what John do + fut now
   'I wonder what John will do at home'.

Here we have a complementizer that is obligatory in embedded interrogatives; moreover, the verb does not show SCI, as we would have expected if the inflected verb had moved to C. Hence, this dialect gives a clear indication that the verb of the embedded interrogative sentence has not moved to the CP layer. Nevertheless, the effect on preverbal subjects is present all the same; if the verb is inflected in its indicative form, a subject in preverbal position would sound very odd; if the verb is inflected for the subjunctive, the conditional, or the future indicative, the preverbal position for the subject becomes acceptable. These data show that the effect on the preverbal subject position is not connected to verb movement to C° but to some other factor. Now, we have two indications that Rizzi's (1991) analysis on embedded interrogatives has to be revised; the first indication is given by standard Italian future indicative, which behaves like the subjunctive, not like the present indicative, in tolerating a preverbal subject. This shows that the wh-feature on the verb is not assigned on the basis of strong versus weak inflection. The second piece of evidence is provided by Paduan, in which there is an obligatory complementizer and no SCI in embedded interrogatives; nevertheless the effect on the subject is entirely similar to that found in standard Italian. These two arguments show that the effect is not connected to V to C at all. Therefore, I discard both of these hypotheses—that there is no nominative case assignment through government and that a pro is obligatorily licensed when the verb moves to C—because the distribution of the subject does not depend on verb movement. But if the factor that bans the subject from the preverbal position in embedded interrogatives is not V to C movement, what is it?

Before presenting my analysis, it is necessary to determine the position of the complementizer in embedded interrogative sentences. We have seen in chapter 3 that in embedded interrogatives many NIDs have obligatory complementizers following the wh-item, and we noticed that the insertion position of this complementizer is in the lowest C° position, C4°. No inversion is possible in embedded interrogative sentences because the complementizer trace blocks V movement to the AgrC° position, where inversion occurs. Moreover, it appears that the complementizer moves up to higher C° heads, as it is adjoined to vocalic clitics.

In chapters 3, 4, and 5, I concentrate on certain particular structures, such as interrogatives and subjunctive clauses, in an attempt to determine how many C positions are needed to explain the dialectal variation found in these contexts. I do not consider the problem of the location of the interrogative CP subdomain inside the CP layer. In chapter 4, I consider a V2 dialect in which interrogative CPs are located lower than V2 CPs. Here, the position of the interrogative complementizer with respect to the declarative complementizer is discussed.

It appears that the position of the complementizer in embedded declaratives is not the same as that found in embedded interrogatives; declarative complementizers are located to the left of dislocated elements, whereas interrogative complementizers are located to their right:

(43)   a. Go deciso che el posto ghe lo dago a to mama.
       have decided that the position to-her it give to your mother
       'I decided that I will give that position to your mother'.

       b. ??Go deciso el posto che ghe lo dago a to mama
       have decided the position that to-her it give to your mother

(44)   a. Ghe go domandà el posto quando che i ghe lo da.
       to-him have asked the position when that SCL to-her it give
       'I asked him when they are going to give him that position'.

       b. ??Ghe go domandà quando el posto che i ghe lo da[14]
       to-her have asked when the position that SCL to-her it give

Rizzi (1997) has already made the same observation for wh-elements that occur to the right of left-dislocated elements, whereas declarative complementizers occur to the left of LD elements. The analysis of NIDs simply confirms Rizzi's hypothesis that wh-elements are located lower than declarative complementizers. What NIDs reveal is the fact that the complementizer may occur in different $C°$ positions inside the CP layer and not only in the highest one. It is only the declarative complementizer that occurs so high in the structure; embedded interrogative complementizers occur lower.

If we combine this observation with the hypothesis discussed in the preceding section, namely, that the subject is located inside the CP layer, it would be plausible to propose an analysis of the effect on the preverbal subject found in main and embedded interrogatives in the following terms: the preverbal subject position is located higher in the CP layer than wh-elements and interrogative complementizers but lower than declarative complementizers. Therefore, sentences like (24) and (27) are impossible because the SpecAgrS position is never available to the lexical subjects in pro drop languages. In other words, there is no structural space for a preverbal subject in embedded interrogatives, just as there is no structural space for it in main interrogatives.

The only preverbal position available to the subject is its usual one, which is higher than wh-elements; in fact, DPs may occur in front of the wh-element-inflected verb sequence in main interrogatives or wh-element-complementizer in embedded interrogatives:

(45)   a. Gianni quando vienlo?
       John when comes-SCL?
       'When is John coming?'

       b. I me ga domandà Gianni quando che el vien.
       SCL me have asked John when that SCL comes
       'They asked me when John is coming'.

Note, however, that QP subjects cannot occur in front of wh-elements:

(46)   *Nessuno quando viene?
       nobody when comes?
       'When is anybody coming?'

This contrast has been interpreted as a consequence of the fact that the subject is left-dislocated in these structures, and QPs, which cannot be left-dislocated, cannot occur there. However, there is another interpretation of this contrast. In section 6.2.2, we saw that to assume that the subject position corresponds to a topic position implies that nontopic subjects occur in an A´ position. It could be the case that the impossibility of having a subject QP in front of the wh-element is due to the fact that the A´ position of the QP is blocked. If the A´ position of the QP is the same as that of the wh-element, the complementary distribution between preverbal QP subjects and wh-elements is directly explained.

Yes/no questions are different in this respect, as a preverbal QP subject is definitely better than in the corresponding wh-interrogative:

(47) Nisuni no te ga parlà de mi?   Venice
      nobody not to-you have spoken about me?
      'Did anybody tell you something about me?'

This appears to indicate that preverbal quantifiers occur in the same position as wh-elements (probably a focus position, as least for some types of wh-items), whereas this is not the case when the wh-operator is a null yes/no operator and not a wh-element. This does not sound so implausible, as a null operator probably requires a type of checking that differs from that required by visible elements like wh-elements.

Moreover, an empty element such as a null operator cannot receive any focus, being phonetically null (cf. Munaro 1997 for a detailed analysis of null operators that occur with wh–in situ elements). I do not enter into a detailed analysis of null operators; here, it is sufficient to assume that they are located in a different position with respect to overt wh-elements to account for the asymmetry between (46) and (47).

Let us thus assume that the subject position is not SpecAgrS but a SpecC position higher than the interrogative subdomain (which includes several projections, as we have seen in chapter 3) and that this SpecC is available only to DPs and not to QPs, which are most probably located lower in the structure in a SpecC position that interferes with wh-items.

How can we explain the variation exemplified in the table in (35), to which we have to add modal interrogative contexts? Modal interrogatives behave like English interrogatives: subject inversion is found in main contexts, and a preverbal subject is grammatical in embedded contexts. I repeat examples (40) and (42) here for convenience:

(48) a. ?Cosa mai avra' Gianni fatto in quel frangente?
         what ever have-fut John done in that occasion?
         'What will John have done on that occasion?'

      b. Cosa mai avrebbe Gianni potuto fare in quel frangente?
         what ever have-cond. John could do in that occasion?
         'What would John have done on that occasion?'

(49) a. ?Me domandavo cossa che Nane fasesse casa   Padua
         me asked what that John do-subj at home
         'I wondered what John was doing at home'.

   b. Me domando cossa che Nane gavaria fato casa.
      me asked what John do-conditional now
      'I wonder what John would have done at home'.

   c. ?Me domando cossa che Nane fara' casa
      me asked what John do + fut now
      'I wonder what John will do at home'.

The hypothesis I propose to account for the data in (48) is that the wh-item and the verb target a projection located higher in modal interrogatives than in nonmodal interrogatives. If this higher landing site for modal interrogatives crosses the subject position, we can explain the phenomenon of inversion in main interrogatives by analogy with English; in main interrogatives the inflected verb moves to a C° position that is higher than the subject position, and this is probably due to a modal feature that it has to check.

   In embedded contexts, as in example (49), the wh-item still targets a SpecC located higher than its usual one and therefore crosses the subject position, whereas the inflected verb does not realize the modal feature checked by the complementizer. Therefore, the subject remains preverbal. In both main and embedded interrogatives, the position of wh-items is higher than the subject position. It is interesting to note that this analysis implies that the "interrogative CP field" analyzed in chapter 3 is not a set of continuous projections. Modal interrogatives have been analyzed in chapter 3 as the highest projection of the field. If this is true, we can admit that the projection for modal interrogatives is not only higher than the other interrogative projections but also higher than the subject position. It also appears plausible that a projection encoding modal features is not contiguous to the other interrogative projections. The structure of the CP layer would thus be the following:

(50) $[_{CP}$ wh che $[_{cpsubj}$ $[_{spec}$ DP$_{subject}$ $[_{cpsubj}$ $[_{CP}$ deictic SCL $[_{AgrCP}$ SCI $[_{CP}$ [pa] che]]]]]]]]

   The same analysis proposed for modal interrogatives may also be applied to Aux to C structures and to absolute participial clauses. In these two contexts, the position that the verb moves to is higher than the subject position, and therefore we see subject inversion. Note that the hypothesis that the verb moves higher in Aux to C constructions than in nonmodal interrogatives is confirmed by the position of left dislocation, which occurs, as we have seen, in front of nonmodal interrogative clauses; however, it can marginally occur to the right of the auxiliary in C.[15]

(51)   a. ?Avendolo il progetto io già proposto in altra sede, siamo andati sul sicuro.
          having-it the project I already presented in another place, (we) are gone sure
          'As I had proposed the project to another committee, we were sure that it was OK'.

       b. ?Avendolo io il progetto proposto in altra sede, siamo andati sul sicuro.
          having I the project presented in another place (we) are gone sure

       c. *Il progetto, avendolo io già proposto in altra sede, siamo andati sul sicuro
          the project having I already presented in another place, (we) are gone sure

Note that the left-dislocated element may be found to the left or to the right of the subject. This could be interpreted as follows: in (51a) the subject is in its SpecC topiclike position, whereas in (51b) it has also been left-dislocated in front of the left-dislocated constituent; LD is not grammatical before the Aux in C (51c). This means that the Aux necessarily has to climb, not only higher than the subject position but also higher than the LD position.[16]

One interesting corollary of the hypothesis presented here is the following. In chapter 4, I accept Rizzi's (1991) proposal that the head of the left-dislocation projection (LDP) is not a suitable host for the verb because it is probably already filled by some feature assigned by the left-dislocated element in SpecLD. The fact that sentences such as (51) are grammatical shows that Aux to C is not an instance of head movement but rather the movement of an XP to a high SpecC position. This assumption solves a problem frequently noted in literature, that is, the fact that the object clitic coindexed with the left-dislocated element moves to a position higher than the left-dislocated element itself. If the object clitic c-commanded the left-dislocated element, this should give rise to ungrammaticality. However, sentences of this type are well formed. If we assume that Aux to C is not head movement but XP movement, the object clitic is embedded under a wider structure and does not c-command the left-dislocated element with which it is coindexed. Therefore, the sentence is correctly predicted to be grammatical.

The other construction in which we assumed a movement of the verb to a location higher than the subject SpecC position is the absolute participial construction:

(52)   Arrivata a casa Maria, i bambini si tranquillizzarono subito.
       arrived at home Mary, the children were immediately quiet
       'As soon as Mary arrived at home, the children became quiet'.

Here it is not possible to insert a LD element either to the left or to the right of the verb:[17]

(53)   a. *A casa arrivataci Maria . . .
          at home arrived-there Mary
          'As soon as Mary got home . . .'

       b. *Arrivataci a casa Maria
          arrived-there at home Mary

Absolute participial constructions show the same intolerance to left dislocation that has been found in Rhaetoromance V2 constructions and for which I proposed that the LD position, occupied by a left-dislocated item, blocks verb movement to higher heads. This suggests that Belletti's (1990) hypothesis about the structure in (52) is correct.[18]

Modal interrogatives also show the same incompatibility with respect to LD:

(54)   a. *A Gianni, cosa mai avrebbe Paolo potuto dirgli in quel frangente?
          to John, what ever might-have Paul could tell him in that occasion?
          'What might John have told Paul on that occasion?'

b. *Cosa mai avrebbe, a Gianni, Paolo potuto dirgli in quel frangente?
   what ever might-have, to John, Paul could tell him in that occasion?

c. *Cosa mai avrebbe Paolo, a Gianni potuto dirgli in quel frangente?
   what ever might-have Paul, to John, could tell him in that occasion?

d. *Cosa mai a Gianni avrebbe Paolo potuto dirgli in quel frangente?
   what ever, to John, might-have Paul could tell him in that occasion?

The incompatibility of modal interrogative with left dislocation shows that modal interrogatives are in reality located higher than nonmodal interrogatives, which are perfectly compatible with a left-dislocated XP to the left of the wh-item.[19]

The discussion on interrogative clauses enables us to answer the questions left open at the end of the previous sections:

1. If the subject is in CP, where is its precise position within the CP layer?
2. If the position of QPs is different from that of DPs, which is the higher one and where precisely are they located?

We did not define precisely which position the subject takes with respect to all other CP elements, although we at least defined a syntactic space inside the CP layer, where a DP subject occurs. Moreover, it appears that the position in which a QP subject occurs is lower than that where DP subjects occur, and it is probably a Spec position inside the interrogative subfield since it interferes with the movement of an overt wh-element. There is a general question that I have not discussed yet, the reason why it is impossible to have a subject in SpecAgrS. Within a strict minimalist framework, the answer would be that AgrS does not exist and therefore it cannot host a subject in its specifier. But the question is only postponed, and we can reformulate it by asking why it appears to be a property of some Romance languages that the SpecT position is not available to a subject. Note that this could not immediately correlate with the pro-drop property, as French appears to have similar properties to Italian in subject inversion structures. As it is not clear what the common property might be, I leave the matter open.

6.4   THE SUBJECT IN CD CONTEXTS

As I pointed out in chapter 5, Giorgi and Pianesi (1997) have shown that speakers split into two classes, those who admit only a pro subject (class I speakers) and those who admit a lexical subject (class II speakers). Here, I examine class II speakers, that is, those who admit a lexical subject:

(55)   a. Credo Gianni arrivi stasera.
          think John arrive-subj tonight
          'I think that John will arrive tonight'.

       b. Credevo nessuno arrivasse in tempo.
          thought nobody arrive-subj in time
          'I thought that nobody would arrive in time'.

   c. *Credevo fosse Gianni arrivato
      thought had John arrived
      'I thought that John had arrived'.

   d. *E' Gianni arrivato?
      is John come?
      'Has John come?'

The subject can be found only in preverbal position. None of the speakers has accepted a structure like the one in (55c) and (55d). According to our hypothesis, in standard Italian and in NIDs, the preverbal subject position is located inside the CP layer, lower than the declarative complementizer and probably also lower than modal interrogatives yet higher than nonmodal interrogatives. The fact that a CD construction, which has been treated as V to C movement, shows a preverbal subject is thus not surprising if we assume that the subject is also inside the CP. Moreover, within the split-CP analysis, the fact that certain speakers accept a preverbal subject, yet no one accepts inverted subjects, shows that the subject position is located higher than the position to which the verb moves inside the CP in CD contexts. We note that in principle, the position where the verb moves in CD cases could be the lowest one of the CP, as this would be sufficient to block the occurrence of a complementizer merged in the lowest C position (and then raised to other C° positions). Hence, the discussion in chapter 5 leaves open a very interesting issue—the exact C° position where the verb moves in CD contexts. The fact that only a preverbal subject is grammatical persuades us that the C° containing the V in CD contexts is situated lower than the subject position (hence lower than LD); lower than the declarative complementizer; and lower than the CP involved in modal interrogatives, and that involved in Aux to C and absolute participial constructions.[20]

    The other interesting case concerning the subject found in chapter 5 has been mentioned in section 6.2 and is illustrated by the following examples:

(56) a. Gnun ch' a s bogia!   Turin
          nobody that SCL moves!
          'Nobody moves!'

      b. Mario ch a s presenta . . .
          M. that SCL presents himself . . .
          'Mario has to go immediately . . .'

      c. Caidun ch a m giuta!   Riva di Chieri
          somebody that SCL me helps!
          'Sommebody helps me!'

      d. Nissugn ch 'i s movi!   Cevia Valle Maggia
          nobody that SCL moves!
          'Nobody moves!'

      e. Qualchedun ch um ma giuta.   Borghetto di Vara
          somebody that SCL me helps!
          'Somebody helps me'.

f. Mario ch u s presenti . . .   Carcare
   M. that SCL presents . . .
   'Mario has to go immediately . . .'

As we have noted, the fact that a subject occurs before a complementizer is an argument in favor of our hypothesis that all preverbal subjects are located in a SpecC position. Moreover, the fact that the complementizer alternates with the verb in other languages has been interpreted as V to C movement in these contexts. Another interesting fact that has not been discussed so far is the presence of a QP subject in front of the complementizer. As we have seen in sections 6.2.2 and 6.3, preverbal QP subjects are located lower than DP subjects. This means that the $C°$ position targeted by the inflected verb in these structures is quite low, at least as low as nonmodal interrogatives. In nonmodal interrogatives, the co-occurrence of a QP subject with the wh-element can be excluded, assuming that they occupy the same A´ position or that the position of the QP subject is lower than the position of the wh and interferes with wh-movement. Note that in (56) the complementizer is located after a QP subject. If the QP subject is in the same or a lower position than wh-items in nonmodal contexts, the position of the complementizer of suppletive imperatives inside the CP layer is probably not very high, most likely lower than modal interrogatives, Aux to C, and absolute participial constructions and probably in the same or a lower position than the SCI in wh-nonmodal interrogatives. The same appears to be true for CD contexts in standard Italian (as we saw in chapter 5, CD contexts are extremely rare in NIDs, with the exception of Tuscan dialects). Hence, in suppletive imperatives and subjunctives, the complementizer targets $C°$ positions located quite low in the CP layer. If these are independent modal projections, different from the interrogative CPs, we have to assume the presence of more than one modal CP projection because the CPs for imperatives and subjunctives are different from the CP for modal interrogatives, which is located higher than the DP subject position.

6.5   CONCLUSION

In this chapter, I have proposed that the preverbal subject position in NIDs and in standard Italian is a SpecC position, although not left-dislocated, and that Spec AgrS (or SpecT in the new minimalist framework) is never accessible to a lexical nonpronominal subject. On this basis, I have reformulated the analysis of Aux to C, absolute participial constructions, main and embedded interrogatives, and suppletive imperatives. If we put together what we have discussed so far with the CP structure of interrogative sentences examined in chapter 3, we obtain the following structure:

(57)   [$_{CP}$ Aux to C/absolute past particle/exclamative clauses [$_{LD}$ LD/invariable
        SCL[CP modal wh [$_{TopP}$ DPsubj.[$_{CP}$ wh-phrases [$_{CP}$ QP?[$_{CP}$ deictic SCLs [$_{AgrCP}$
        SCI [$_{CP}$ ch/lo]]]]]]]]]

This structure is underdetermined, as it is not clear whether Aux to C, absolute participial constructions, and exclamatives are located on the same projection or not. In a general perspective that encodes a single feature on each functional head, such as the one adopted by Cinque (1999), one could assume a distinct projection for each of these constructions. However, at the moment I do not have any empirical evidence to support such a claim. Another problem concerns the position of QP subjects, which could be the same as that of wh-elements or a lower one. As I have no empirical basis to enable me to choose one or the other option, I leave the issue open.

As we have seen, the highest positions are reached by the verb in Aux to C, absolute participial, and exclamative constructions. They are located higher than the LD position [see Benincà 1996 for exclamative clauses and examples (47) for Aux to C]. In a position located lower than LD, there is the projection that contains modal interrogatives, which are still higher than the DP subject position since they trigger subject inversion. From this point on, we have the interrogative structure already discussed in chapter 3 for interrogative clauses.[21] If the basic idea put forth in this chapter is correct, that the preverbal subject position is in the CP layer and not in IP, the consequences for the languages considered here (standard Italian, French, and NIDs) and for other Romance languages are far-reaching. The first problem has already been mentioned in section 6.3: we have to assume that the IP position (SpecAgrS or SpecT) for subjects is not available in certain Romance languages. But our question is, why not? Moreover, is this valid for all Romance or is there variation within this language group? The other question regards the position of the subject SpecC with respect to the other projections contained in the CP layer. Is this position connected to the SCI position and to some agreement phenomena or not? If it is true that the subject is in CP in Romance, what about Germanic V2 languages? It has recently been proposed that subject-initial main clauses in Dutch and Germanic languages in general (cf. Zwart 1993) are AgrSPs, not CPs. This hypothesis could be reformulated on the basis of data about Romance V2, discussed in chapter 4, and the evidence reported here, in the following way: subject-initial V2 clauses are different from clauses beginning with a focalized object or adverb. However, they are still CPs, even though the projection occupied by the subject inside the CP is different from the focus projection that is, in turn, different from the projection occupied by scene-setting adverbs.

There are several more general consequences of the analysis presented here. These are discussed in the following, and concluding, chapter.

SEVEN

A Brief Summary

7.1 INTRODUCTION

In this conclusive chapter, I present a summary of the results of our inquiry into NIDs and discuss some of the general perspectives that have been opened by the present investigation. I point out the problems that remain to be solved and the possible lines of research that may lead to interesting developments, based on the conclusions we have reached concerning the way in which functional projections are layered and the kinds of connections among them. The analysis of syntactic phenomena found in NIDs in the structural space that is usually defined as AgrSP and CP has led us to split these two projections into a complex set of FPs, each corresponding to a distinct semantic feature.

The choice of a number of closely related dialects has already been justified in chapter 1; this choice has enabled us to restrict the number of variables in our experiment. The analyses presented here are all based on the general assumption that the syntactic structure of NIDs is the same for all the dialects. Cinque (1999) considers the structure of the clause as a UG property that the child does not have to acquire. Hence, all languages have the same structure. I do not take a position on this question. In this work, it has been assumed that all NIDs have the same structure, a much weaker claim.

On the basis of syntactic tests, such as the position of SCLs with respect to the preverbal strong negative marker (in Zanuttini's 1997 terms), their behavior in different types of coordination, and their relation to typical CP elements like the complementizer and wh-elements, I have shown that four types of SCLs have to be distinguished. The analysis of these four types has led us to assume the existence of an agreement field, where SCLs are merged; invariable and deictic subject clitics are located inside the CP field and interact with the complementizer and wh-elements, whereas number and person clitics do not interact with CP elements and are closer to the inflected verb:

(1) [$_{LDP}$ inv SCL$_i$ [$_{CP}$ deic SCL [$_{WHP}$ t$_i$ [$_{IP}$ [$_{NegP}$ [$_{NumbP}$ SCL [$_{HearerP}$ SCL [$_{SpeakerP}$ inflV [TP]]]]]]]]]

Thus the agreement field is located half in the IP layer and half in the CP layer. Invariable and deictic clitics are always located higher than the strong preverbal negative marker; number and person clitics can be located lower than the NegP projection, but there are cases in which they appear to the left of the negative marker. I interpret some of these cases of prenegative person and number SCLs as movement of the SCL to a higher position. The lowest position of the agreement field is occupied by the inflected verb. If we assume that SCLs are located in projections that correspond to the feature they express, we find an interesting and complex structure that encodes the so called phi features of the subject; the highest position (the one occupied by invariable SCLs) has to do with the topic/focus organization of the clause. Deictic SCLs are located immediately below and express a feature that distinguishes between deictic and nondeictic persons (essentially first and second person versus third person). Inside the IP layer, a projection expresses the features of number (and gender), and the lowest features are those corresponding to person. It appears that person is not a single feature expressed as a whole, as it is split into two positions (the lowest SCL position and the position of the inflected verb): the lower position corresponds to a [speaker] feature and the higher to a [hearer] feature. The third person results from a negative setting of both features. The reason that NIDs do not have morphologically distinct first-person SCLs (only deictic SCLs are possible, and they do not distinguish between first and second person) can thus be seen as the result of the complementary distribution of the inflected verb.[1]

This complex agreement structure probably reflects on the way DPs are legitimized inside the structure. As we have seen in chapter 6, the position of preverbal subjects is not always the same. It varies according to the type of XP: DPs and QPs occupy different positions, and it is probable that even inside the two classes of DPs and QPs there are different positions that have to do with a distinct interpretation of DPs. A great deal of work in this direction must still be done and will probably show that the standard notion of "nominative case" assigned through Spec-head agreement by a single functional head (AgrS° or T° in the minimalist framework) needs further elaboration.

Another general observation concerns the fact that the functional projections of the agreement field are not contiguous: two[2] of them are still in the IP layer, and two are in the CP space, higher than the position where the complementizer is merged in the structure. Nevertheless, there seems to be a connection between the two "subfields" that host SCLs, the one in IP and the one in CP, because SCLs have been shown to move from one subfield to the other (cf. chapter 2.5.1), crossing the nonclitic positions, as well as those of the negative marker and the complementizer. Therefore, it appears that SCLs do not move through a head-to-head mechanism (unless we permit incorporation and excorporation to the Neg° and lowest C° heads) but simply "jump over" those heads that do not belong to the agreement field. It appears that the projections that belong to the relevant field are the only ones that are visible to the moving SCL, as if there were a sort of relativized minimality at work, which makes all the positions that cannot host a SCL invisible and counts only those heads that are possible hosts for SCLs. This view of syntactic fields, constituted by nonadjacent FPs, opens many questions, which remain open for future research.

In the third chapter, four CP projections have been postulated to account for dialectal variation in the empirical domain of interrogative sentences. We have seen that there are seven types of structures in main interrogatives spread across the domain and that some of them show that more than one FP is activated. The structures found for nonsubject wh-items are the following:

1. Wh-SCL V: the only difference from a declarative clause is the presence of the wh-element at the beginning of the sentence.
2. Wh-complementizer SCL V: a C° position is occupied by a complementizer.
3. Wh-V + SCL: a C° position is occupied by the verb plus the enclitic pronoun.
4. Wh-V + SCL + particle: a particle occurs at the right of the V + SCL. We have to postulate at least two positions: one for the V + SCL and one for the particle.
5. Wh-deictic SCL V + SCL: a deictic clitic occurs in front of the V + SCL, showing that the position of deictic SCLs is higher than the position of inversion but lower than the position in which some types of wh may occur.
6. Wh-complementizer deictic V + SCL (only in those dialects that have two complementizers in embedded clauses): the complementizer occurs in front of a vocalic clitic, which in turn is higher than the position of inversion.

These types of examples show that there are three head positions involved in interrogative structures.

On the basis of this variation we have postulated the following "interrogative field":

(2) $[_{C1}$ ch $[_{C2}$ deictic SCL $[_{AgrC3}$ SCI $[_{CP4}$ [$_{SPECC4}$ pa] $[_{C°4}$ ch/lo]]]]]

The activation of each of these FPs corresponds to a distinct interpretation of the question: the highest CP encodes modal interrogatives; the one where deictic SCLs are realized, a "surprise" interpretation; the position where the complex form V + SCL occurs, an "out-of-the-blue" question; and the lowest position, where particles occur, a rhetorical interpretation.

I have assumed that the doubly filled Comp filter prevents a specifier and a head from occupying the same projection, unless they undergo a process of Spec-head agreement. Wh-elements may occur in different SpecC positions, depending on their interpretation and status. If they are weak pronouns (in the sense of Cardinaletti and Starke 1999), they have to occur in a position in which they can enter a Spec-head relation with a suitable head that has the same features, such as the inflected verb or the complementizer. The specifier position of deictic SCLs is not a position where Spec-head agreement can occur because the deictic SCL has only subject (and not wh-) features and therefore its Spec position has to remain empty. Unlike weak wh-items, tonic wh-items are not bound to a Spec-head configuration and occur in the specifiers of empty heads, their distribution limited only by the interpretation of the question that corresponds to the activation of different head positions. Connected to this is the observation about the types of wh-elements: it appears that argumental wh-words become weak (and even clitic head) pronouns much more frequently than nonargumental wh-words (like "when" or "why"). This suggests a possible line of research that ties the mechanism of cliticization to the part of the VP structure where subcategorized arguments are merged.

Structure (2) also shows that V to C and the requirement for weak wh-elements to be in a Spec-head relation with a head marked [+wh] are independent phenomena; V to C targets a specific position inside the interrogative field, whereas wh-elements may be located in the specifier position of a projection, whose head does not contain the inflected verb. Therefore, it appears that Rizzi's (1991) wh-criterion does not account for verb movement to the CP layer in NIDs. I tentatively suggest that V to C occurs as a consequence of feature checking of the inflected verb itself. Moreover, the Spec-head relation between the wh-item and a head is only necessary for weak wh-items and not for strong forms.

The interrogative field has an interesting property that is similar to the agreement field: it does not consist of a set of contiguous projections because the projections where modal interrogatives are checked are separated from the other three by the DP subject position (see chapter 6.3 and below).

In chapter 4, I analyze the phenomenon of Central Rhaetoromance V2—which can also be accounted for in terms of split CP—adopting a solution that places the verb higher in V2 structures than the interrogative projections (as the declarative/ interrogative asymmetry with respect to left dislocation shows). Moreover, I propose to further split the "projection" into a "V2 field," separating the position where scene-setting adverbs occur[3] and the positions where strongly focalized adverbs and objects occur from the position where focalized circumstantial adverbs occur.[4]

(3)   [scene-setting [$_{emb\ CP}$XP + foc [$_{embCP}$?SubjP XP circ. adv.   SubjP? LD   WH]]]

As for V2, there is no evidence that the set of V2 projections consists of non-contiguous projections. The results obtained through analysis of Rhaetoromance V2 are not much more than a way of expressing descriptive generalizations observed in the data. However, the analysis of this Romance language is interesting, as it gives us a basis for a comparative work with Germanic V2. Moreover, the observation that some XPs can be moved only to an embedded V2 position when the selecting verb belongs to a particular class opens up the possibility of different verbal classes selecting different types of CPs. In other words, the selection restrictions observed for many verbal classes may be directly encoded in the syntax by assuming that they select different CPs with different semantic properties; implicational restrictions may be observed so that when a higher CP is selected, the lower ones are also automatically selected.

Chapter 5 analyzes cases of complementizer deletion as V to C movement. Here, I propose an extension of V to C movement to disjunctive sentences and hypothetical, optative, and counterfactual clauses. As all these types of clauses show SCI, this means that the verb can reach the AgrCP projection, where the complex form V + SCL checks its features [as discussed in chapter 3 and illustrated in (2) above]. Moreover, the phenomenon of V to C is also found in standard Italian embedded clauses selected by a bridge verb. I propose that the feature that triggers V to C in CD contexts is a modal one, which would have to be kept distinct from the case of modal interrogatives [which are located higher in the structure, as shown in (2)].

The last case of activation of the CP layer is the suppletive imperative with a subjunctive verb. This may be +deictic or –deictic, in the sense that the order (or permission) can be given directly to the person who has to perform it [+deictic] or to somebody else [–deictic]. The two projections where +deictic and –deictic imperatives are realized appear to be located inside the CP layer in the following order:

(4)   [-deictic imperative FP [che/V]   [+deictic imperative FP [che/V]]]

This order accounts for the typological implication, discussed in chapter 5, which states that a given dialect has a complementizer with deictic suppletive imperatives only if it always has a complementizer for nondeictic suppletive imperatives. Moreover, the fact that in Ligurian dialects the deictic complementizer is morphologically different from the nondeictic one is also accounted for by a structure like (4), where the two positions are distinct.

We can sum up the findings in chapter 5 by assuming that there is a portion of the CP layer that encodes a modal feature of sentential complements of bridge verbs and +deictic and –deictic features of suppletive imperatives. Moreover, in some dialects, counterfactual, disjunctive, and optative clauses show movement of the inflected verb to the CP layer.

Another interesting observation is the fact that the AgrCP projection (corresponding to SCI) may be used as a landing site of the verb in different types of structures, such as interrogatives, counterfactuals, and optative and disjunctive sentences. This can help us to better characterize this projection as not uniquely interrogative. However, if we were to characterize it as simply indicating the "sentence type," this would be misleading, as we have seen that imperatives do not mark this projection (the same is probably also true for at least some types of exclamative clauses; see Benincà 1996 and Portner and Zanuttini 1996). The best characterization of the AgrCP projection is probably given in relation to the following feature: when AgrC is activated, there is an operator in its specifier position (a wh-element, as in interrogative clauses; a disjunctive operator or a modal operator, as in optative and counterfactual clauses). Thus AgrCP is the structural correlate of the wh-criterion proposed by Rizzi (1991), as in chapter 3; the projection is occupied by operators that need a specifier-head relation with a head. Nevertheless, it appears that not all wh-elements need this relation, as is probably also true for other types of operators. Another possible line of research will consider the subset of operators that need this special relation and their properties. In chapter 6, I analyze preverbal subject DPs and QPs in non-V2 varieties.[5] I put forth the hypothesis that DPs and QPs have distinct preverbal positions.

The position of DP subjects is higher than the positions where wh-elements are moved in "out-of-the-blue" interrogatives but lower than the position where wh-elements are moved in modal interrogatives and in exclamative clauses. The subject position is lower than auxiliaries in Aux to C constructions and lower than past participles in absolute constructions. The relevant structure is illustrated in (5):

(5)   [$_{CP}$ Aux to C/absolute past particle/exclamative clauses [$_{LD}$ LD/invariable SCL[CP modal wh [$_{TopP}$ DPsubj.[$_{CP}$ wh-phrases [$_{CP}$ QP?[$_{CP}$ deictic SCLs [$_{AgrCP}$ SCI [$_{CP}$ ch/lo]]]]]]]]

In this way, we have obtained a "map" of the FPs located in the syntactic space traditionally defined by AgrSP and CP. The relative order of some positions remains to be seen; one problem concerns the positions of QP subjects, which are incompatible with wh-elements (but not with null operators of yes/no questions) and could be located in the same position or excluded because of a minimality effect. Another point in the structure that remains underdetermined is the exact position of the subject in V2 languages, which appears to occur lower than nonfocalized circumstantial adverbs and focalized objects and higher than wh-elements and left dislocation; however, there are no clues to the order of focalized circumstantial adverbs.

Moreover, in (5), many constructions have been squeezed into a single projection; this means only that NIDs do not give any evidence of a more fine-grained structure because Aux to C and absolute participial constructions are very rare in this domain. We do not know whether Aux to C and absolute participial and exclamative clauses are located higher or lower than V2 phenomena; I was not able to find any evidence of a possible ordering.

The data examined in this work confirm and refine Rizzi's (1997) hypothesis of a fine structure of the left periphery: wh-elements are generally located lower than left dislocation (but can move higher in exclamative contexts); deictic SCLs are also located lower than left dislocation and interact in an interesting way with wh-elements; V2 phenomena, Aux to C, and absolute participial constructions are located higher than left dislocation.

7.2   SOME GENERAL PROPERTIES OF FUNCTIONAL STRUCTURE

It has been assumed in some recent works (Chomsky 1995 and Cinque 1999) that FPs can be of two types: those that are semantically content-significant such as tense, mood, aspect, and so on, and those that have only a structural nature, being essentially agreement projections. Chomsky proposes to get rid of this second type of projection, transferring the case properties traditionally attributed to agreement projections to V° and T° (for accusative and nominative, respectively). It is a fact that in NIDs subject clitic heads need a structural position because they cannot all be adjoined to T°. Therefore, I have used the traditional terminology of agreement projection(s), although the positions where SCLs occur are not all identical, as they realize distinct features (number, speaker, hearer, etc.). Moreover, what we call agreement projections could have more to do with semantics than is normally assumed, if Beghelli's (1995) work on the distinct positions of dif-

ferent types of quantifiers is on the right track. In recent literature, AgrSP has
often been proposed to be a set of projections, NumberP, PersonP, and GenderP
(cf. Shlonsky 1990 and Tortora 1998); the empirical domain of SCLs confirms
this hypothesis. Moreover, it appears that the concept of person is a morphological one, whereas several more basic features are encoded into the syntax;
their combination gives rise to the interpretation of first, second, or third person. On the other hand, gender is not expressed in the verbal system as an independent head, or at least I have not found any evidence of a GenderP. As gender is a nominal feature, it might be that it can only appear as "parasitic" to
another feature (such as number) in IP (which constitutes the extended projection of the verb), whereas it can have an autonomous realization in the DP structure. Thus, the picture that emerges from the examination of SCLs is not immediately comparable to the proposals mentioned above because gender and number
occur on the same FP and person is split into two FPs. Moreover, the deictic
feature that occurs in the CP layer shows that, on the one hand, the agreement
in Comp phenomena are not an exclusive property of verb second languages
and, on the other, that it is not possible to consider agreement in Comp as a pure
copy of the agreement features of the IP layer.

The structure of the CP layer presented here is only a proposal based on a
restricted number of languages from the same typological and genetic group. When
we have compared this structure with the structure found in other languages, a
regularity will probably emerge, even though it may not be similar to the one found
in the IP layer.

In this work, I have attempted to maintain the traditional distinction between
IP and CP, assuming as a basis that the CP layer begins where we see a complementizer. However, it might be that the functional part of the sentence structure is
a single set of FPs and that there is no need to distinguish between IP and CP. As
we have seen, the inflected verb can indeed move to the CP layer, whereas an
auxiliary cannot be directly merged in a C° position but can only move from a
lower position. The element directly merged in C is the complementizer, not a
verbal element like the auxiliary, as is normally the case in the IP layer. If Kayne's
(1998) proposal that the IP is not the complement of a C° head is correct, and if
the order complementizer IP is obtained by movement on the IP to the SpecC
position and is followed by the movement of the complementizer to a higher position, we will have to restructure the whole system. However, what remains valid
are the number and the serialization of the functional projections that have been
determined and their properties, whatever their name is. Here, I have slightly
modified the traditional interpretation of the complementary distribution between
the verb and the complementizer; that is, I have assumed that the complementary
distribution means that the verb and the complementizer have passed through the
same position, which is the lowest C° head. The complementizer is merged in that
position and then moves to higher C° heads, depending on the features it has to
check. The inflected verb can also move to a higher C° position, after having
reached the lowest C°. Hence, the complementary distribution does not necessarily mean that the two elements are in the same position at PF but only that their
movement paths have crossed each other. The proposal that the complementizer

is a sort of "wild card" for many C° positions can also account for the fact that the same form occurs in all embedded contexts, including relatives, clefts, and embedded interrogatives, which clearly have different properties from declarative complement clauses.

An alternative hypothesis to the split of functional projections into two domains, IP and CP, is already sketched here in the split of the sentence structure into a series of fields—such as the agreement, interrogative, V2, and modal fields—which are not necessarily made up of adjacent projections, though they have common properties and are connected through both head and XP movement. While studying the variation among dialects, I have found that a general condition emerges that is operative in all the fields examined in this work. It states that whenever a given field is activated (i.e., whenever its FPs are occupied by a head or a specifier), the activation process starts from the lowest FP to the highest one. It is not possible to fill an FP without having first filled the lower ones. This is particularly evident for the case of the agreement field, where the occurrence of higher SCLs implies the occurrence of lower SCLs in a given dialect, and for the interrogative field, where the occurrence of higher heads implies the realization of lower heads. This condition can also be satisfied through the movement of a single head to the higher FPs, which is what occurs inside the CP layer, where the verb or the complementizer can move from a lower to a higher position. In Giorgi and Pianesi's (1997) terms, when certain features are scattered through the structure, they are always scattered first from the lowest position [cf. the condition formulated in (60) in chapter 2]. As noted, the condition stated here corresponds to a bottoms-up procedure, which is also perfectly compatible with the minimalist account of merging in order to create structure.

The last point I want to mention concerns the very general problem of the theoretical framework we adopt to account for dialectal variation. For the data that have been discussed in this work, it becomes evident that dialectal variation cannot be accounted for by following a parametric approach, at least in the usual meaning of the term. Parameters are usually defined as a single choice for a given abstract property, which has the effect of accounting for a set of characteristics that always go together in a given language. The domain of dialectal variation is too narrow to enable an account in parametric terms, as the system of parameters is too rigid to account for the very little and nevertheless systematic differences found by comparing very similar languages. Here, I try to account for the differences found in the sample of dialects, chosen by assuming a more complex sentence structure than that which had been assumed before; dialectal variation has been exploited to show that sentence structure is very complex. However, a residue of variation in the number of FPs activated by a given dialect and in the element that checks the features of the active FPs has remained. This residue can be analyzed in terms of lexical properties of the relevant checking elements, which can support only a given number of features; it is this number that varies from dialect to dialect. More research is needed on this point, as on many others that have only been very briefly outlined here.

Notes

CHAPTER 1

This work has been made possible with the help of a research program in which extensive use has been made of data belonging to more than 100 varieties, and many others have been considered for single features. Data have been collected from ASIS (Syntactic Atlas for Northern Italy), which is currently in preparation at the Linguistics Department of the University of Padua. They are available on a database at the following internet site: http://asis-cnr.unipd.it.

1. This is clearly an alternative view to CP (or IP) recursion, as each FP is different from all the others and they are all ordered in the same way. Therefore, recursion is not used to analyze the phenomena described here.

2. It is assumed here that right adjunction is generally excluded and only left adjunction is possible (cf. Kayne 1994 for a principled account).

CHAPTER 2

1. As G. Graffi has pointed out, this division of persons has already been proposed by Benveniste (1966).

2. There are reasons to believe that the vowel here is epenthetic; cf. Vanelli (1992).

3. Provençal and Franco-Provençal varieties are an exception, as they have a complete system for person SCLs. Nevertheless, it can be shown that these dialects have a different system, which is more similar to the French SCL system. If we adopt Cardinaletti and Starke's (1999) theory, these SCLs are weak pronouns and not clitics, they are located in a specifier position, and they are not heads, as are the other clitics we are examining here. Therefore, data from Provençal and Franco-Provençal dialects are not considered here.

4. Second-person singular can also occur in this paradigm, as in this case it is opposed to second-person plural and realizes a [–plural] feature. However, it should be noted that second-person plural is quite rare in the corpus, as it is only present in a few Tuscany dialects around Florence and in Franco-Provençal.

5. Following Cardinaletti and Starke (1999), I assume that French SCLs are not heads, but rather weak pronouns, and therefore located in a specifier position. Hence, they are radically different from the SCLs we are examining here.

6. The coordinations involving verb pairs like 'eat and drink' and 'dance and sing' are not the best candidates for this test as they may be interpreted as a single action, hence as an instance of type 3 coordination, or as two distinct actions, hence of type 2 coordination. Because informants could vary in the interpretation of these pairs, less ambiguous verbs have been taken for these tests.

7. As for the second sentence, Benincà and Cinque assume that there has been a spreading of the tense node onto the two verbs. The same could be true for the first example. In this case, we would have an aspect node (the *ri* prefix is an aspect marker, indicating iteration of an action).

8. Several dialects provide an apparent counterexample to this generalization. These facts are analyzed in section 2.5.

9. A number of dialects provide an apparent counterexample to this generalization. These facts are analyzed in section 2.5.

10. Lori Repetti pointed out that the clustering process could also be a purely phonological fact. However, I do not believe that this is correct, as the contrast between (21) and (22) would remain unexplained.

11. Benincà first noticed these facts for the Paduan dialect; Brandi and Cordin (1981) then showed that the same pattern occurs in Florentine.

12. This sentence becomes grammatical with a strong pause and an intonation break after the focalized element. As P. Benincà suggests, this might indicate that the structure is much more complex in this case. Therefore, it is not considered here.

13. Type 2 coordination is not considered here, as it does not single out any SCL class. It merely gives the same results that are given by coordination of type 1. Incidentally, this confirms Kayne's (1994) proposal that coordination of type 2 has the same structure as coordination of type 1.

14. It is to be noted that deictic and invariable SCLs are omitted in type 3 coordination, which is just what we expect, given the structural hypothesis proposed here plus the assumption that higher clitics may be left out in coordination structures in which lower SCLs have to be repeated.

15. Type 3 coordination has been analyzed by Kayne (1994), who proposes that object clitics can be omitted in the second conjunct because they climb to a position higher than the coordinated structural portion. When the second-person singular SCL is present in Venetian, it is not possible to omit the object clitic, and the whole clitic cluster has to be repeated:

(i)   Ti lo lesi e ti lo rilesi tuto el giorno.   Venetian
       SCL it read and SCL it reread all the day
       'You read it and reread it all day long'.

(ii)   *Ti lo lesi e ti rilesi tuto el giorno
       SCL it read and SCL reread all the day

(iii) lo leso e rileso tuto el giorno.
       it read and reread all the day
       'I read it and reread it all day long'.

(iv)   *ti lo lesi e rilesi tuto el giorno
       SCL it read and reread all the day
       'You read it and reread it all day long'.

When there is no second-person SCL [as in (iii)], it is possible to let the object clitic climb out of the coordinated portion of the structure. When the second-person SCL is present, the object clitic also needs to be repeated [cf. the ungrammaticality of (ii)]. The SCL thus seems to constitute a barrier for the object clitic's climbing out of the coordinated structure.

16. See chapter 3 for a detailed discussion of why the enclitic and proclitic series are morphologically different from each other.

17. For languages that have inclusive and exclusive persons, the structure should be even more complex than that which is assumed here. For languages that have six persons as the NIDs, we can assume that the whole paradigm is given by the following combinations:

	Speaker	Hearer	Number
1st	+	–	0
2nd	–	+	–
3rd	–	–	–
1st pl.	+	+	0
2nd pl.	–	+	+
3rd pl.	–	–	+

Second- and third-person plural are not distinguished from second- and third-person singular. The distinction between singular and plural is most likely encoded in the Numb° position. As for first-person singular, first-person plural is already distinct from singular, as it has a + both for speaker and hearer, which is exactly what first-person plural means (as R. Kayne noted, first-person plural is not a plurality of first persons but the speaker plus the hearer). This argument is not pursued further here.

18. Benincà and Vanelli examine only the present indicative and subjunctive, although these phenomena are also found in both the indicative and subjunctive imperfect.

19. In the variety considered here, this agglutination seems optional, although it is not clear whether it is subject to constraints or not.

20. The varieties that have second-person agglutination also have first-person agglutination; hence verb movement proceeds correctly from the lower to the higher position.

21. However, this is not possible if the negative marker is not represented by a discontinuous type of negation *ne . . . mina*, as in (34), but by a purely preverbal negative marker, which is *no* in this variety:

(i)   N'i vien.
       not SCL come
       'They are not coming'.

(ii)   *I m'ha dito ch'i no vien
       SCL to-me have told that SCL not come
       They told me that they are not coming'.

This could lead us to the hypothesis that it is not the SCL that moves but rather that we are dealing with two types of preverbal negation in this context; that is, the strong and the weak negative marker of Zanuttini's account (58b) should have a weak negative marker, and (58a) should have a strong negative marker located on an independent head above the one where the inflected verb is located. Several arguments show that this is not the best solution to account for (57) versus (58). As already mentioned, the prenegative SCL occurs only in embedded contexts, whereas the difference between strong and weak negative markers is present in both embedded and main clauses. In other words, the main versus embedded asymmetry points toward a solution in terms of CP and not of NegP. Moreover, if the difference lies in the position of the negative marker and not in the SCL position, it remains a puzzle why in this case the prenegative SCL has to cluster with the complementizer, whereas this is not usually the case for [+/–plural] SCL, as the clitic in (35) is. Therefore, the prenegative position of the SCL is interpreted as SCL climbing to a higher position and not as a different position of the negative marker.

22. The subject clitic *i* is not a vocalic clitic but a number clitic.

23. Note that even though this is a case of long head movement, clitics usually move in this way in the syntax, jumping over other heads. Our hypothesis postulates SCL climbing from a clitic position to another clitic position (one of the two containing vocalic SCLs), hence it is not deviant in any way from standard analyses.

24. For the position of the tonic pronoun, see chapter 6, where preverbal subjects are analyzed as occupying a very high position in the CP domain.

25. The first generalization is contradicted by several varieties, such as the Tuscany dialect of Colle Val d'Elsa, which shows only a vocalic clitic of the invariable class, at least in the indicative mode. This means that it is not entirely impossible to fill the highest position of the agreement field, leaving the others empty. However, the fact that the overwhelming majority of varieties obeys the generalization is significant and must be accounted for.

26. The comparison is complete if we exclude the case of fifth person, which is quite rare and has most likely not been taken into account by Renzi and Vanelli (1983), as they consider a more limited set of dialects.

27. The condition that establishes that the lowest SCL position is not valid for invariable SCLs, which is the only type realized in Colle Val d'Elsa, as we have already seen. It must be kept in mind that invariable SCLs are different from other SCLs because they relate to the informational structure of the sentence and do not encode any semantic feature of the subject, only signaling that there is a subject.

CHAPTER 3

1. See chapter 4 for a more detailed discussion of the V2 phenomenon and the references quoted there.

2. Munaro provides two arguments in favor of this choice. First, he comments on Renzi and Vanelli's (1983) generalization 5, which states that the number of interrogative SCLs is equal to or greater than the number of declarative SCLs in the dialects examined. His argument is the following: if interrogative SCLs are more numerous than declarative SCLs, this would mean that they manifest a more complete morphological specification of the subject agreement features for declarative SCLs. Hence, they must be located inside IP. However, one could also make the opposite claim, namely, that interrogative SCLs, being different from declarative clitics, are located in CP, not in IP. Looking across the paradigm of interrogative SCLs, we find that the neutralizations between the first-person singular and plural found in declarative SCLs (cf. section 2.2) is also observed in interrogative SCLs. Hence, interrogative clitics do not encode more agreement subject features than declarative clitics. Moreover, in northern Italian varieties, verbal morphology is not weak at all, which probably means that the reason that subject clitics are there is not at all connected with the morphological necessity to express all subject features but probably with a different syntactic mechanism. Munaro's second argument regards interactions with negation, as SCI and strong preverbal negative markers are not compatible (see Portner and Zanuttini 1996 and Zanuttini 1997). Munaro proposes that the complex V + SCL and the negative marker are located on the same head, namely, Type°, and both define a sentence type, such as interrogative or negative, respectively. It seems to me that the strong preverbal negative marker and interrogative clitics are better kept separate for the following reason. Munaro assumes that the head of TypeP is saturated in embedded contexts by

the feature imposed by the selecting main verb. Therefore, the head of TypeP can only be morphologically specified in matrix contexts. This accounts for the fact that SCI is restricted to main contexts. However, preverbal negation is by no means restricted to main contexts because it is also possible to negate embedded clauses with this type of negative morpheme. Thus, the head of TypeP must be accessible to preverbal negative morphemes even in embedded contexts, whereas it is not accessible to SCI. It appears to me that it would be better to keep SCI and preverbal negation on two distinct heads and that the incompatibility between SCI and preverbal negative markers can be accounted for in terms of a negative head-blocking verb movement to the C° position, where SCI occurs, as proposed by Zanuttini.

3. There is another possible analysis of the order V + SCI + *pa*, depending on the assumption that *pa* could be used as a bound morpheme and not as an independent element. In this case, first the verb could move to the position of the SCL adjoining to its left; then the complex V + SCL could left-adjoin to the interrogative bound morpheme *pa*, yielding the correct word order. The reason that I think this analysis is not viable is illustrated by the following example:

(i)   Olà pa?   Pera di Fassa
      where interr. marker
      'But where?'

Because *pa* can occur in this context, it cannot be considered to be a bound morpheme. Therefore, I discard this hypothesis. Moreover, cases like (53), where an interrogative bound morpheme is used, show exactly the opposite order, namely, V + interrogative morpheme + SCL, showing that the position of interrogative markers is lower than that corresponding to SCI.

4. As far as I know, the combination of a complementizer and *pa* is never possible in Rhaetoromance varieties.

5. An exception is Spec-head agreement, where the features of the two elements are shared by the specifier and the head. Note that in the case of *pa* and the complementizer, there appears to be no overt feature sharing. I discuss this in detail below.

6. As already mentioned, SCI occurs not only in interrogative sentences but also in contexts where postulating verb movement to C° is not so obvious. In some varieties, even embedded subjunctives show inversion, as in the following example:

(i)   Se gaves-tu fam. . .   Tuenno (Trentino)
      if had + subjunctive-you hunger
      If you were hungry. . .

We examine these cases in chapter 4, where I discuss complementizer deletion in standard Italian and interpret it as a case of V to C°, as well as in other contexts, such as suppletive imperatives. I attempt to reduce all these cases to verb movement to the same position within the CP domain.

7. For the present discussion, it is irrelevant to postulate that the clitic morphemes are generated directly in the syntactic position, where the verb moves as in the traditional analysis (e.g., Pollock 1989), or to assume that the forms verb + SCL are directly extracted from the lexicon and a checking process applies to the form once it reaches the relevant position, as in the minimalist framework.

8. I am adopting the terminology of Shlonsky (1994), who proposes that an AgrC position is present in West Flemish, but in the following discussion I use the terms AgrCP and CP3 as synonymous.

9. Some additional evidence in favor of this hypothesis can be found in those dialects that show agreeing complementizers. Brovedani (1981) reports that in the Friulian variety of Clauzetto, complementizers show the following morphological modifications across the verbal paradigm:

(i)

1	2	3	1pl	2pl	3pl
so	su	s	so	so	s
ko	ku	k	ko	ko	k

The cases of first-person singular and plural and second-person plural could be analyzed as involving clustering of the SCL with the complementizer, a phenomenon that has already been described in chapter 2 for deictic clitics, and these are indeed instances of deictic clitics. However, the second-person singular cannot be treated as a clustering of the second person SCL, as (ii) shows:

(ii)   . . . ku tu ven
        . . . that you come/. . . that you are coming

The SCL occurs after the complementizer, and there is a sort of vowel harmony between the complementizer and the subject clitic. This shows that the data presented in (i) are really to be interpreted as a case of agreeing complementizer and not as an SCL clustering on the complementizer. These data could be accounted for in the same way in which they have been interpreted in Germanic languages. Shlonsky (1994) proposed that the complementizer moves to the position of the agreement morpheme, incorporating to the left of it. If it is true that the complementizer moves to an AgrCP inside the CP layer, we will be forced to postulate that this AgrCP is higher than the lowest complementizer position, exactly as Shlonsky does.

10. This is not always true. Note that proclitics also use the same morpheme for the fifth person, but this is not true for enclitics.

11. See chapter 5 for an analysis of SCI in disjunctive, optative and counterfactual clauses, where an empty operator is probably realized in some SpecCP.

12. Fassano dialects vary in this feature. In Moenat, for instance, *pa* is obligatory in all main interrogatives, as in Gardenese, whereas in the most conservative varieties, such as Alba or Canezei, we find main interrogatives with a complementizer.

13. In the descriptive grammars of Rhaetoromance, *pa* is defined as a "question-reinforcing" element; this feeling of reinforcement can be translated in more formal terms by assuming that *pa* corresponds to the rhetorical interpretation.

14. Standard German also uses a particle, *denn*, at the end of the question to mark this context. Fassano informants usually translate *pa* with *denn* when they are asked to explain the meaning of *pa*. Even standard Italian has a morpheme that signals that the question entails a presupposition. This corresponds to the adversative particle *ma*, occurring before the wh and even before a subject:

(i)   Ma Gianni dove va?
       but John where goes?
       Where is John going?

15. Both Badiotto and Gardenese are V2 varieties, but Fassano is not. I do not know if there is a connection between the realization of the CP4 and verb movement in declarative clauses, and I do not explore this possibility here.

16. In Badiotto, this is true only for wh-questions but not for yes/no questions that behave as in Fassano. This suggests a difference between wh- and yes/no questions that is not dealt with here.

17. It is always possible that even this structure is used to convey particular presuppositions if the intonation is not flat but, for instance, if a pitch accent is realized on the wh-item. However, when this structure is possible in a given variety, it is always the one used for an out-of-the-blue interrogative.

18. In this dialect, the phenomenon is restricted to yes/no questions, but this is not the case in Friulian.

19. It is interesting to note that this structure is never found with auxiliaries. This could be interpreted as a difference in the raising possibilities of auxiliaries to the position of deictic clitics. However, as most auxiliary forms begin with a vowel, the process might be only phonetic, as data must still be checked with other forms.

20. It is not clear whether the loss of SCI is simply the loss of the morpheme in AgrC° and the inflected verb still moves to AgrC°, although the movement is not visible anymore, or if the loss of the morpheme has to be interpreted as loss of verb movement.

21. The same type of modal interpretation is found in standard Italian, when the verb is inflected in its future form, even though no complementizer is present.

22. Note, however, that there is no SCI, and the verb is inflected in its subjunctive form. The fact that SCI is incompatible with present subjunctive is discussed in detail in chapter 5.

23. As mentioned, SCI can also be found in noninterrogative contexts such as disjunctive or counterfactual clauses, although it is not clear whether the verb remains in AgrC° or climbs higher inside the CP layer in these structures.

24. The wh-feature is realized by the complementizer even in modal interrogatives, although this is a nonselected context.

25. Note that in embedded sentences there is one single position that can be targeted by all wh-items, that is, SpecC1.

26. It is interesting to note that wh-items such as *co* and *che* may occur with a complementizer. This fact favors the hypothesis that the complementizer can undergo an agreement process with a wh-item.

27. Some speakers find these sentences acceptable with a pitch intonation on the wh-item. This changes the interpretation of the question, which becomes of this type: "Tell me exactly how you do it or what you buy."

28. This position within CP could contain a null operator in the cases of wh–in situ, discussed above (cf. Poletto 1993b).

29. Another gap found in the structures could be purely coincidental, that is, the lack of a variety in which all four projections are visible, because we have seen that CP4 is usually occupied by the trace of verb movement and only in some varieties is there a specifier or a bound morpheme that permits the movement of the verb through the CP4 head.

30. Note that if the movement of the complementizer is due to checking, we may expect variation across different varieties, as the features of the C° heads that attract the complementizer could be strong in one language but weak in others. Therefore, the complementizer could remain lower in some dialects than in others.

31. For a more detailed discussion on the distribution of the two structures, see Poletto and Vanelli (1994: 147).

CHAPTER 4

1. Object clitics are not possible first-position elements because they are heads and not XPs. No Tobler-Mussafia effects are found in these contexts. Therefore, cases of V3 are virtually possible with an object clitic. Similar cases are also found in Old Germanic languages (see van Kemenade 1987 for English and Tomaselli 1995 for German).

2. Indirect objects are always doubled by a clitic in this variety, as in many other northern Italian varieties. This applies even to the case in which the indirect object is represented by a wh or by a quantifier. Thus, a doubling of the indirect object cannot be interpreted as left dislocation because wh and quantifiers can never be left-dislocated.

3. We are abstracting away from parenthetical adverbs, which are possible in these structures, although with a different status.

4. Moreover, agreement is the only structural relation that makes it possible to bypass the general restriction known as doubly filled Comp filter. In chapter 3, this filter has been reformulated as a general restriction, which prevents a head and its specifier from being filled at the same time if they do not enter a Spec-head relation. This restriction might ultimately stem from an economy principle, which prevents the features of an FP to be checked both by the head and by the specifier.

5. One might object that this is not a unitary account of V2. However, the obligatory presence of a topicalized or focalized XP in the CP layer could reflect a more general requirement on the organization of the theme/rheme relations in the following terms: V2 languages always require a theme/rheme specification. Therefore, there is always an active CP projection (even though it is not always the same) in these languages. I do not speculate further on the ultimate trigger for V2.

6. An alternative analysis has been suggested by A. Tomaselli (personal communication). One could assume that left dislocation and V2 are incompatible because they are alternative ways of creating a topic/comment structure. It must be noted, however, that this would exclude only V2 elements that are topics and not focalized V2 items, which should behave as wh-items and be compatible with left dislocation. Therefore, an analysis in terms of split CP is maintained.

7. It might be argued that preverbal subjects are not V2 structures at all, but I show in section 6 that this is not the case for the S. Leonardo variety.

8. Alternatively, in cases like (20), the adverb could have moved from a position higher than that where negation is interpreted. However, Cinque (1999) excludes the possibility that adverbs move if they are not focalized. (see Cinque for a more detailed discussion on adverb movement and scope interactions).

9. Cf. Cinque (1999), who defines lower adverbs as those that may be found in the structural space of the past participle movement in Romance.

10. The VP topicalization is probably not the movement of the VP itself but of a larger portion of the lower functional structure, as the inclusion of adverbs seems to indicate.

11. Other Rhaetoromance varieties show V2 even in embedded interrogatives (e.g., Gardenese). These are not considered here.

12. It should be noted that there is a difference between restrictive relative and appositive relatives. In restrictive relatives V2 is marginal, whereas it is completely excluded in appositive relatives. As the data are quite complicated, this analysis includes only declarative sentences in which embedded V2 is clearly possible.

13. Note that extraction of the adverb from the lower clause is possible, though the adverb is again obligatorily focalized, even if it occupies the first position of the main clause:

(i) a. DUMAN m a-al dit c al vagn.
         tomorrow me has-he told that he comes
         'He told me that he is coming'.

     b. DUMAN m a-**al** dit c al n vagn nia.
         tomorrow me has-he told that he not comes not (interpretation not tomorrow)
         'Tomorrow he told me that he is not coming'.

14. A potential problem occurs in sentences like (i), which is grammatical in standard Italian. However, the difference might stem from the non-V2 status of standard Italian:

(i)   Credo che domani venga.
      think that tomorrow comes
      'I think that he will come tomorrow'.

Example (i) has no focus on the adverb. The grammaticality of (i) could be due to a different position of the adverb in standard Italian than in Rhaetoromance.

15. This is also true in the variety we are examining. Embedded wh-interrogatives always require a complementizer after the wh-element, as the following example illustrates:

(i)   Al ma demanee can c al vagn.
      he me asked when that he comes
      'He asked me when he is coming'.

This implies that there are more projections than those illustrated in (39), but there may be other independent arguments to assume that they exist.

16. In both cases, they take a CP containing a complementizer, but as we have seen, this does not mean that they take the same CP.

17. It should be noted, however, that the embedded sentences cannot be analyzed as AgrSPs, with the subject occupying the SpecAgrS position, as left dislocation is not possible in front of a preverbal subject, similar to that which occurs in main clauses:

(i)   *Al m a dit c l liber Giani l lii
      he me has told that the book John it reads
      'He told me that John reads the book'.

(ii) *Al m despleej c l liber Giani l lii
      I am sorry that the book John it reads
      'I am sorry that John reads the book'.

Hence, preverbal subjects in embedded contexts are always in the CP field, as in main contexts.

18. In chapter 6 the preverbal subject position in non-V2 dialects is considered, and it is argued that in non-V2 languages the subject position is lower than the left-dislocation position.

19. The same contrast occurs in several Bavarian dialects, known as Cimbro, spoken in northern Veneto and Trentino. These dialects maintained their V2 structure until the last century but have lost the SOV order typical of the German that acquires SVO (see Benincà and Renzi 1998; Poletto and Tomaselli 1998).

20. Even though there are several CP projections, the V2 constraint holds and is a consequence of the Spec-head relation that the V2 constituent and the inflected verb must enter. In other words, only one CP projection can be used in each sentence, as there is only one inflected verb that can satisfy the Spec-head agreement relation required by both the V2 constituent and the inflected verb.

21. This analysis is obviously not justifiable in Chomsky's (1995) framework, where he simply eliminates head government.

22. The position of the subject is not fully determined, and this has been identified by a question mark in (51). The head positions for the complementizer in embedded context have been omitted.

23. Altmann notes that this sentence is grammatical if the first of the two XPs is a hanging topic but not in the case in which both XPs are left-dislocated.

24. Cf. Vikner (1995: sec. 4.1) for a detailed discussion of Icelandic and Yiddish data. V2 in embedded interrogative sentences is only possible with wh-elements that are presumably generated in CP and not moved from the inside of the clause. Vikner interprets this as a consequence of a minimality constraint, which bans the movement of both a topicalized element and a wh-item into the CP domain.

CHAPTER 5

1. I have already examined a case of complementizer plus SCI and double complementizers in Piedmontese (cf. chapter 3). Several more cases of double complementizers are discussed in chapter 6.

2. See 3.2 for the general criteria for determining whether SCI corresponds to V to C or not.

3. These sentences have been used to elicit the corresponding data in the sample of varieties examined.

4. Note that in the case of lexical verbs we do not have any evidence of where the subject is located, as it could well occupy the postverbal subject position. However, I assume that the structure with lexical verbs is similar to the one with auxiliaries, although the data regarding the subject positions are not very clear. In the structure with lexical verbs, the subject may occur before objects:

(i)   Lavasse Giorgio i piatti, faremmo prima.
      washed Giorgio the dishes, do + cond. earlier
      'If Giorgio washed the dishes we would finish earlier'.

(ii) Lavasse i piatti Giorgio, faremmo prima.
      washed the dishes Giorgio, do + cond. earlier

In (i) the subject occurs before the object, whereas in (ii) it occurs after. In the case of auxiliary structures, there are three subject positions:

(iii)   a. Avesse Giorgio lavato i piatti . . .
           'Had Giorgio washed the dishes . . .'

        b. Avesse lavato Giorgio i piatti.
           had washed Giorgio the dishes . . .

        c. Avesse lavato i piatti Giorgio.
           had washed the dishes Giorgio . . .

The highest subject position precedes the past participle in (i), an intermediate subject position probably connected with focus is found after the past participle but before the object, and a third position is found after the object. Hence, in the case of lexical verbs, it is not a simple matter to find a test that shows that the subject is in AgrS and not lower. It could even be the case that the subject does not occupy the SpecAgrS position at all when there is only a lexical verb and the verb has moved to C nevertheless, preventing the merging of the complementizer.

5. For some speakers, CD is only possible with a subjunctive, not with a future indicative or a conditional. Even for speakers who accept (28) and (29), they are stylistically more marked than (27b). This seems to suggest that there is a difference between the two types of CD.

6. Note that future morphology does not distinguish between indicative and subjunctive forms.

7. We specify the class in question in the next section.

8. Cf. Cinque (1989) for similar conditions on embedded V2.

9. I do not discuss languages that have unrestricted V2 in embedded contexts, limiting the comparison to German and mainland Scandinavian, which restrict the context of embedded V2 to the class of verbs we are considering. In this work, I use German for the examples concerning Germanic languages.

10. From an observational point of view, CD is thus more a V1 than a V2 phenomenon, as the inflected verb moves to C° but the SpecC position is (at least phonetically) empty. Note that even in V2 languages there are some restricted cases of V1: in German there are only cases in which a null operator may be plausibly assumed in SpecC, such as yes/no interrogatives or imperatives. In other languages (generally Old Romance and Old Germanic languages) V1 can be found in so-called narrative contexts, where the null operator analysis is less obvious, even though it has been proposed. In CD structures, the verb may be the first element of the embedded clause.

11. The internal structure of each FP has been omitted for reasons of space.

12. Cinque proposes that the verb can stop in a head position if it is marked strong for the feature that corresponds to the head.

13. Not all epistemic adverbs are grammatical in this position; for instance, an adverb like *probabilmente* 'probably' yields ungrammaticality. This might be due to some independent factor. It is important to note, however, that all epistemic adverbs give an ungrammatical result if they are placed in front of the verb when CD applies.

14. Speech-act adverbs like *francamente* 'frankly' appear to resist embedding:

(i)   *Credo che francamente lo farà
      think that frankly it do + fut.
      'I think that frankly he will do it'.

The adverb appears to be oriented to the subject of the main sentence and not to the subject of the embedded sentence. For this reason, this type of adverb has not been taken into consideration for our test.

15. The adverb *fortunatamente* 'luckily' can be found in a right-dislocated position with the typical pause intonation. I do not consider this case.

16. On the basis of a Tyrolean German dialect, Alber (1994) has also proposed a complex structure for the CP domain.

17. This position could correspond to one of the positions of the interrogative domain, namely, the highest one, which encodes a modal feature, or it could be a different position. Since modal interrogatives do not have a nonrealis, but rather an epistemic, interpretation, I keep the modal epistemic CP of interrogative clauses distinct from the modal CP activated in the CD contexts examined here, even though the type of verbal inflection in the two cases is the same.

18. This analysis could be applied to Germanic languages as well, distinguishing between the core V2 cases found in matrix clauses—where V movement would be triggered by an agreement feature in the Comp domain (as proposed by many authors; cf. section 5.2)—and embedded V2 under bridge verbs, which would be triggered by a [-realis] feature inside the Fin° head. I do not pursue this idea any further.

19. Speakers who admit a pro subject also find that the second-person pronoun is possible in the preverbal position. However, this pronoun has a particular distribution in subjunctive contexts, as it is obligatory and no pro drop is licensed. I do not pursue this matter any further, although it is clear that the second-person pronoun in these contexts is different from tonic pronouns normally found in standard Italian (cf. Cardinaletti 1997).

20. The difference between standard Italian and NIDs is analogous to the difference between German and Dutch: in German, embedded V2 is possible under bridge verbs, whereas this is not the case for Dutch.

21. We are forced to admit that percolation of the selection features from the matrix verb to the relevant C position, where they are encoded, could only occur if the higher heads are not phonetically realized. This is not an obvious assumption and should be demonstrated independently.

22. The solution of this problem could come from studies on the Germanic domain, as Dutch does not have embedded V2, although German does. The analysis proposed for this difference could also be adopted for explaining the difference between NIDs and standard Italian.

23. These sentences have been used to elicit the corresponding data in the sample of varieties examined.

24. The only exception is Colle Val d'Elsa:

(67)   b. Mario si presenti subito dal direttore.   Colle Val D'Elsa
           M. himself presents immediately to the director
           'Mario has to go immediately and see the director'.

25. In Veneto and Trentino dialects, the complementizer is generally not realized in deictic suppletives (apart from Verona) and with QP preverbal subjects. In Friulian, the complementizer is always realized with deictic suppletives and is optional with preverbal QPs; the same is true in Lecco, a Lombard dialect. Generally, in Western Lombard the complementizer is optional with deictic suppletives. Emilian works like Western Lombard. In Northern Lombard, spoken in Switzerland, the complementizer is always realized except in the variety of Brione. In Eastern Lombard, no complementizer is realized with deictic and preverbal QP subjects. Ligurian is like Friulian; that is, the complementizer is always realized with deictic suppletives and is optional with preverbal QP subjects. Many Piedmontese dialects have this interesting property (discussed in the next chapter), showing the QP or DP subject in front of the complementizer.

CHAPTER 6

1. The term *postverbal* indicates here a position after the auxiliary verb, not the postparticipial position(s) typical of free inverted subjects.

2. In Poletto (1993), I simply make a distinction between DPs and QPs, though it is most likely that there is a difference between specific and nonspecific DPs, possibly involving other semantic differences, too, such as the possibility of an existential interpretation or d-linking. I do not pursue this matter here because I do not have a methodical set of data for all varieties to support this claim at present.

3. Some varieties appear to distinguish between different person tonic pronouns since they show obligatory doubling with the second-person singular but not with the third-person singular and plural (see Poletto 1993). It is a fact that urges us again to analyze person as a complex category, as has been done in chapter 2.

4. Many Friulian varieties show a so-called "subject for object clitic phenomenon," namely, the absence of the subject clitic if an object clitic or the preverbal negative marker is realized. Therefore, sentence (8a) with an object clitic is not a good test for determining clitic doubling with quantifiers. I have included (8b), which is another sentence of the common questionnaire, even though this might not be completely comparable to (8a). It is a fact that doubling extends from quantifiers like *tutti* all, which can more easily be d-linked, through to quantifiers like *qualcuno* somebody, which can be more easily inter-

preted as specific to the negative quantifier *nessuno*, the last one that occurs with doubling. As already noted, the variation does not always cut between pronouns and DPs or DPs and QPs, whereas it does inside each class. The data I discuss here are a simplification of the real situation found in the field, but they can serve as a basis for understanding the factors to which the doubling phenomenon is sensitive. It also appears that the doubling phenomenon is sensitive to the tense and mood used in the sentence, and this might be a reflex of the fact that the quantifier is interpreted differently if the tense of the sentence varies.

5. An exception is again the second-person singular pronoun, which appears to require the clitic.

6. Note that we are introducing an additional position in the agreement field that encodes the [+/–human] feature. In chapter 2, I show that some SCLs can move to a prenegative position. One could explore the idea that this prenegative position corresponds to the one in which the [+/–human] feature is checked. I do not develop this idea any further here.

7. Therefore, the inflected verb would occupy the head position of number SCLs if we assumed that NIDs and standard Italian had the same set of agreement projections. Alternatively, one may assume that standard Italian has only one AgrS projection, where all features are realized and the inflected verb occupies that position.

8. In some dialects, QPs may be morphologically distinct for singular and plural, and this correlates with the + or – specific interpretation of the quantifier.

9. Another Romance dialect that shows that the CP domain has to be split into more than one structural position is the Salentino variety studied by Calabrese (1993). He reports [in his (36)] that in Salentino two complementizers, *ka* and *ku*, occur on two different sides of the preverbal subject. *Ka* is found before the subject, and *ku* must follow it:

(32)   a. Oyyu ka lu Marju bbene krai.
            want that the Mariu comes tomorrow
            'I want that Mario comes tomorrow'.

       b. Oyyu lu Marju ku bbene krai.
            want the Mariu that comes tomorrow

Although the two complementizers do not co-occur, it is possible to state that they are in different positions, as one occurs before and the other after the subject.

10. Certain dialects appear to possess doubling of an invariable SCL with preverbal DPs and QPs or with preverbal QPs only (see Vassere 1993). These cases are better analyzed as deictic SCLs, which are homophonous to the invariable series. Vassere himself notes that the same form may have different functions in northern Lombard dialects.

11. Note that the subject position needs to be located quite high in CP as it occurs higher than SCI and higher than the position where the interrogative complementizer is inserted. I come back to this topic when I examine the occurrences of preverbal subjects in main and embedded interrogative clauses.

12. This property is reminiscent of V2 languages. I assume, following Schwartz and Vikner (1996), that all V2 clauses are CPs, even those whose XP in first position is the subject. One interesting corollary of this observation concerns the diachronic development of NIDs, which were originally V2 languages in the medieval period and have subsequently lost this property with the development of the system of SCLs (analyzed in chapter 2). One could consider the development of SCLs as a consequence of the loss of V2 because they appear to occupy the structural positions the verb does not move to any more, namely, CP and the highest IP portion. Hence, these dialects would still be V2 in a

deeper sense; that is, they still occupy the heads of the CP layer, and they still have preverbal subjects inside CP, although the element that fills these positions is no longer the inflected verb but rather a subject clitic. This hypothesis is intriguing because it formally encodes an interesting and well-known observation—that only the varieties that possessed the V2 property with a main versus an embedded asymmetry (French and NIDs) developed subject clitics when they lost V2, whereas other Romance languages that had a different type of V2 (most probably involving lower functional positions), and did not show main versus embedded asymmetries, did not develop subject clitics. Moreover, it gives us a better understanding of why vocalic SCLs have much in common with West Flemish subject clitics and in general with Germanic agreement phenomena inside the CP layer. An analysis of the diachronic syntax of NIDs would take us too far from our present discussion, as it constitutes the field of inquiry for another work.

13. These structures have been analyzed as T to C by Roberts (1993c), always in a perspective that differentiates case assignment through Spec-head agreement and case assignment through government. Because T would assign case through government, it is possible to find structures with inversion of the subject. Note, however, that here the verb is not an infinitival form but a subjunctive form; hence, it can hardly be considered to be a bare T.

14. This sentence becomes more acceptable if the wh-element is strongly focalized since the interpretation becomes one of correction, as the wrong information has been given; that is, I am asking when and not how.

15. It is interesting to note that the Aux to C construction behaves differently with respect to left dislocation whether a subject is realized or not. If no subject is phonetically realized, a left-dislocated item is ungrammatical, whereas if the subject is present, left dislocation becomes possible. See Poletto (1993) for a discussion of these facts.

16. This sentence is grammatical if the LD element is construed as the hanging topic of the other clause.

17. G. Cinque pointed out to me that certain examples are grammatical:

(i)   Giuntigli a Gianni due pacchi . . .
       arrived-to him to John two packets . . .
       'As John had received two packets . . .'

In this case, absolute participles behave as Aux to C structures, and the analysis can be the same.

18. There is another possible explanation for the difference between modal and nonmodal interrogatives. It could be that the modal feature of these verbal forms is not checked in CP but rather inside IP. Cinque's (1999) analysis of the functional projections of the clause admits several modal projections (see chapter 5 for more details), and the modal feature of the verb in modal interrogatives could be checked in one of those projections. The verb would then raise to C in main contexts and remain in the modal head in embedded modal interrogatives. This opens the opportunity to exploit this modal projection to explain the presence of a subject in modal interrogatives. The difference between modal and nonmodal interrogatives with respect to the subject would thus not be attributed to the fact that the wh-element in modal interrogatives moves to a higher SpecC position and crosses the subject position, triggering the order wh-element subject (the preverbal or postverbal status of the subject depends on verb movement in main versus embedded interrogatives). Rather, it would be a consequence of the activation of the modal IP projection that makes a new specifier position available, namely, SpecMod, where the subject may be located. Nonmodal interrogatives do not have modal features. They do not

activate the modal projection; hence its specifier position is not available. Note, however, that this hypothesis does not explain the incompatibility of modal questions with left dislocation.

19. Note that this type of structure could also directly account for French complex inversion if we assume that even in this case the wh rises to SpecC1, whereas the inflected verb moves only to the SCI position AgrC. We do not necessarily expect complex inversion in French to have a modal flavor, as we have seen that in many NIDs all the four interrogative CP positions can be used with the interpretation of an out-of-the-blue interrogative.

20. I do not deal with the issue of why there are two classes of speakers and in what ways their grammar differ. I refer to Giorgi and Pianesi (1997) for a proposal on this question.

21. There could be an additional distinction splitting the position of null operators from the position of overt wh-elements on the basis of the difference found when a QP subject is realized because yes/no questions tolerate preverbal QP subjects but wh-interrogatives do not.

CHAPTER 7

1. First person SCLs are found only in Lombard and Rhaetoromance dialects; they appear as enclitic to the inflected verb, thus confirming the idea that the position occupied by the inflected verb is that where first-person features are realized.

2. Three if we include the position reached by the inflected verb in most dialects.

3. This position is available only in main V2 clauses.

4. The first of the two positions is available only under bridge verbs in embedded V2, whereas the second is available under all types of selecting verbs.

5. As shown in chapter 4, the V2 dialects have a different position for the preverbal subject, a position located inside the V2 field.

Bibliography

Adams, M. (1987). From Old French to the Theory of Pro-drop. *Natural Language and Linguistic Theory*, 5: 1–32.

AIS Sprach und Sachatlas Italiens und der Sudschweiz (Language and Object-Atlas of Italy and Southern Switzerland). (1928–1940). Rengien et Co., Zofingen.

Alber, B. (1994). Indizi per l'esistenza di uno split-CP nelle lingue germaniche (Clues for the Existence of a Split CP in Germanic Languages). In G. Borgato, ed., *Teoria del linguaggio e analisi linguistica—XX Incontro di Grammatica Generativa* (Language Theory and Linguistic Analysis—XX Generative Grammar Meeting), pp. 3–23. Unipress, Padova.

Alberton, S. (1990). Enclise du pronom object en francais et en italian antique ou la loi Tobler-Mussafia (Enclis of the Object Pronoun in Old French and Italian or the Tobler-Mussafia Law). Memoire de Licence (b.a. thesis), University of Geneva.

Altmann, H. (1981). *Formen der Heraustellung im Deutschen.* Niemeyer, Tübingen.

Aly-Belfadel, A. (1933). *Grammatica Piemontese* (Piedmontese Grammar). Guin, Noale.

Ambar, M. (1988). Para uma sintaxe da inversão sujeito verbo em português (For a Syntax of Subject-verb Inversion in Portuguese). Ph.D. thesis, University of Lisbon.

Antinucci, F., and G. Cinque. (1977). Sull'ordine delle parole in italiano: L'emarginazione (On Word Order in Italian: Emargination). *Studi di Grammatica Italiana* (Studies of Italian Grammar), 6:121–146.

Apollonio, B. (1930). *Grammatica del Dialetto Ampezzano* (Grammar of the Ampezzano Dialect). Arti Grafiche Tridentum, Trent. Reprinted in 1987 by Cooperativa di Consumo di Cortina d'Ampezzo.

ASIS, Atlante Sintattico dell'Italia Settentrional (Syntactic Atlas of Northern Italy). (1991–1998). Unpublished material, CNR, Centro di Studio per la Dialettologia Italiana, University of Padua.

ASLEF, Atlante Storico Linguistico Etnografico Friulano (Historical Linguistic Ethnografic friulian Atlas). (1981). Tipografia Antoniana, Padova.

Authier, J. M. (1992). Arbitrary Null Object Languages in a Parametric Theory of Linguistic Variation. In A. J. Lakarra and J. O. de Urbina, eds., *Syntactic Theory and Basque Syntax.* Supplements of the Annuario del Seminario de Filologia Vasca "Julio de Urquijo," *International Journal of Basque Linguistics and Philology*, 27.

193

Azaretti, E. (1982). *L'evoluzione dei dialetti liguri* (The Evolution of Ligurian Dialects). Edizioni Casabianca, Sanremo.

Azaretti, E., and G. Petracco Sicardi. (1989). *Studi Linguistici sull'Anfizona Liguria-Provenza* (Linguistic Studies on the Borderline Liguria-Provenza). Edizioni dell'Orso, Alessandria.

Baker, M. (1988). *Incorporation: A Theory of Grammatical Function Changing*. University of Chicago Press, Chicago.

Baker, M., and K. Hale. (1990). Relativized Minimality and Pronoun Incorporation. *Linguistic Inquiry*, 21: 289–297.

Barbosa, P. (l997). Subject Positions in the Null Subject Languages. *Seminàrios de Linguìstica Universidade do Algarve,* 1: 39–63.

Battisti, C. (1914). *Testi dialettali italiani* (Dialectal Italian Texts). Niemeyer, Tübingen.

Bayer, J. (1984). Comp in Bavarian Syntax. *The Linguistic Review*, 3: 209–274.

Beghelli, F. (1995). The Phrase Structure of Quantifier Scope. Ph.D. thesis, UCLA.

Beghelli, F., and T. Stowell. (1997). Distributivity and Negation: The Syntax of *Each* and *Every*. In A. Szabolcsi, ed., *Ways of Scope Taking*. Kluwer, Dordrecht.

Belletti, A. (1988). The Case of Unaccusatives. *Linguistic Inquiry*, 19: 1–34.

Belletti, A. (1990). *Generalized Verb Movement*. Rosenberg and Sellier, Turin.

Belletti, A., and L. Rizzi. (1988). Psych-verbs and Theta Theory. *Natural Language and Linguistic Theory*, 6: 291–352.

Benincà, P. (1983). Il clitico "a" nel dialetto padovano (The Clitic "a" in the Paduan Dialect). In *Scritti linguistici in onore di Giovan Battista Pellegrini* (Linguistic Papers in honor of G. B. Pellegrini), pp. 25–32. Pacini, Pisa. Reprinted in Benincà (1994a).

Benincà, P. (1984). Un'ipotesi sulla sintassi delle lingue romanze medievali (A Hypothesis on the Syntax of Medieval Romance Languages). *Quaderni Patavini di Linguistica* (Paduan Working Papers in Linguistics)*,* 4: 3–19. Reprinted in Benincà (1994b).

Benincà, P. (1985/6). L'interferenza sintattica: di un aspetto della sintassi ladina considerato di origine tedesca (Syntactic Interference: an Aspect of Rhaetoromance Syntax considered of Germanic Origin). *Quaderni Patavini di Linguistica* (Paduan Working Papers in Linguistics), 5: 3–15. Reprinted in Benincà (1994b).

Benincà, P. (1986). Punti di sintassi comparata dei dialetti italiani settentrionali (Notes of Comparative Syntax on Northern Italian Dialects). In G. Holtus and K. Ringger, eds., *Raetia Antiqua et Moderna, W. Th. Elwert zum 80. Geburtstag* (Old and Modern Raetia. For the 80. Birthday of W. Th. Elwert), pp. 457–479. Niemeyer, Tübingen. Reprinted in Benincà (1994b).

Benincà, P. (1988). L'ordine degli elementi della frase e le costruzioni marcate (The Order of Elements in the Sentence and Marked Constructions). In L. Renzi, ed., *Grande Grammatica Italiana di Consultazione* (Italian Reference Grammar), pp. 129–194. Il Mulino, Bologna.

Benincà, P. (1989). Friaulisch (Friulian). In G. Holtus, M. Metzeltin and Ch. Schmitt, eds., *Lexikon der Romanistischen Linguistik* (Lexicon of Romance Linguistics)*,* vol. 3, pp. 563–585. Niemeyer, Tübingen.

Benincà, P. (1994a). I dati dell'ASIS e la sintassi diacronica (The ASIS Data and Diachronic Syntax). In E. Banfi et al., eds., *Italia Settentrionale:Crocevia di idiomi romanzi* (Northern Italy: Crossroad of Romance Varieties)*,* pp. 133–144. Niemeyer, Tübingen.

Benincà, P. (1994b). *La variazione sintattica* (Syntactic Variation). Il Mulino, Bologna.

Benincà, P. (1995a). Agglutination and Inflection in Northern Italian Dialects. In C. Parodi, C. Quicoli, M. Saltarelli, and M. L. Zubizzareta, eds., *Aspects of Romance Linguistics*. Selected Papers from the Linguistic Symposium on Romance Languages 10–13 marzo 1994). vol. 24, pp. 59–72. Georgetown University Press, Washington, D.C.

Benincà, P. (1995b). Complement Clitics in Medieval Romance: The Tobler-Mussafia Law. In A. Battye and I. Roberts, eds., *Clause Structure and Language Change,* pp. 296–325. Oxford University Press, Oxford.

Benincà, P. (1996). La struttura della frase esclamativa alla luce del dialetto padovano (The Structure of the Exclamative Clause through the Paduan Dialect). In P. Benincà, G. Cinque, T. De Mauro, and N. Vincent, eds., *Italiano e dialetti nel tempo: Saggi di grammatica per Giulio C. Lepschy* (Italian and Dialects in Time: Grammar studies for G. C. Lepschy), pp. 23–43. Bulzoni, Rome.

Benincà, P. (1997). Syntactic Focus and Intonational Focus in the Left Periphery. In G. Cinque and G. Salvi, eds., *Current Studies in Italian Linguistics Offered to Lorenzo Renzi.* Foris, Dordrecht.

Benincà, P., and G. Cinque. (1985, August). Lexical Subjects in Italian and the Pro-drop Parameter. Paper presented at the Comparative Generative Grammar Fiesta, Salzburg.

Benincà, P., and G. Cinque. (1993). Su alcune differenze tra enclisi e proclisi (On Some Differences between Enclis and Proclisis). In *Omaggio a Gianfranco Folena* (In Honor of G. Folena). pp. 2313–2326. Editoriale Programma, Padova.

Benincà, P., and C. Poletto. (1994). Bisogna and Its Companions: The Verbs of Necessity. In G. Cinque et al., eds., *Paths Towards Universal Grammar: Studies in Honor of R. Kayne,* pp. 35–58. Georgetown University Press, Washington, D.C.

Benincà, P., and C. Poletto. (1997). *Quaderni di lavoro dell' ASIS.* 1. Centro Stampa Maldura, Padova.

Benincà P., and C. Poletto. (1998). A Case of Do-support in Romance. *Venice Working Papers in Linguistics,* vol. 8, pp. 27–64. CLI, Venice.

Benincà, P., and L. Renzi. (1998, October 1–3). Struttura della frase interrogativa nei due Catechismi cimbri del 1602 e del 1813 (The Structure of the Interrogative Sentence in the Two Cimbri Cathetisms of 1602 and 1803). Talk delivered at the Conference "Fragen über Fragen" Innsbruck. To appear in *Romanistik in Geschichte und Gegenwart.*

Benincà, P., and L. Vanelli. (1975). Morfologia del verbo friulano: Il presente indicativo (Morphology of the Friulian Verb: The Present Indicative). *Lingua e Contesto* (Language and Content), 1: 1–62.

Benincà, P., and L. Vanelli. (1982). Appunti di sintassi veneta (Notes of Veneto Syntax). In M. Cortelazzo, ed., *Guida ai dialetti veneti* (Guide to the Veneto Dialects), vol. 4, pp. 7–38. CLEUP, Padova. Reprinted in Benincà (1994b).

Bennis, H., and L. Haegeman. (1984). On the Status of Agreement and Relative Clauses in West Flemish. In W. de Geest and Y. Putseys, eds., *Sentential Complementation,* pp. 35–55. Foris, Dordrecht.

Benucci, F. (1990). *Destrutturazione* (Destructuring). Unipress, Padova.

Benveniste, E. (1966). Relationship of Person in the Verb. In *Problèmes de linguistique générale,* pp. 195–204. Gallimard, Paris.

Besten, den, H. (1984). On the Interaction of Root Transformations and Lexical Deletive Rules. In W. Abraham, ed., *On the Formal Syntax of West Germania,* pp. 47–131. Benjamins, Amsterdam.

Biondelli, B. (1853). *Saggio sui dialetti Gallo-Italici* (Study on the Gallo-Italian Dialects). Bernardoni, Milano.

Borer, H. (1989). Anaphoric Agr. In O. Jaeggli and K. Safir, eds., *The Null Subject Parameter,* pp. 69–110. Kluwer, Dordrecht.

Bracco, C. L., Brandi, and P. Cordin. (1981). Sulla posizione soggetto in italiano e in alcuni dialetti (On the Subject Position in Italian and in Some Dialects). In A. Franchi de Bellis and L. M. Savoia, eds., *Sintassi e morfologia della lingua italiana d'uso. Teorie e applicazioni descrittive* (Syntax and Morphology in the Italian Language. Theories and Descriptive Applications), pp. 185–209. Bulzoni, Roma.

Brandi, L., and P. Cordin. (1981). Dialetto e Italiano: Un confronto sul parametro del soggetto nullo. *Rivista di Grammatica Generativa*, 6: 33–87.

Brandi, L., and P. Cordin. (1989). Two Italian Dialects and the Null Subject Parameter. In O. Jaeggli and K. Safir, eds., *The Null Subject Parameter,* pp. 111–142. Kluwer, Dordrecht.

Brovedani, L. (1981). La formazione delle frasi interrogative e relative nella varietà friulana di Clauzetto (The Formation of Relative and Interrogative Sentences in the Friulian Dialect of Clauzetto). Tesi di Laurea, University of Padua.

Brugger, G., and C. Poletto. (1993). On Negation in German and Bavarian. *Working Papers in Linguistics*, vol. 151, pp. 41–79. Università di Venezia. Reprinted in *Rivista di Grammatica Generativa*, 1995: 111–159.

Burzio, L. (1986). *Italian Syntax.* Reidel, Dordrecht.

Calabrese, A. (1980). Sui pronomi atoni e tonici dell'italiano (On Tonic and Clitic Pronouns in Italian). *Rivista di Grammatica Generativa* (Generative Grammar Review), 5: 65–116.

Calabrese, A. (1982). Alcune ipotesi sulla struttura informazionale della frase in italiano e sul rapporto con la struttura fonologica (Some Hypotheses on the Informational Structure of the Sentence in Italian and on its Relation with Phonological Structure). *Rivista di Grammatica Generativa* (Generative Grammar Review), 7: 3–78.

Calabrese, A. (1993). The Sentential Complementation of Salentino: A Study of a Language Without Infinitival Clauses. In A. Belletti, ed., *Syntactic Theory and the Dialects of Italy*, pp. 28–98. Rosenberg and Sellier, Turin.

Campos, H. (1986). Inflectional Elements in Romance. Ph.D. thesis, UCLA.

Cardinaletti, A. (1991). On Pronoun Movement: The Italian Dative *loro*. *Probus*, 3: 127–153.

Cardinaletti A. (1997). Subjects and Clause Structure. In L. Haegeman, ed., *The New Comparative Syntax*, pp. 33–63. Longman, London.

Cardinaletti, A., and M. Starke. (1999). The Typology of Structural Deficiency: On the Three Grammatical Classes. In H. van Riemsdijk, ed., *Clitics in the Languages of Europe, Vol. 8.* of *Empirical Approaches to Language Typology*. Mouton de Gruyter, Berlin.

Chenal, A. (1986). *Le franco-provençal valdotain* (The Franco-Provençal Spoken in Val d'Aosta). Musumeci, Aosta.

Chomsky, N. (1981). *Lectures on Government and Binding.* Foris, Dordrecht.

Chomsky, N. (1986). *Barriers.* MIT Press, Cambridge, Mass.

Chomsky, N. (1993). A Minimalist Program for Linguistic theory. In K. Hale and S. J. Kayser, eds., *The View from Building 20*, pp. 1–52. Moyer Bell, Wakefield, London.

Chomsky, N. (1995). *The Minimalist Program.* MIT Press, Cambridge, Mass.

Cinque, G. (1989). On Embedded Verb Second Clauses and Ergativity in German. In D. Jaspers and W. Klooster, eds., *Sentential Complementation and the Lexicon. Studies in Honor of Wim de Geest*, pp. 77–96. Foris, Dordrecht.

Cinque, G. (1990). *Types of A-bar Dependencies, Vol 17. Linguistic Inquiry Monographs.* MIT Press, Cambridge, Mass.

Cinque, G. (1995). *Italian Syntax and Universal Grammar.* Cambridge University Press, Cambridge.

Cinque, G. (1999). *Adverbs and Functional Heads.* Oxford University Press, Oxford.

Comrie, B. (1989). *Language Universals and Linguistic Typology.* Blackwell, Oxford.

Cordin, P. (1993). Dative Clitics and Doubling in Trentino. In A. Belletti, ed., *Syntactic Theory and the Dialects of Italy*, pp. 130–154. Rosenberg and Sellier, Turin.

Cortelazzo, M. (1975). *Profilo dei dialetti italiani* (Overview of Italian Dialects). Pacini, Pisa.

Cuneo, M. (1997). L'elemento interrogativo "koelu" (The Interrogative Element 'Koelu'). *Quaderni di lavoro dell'ASIS* (ASIS Working Papers), 1: 31–61.

D'Aronco, G. (1960). *Nuova Antologia della Letteratura Friulana* (New Anthology of Friulian Literature). Edizioni Aquileia, Udine-Tolmezzo.

Diesing, M. (1990). Verb Movement and the Subject Position in Yiddish. *Natural Language and Linguistic Theory*, 8: 41–81.

Dobrovie-Sorin, C. (1990). Clitic Doubling, Wh-Movement and Quantification in Romanian. *Linguistic Inquiry,* 21: 351–397.

Elwert, W. Th. (1943). *Die Mundart des Fassa-Tals* (The Dialect of the Fassa Valley). Winter Verlag, Heidelberg.

Fava, E. (1993). Sulla pertinenza della pragmatica nell'analisi grammaticale: un esempio dalla cosiddetta coniugazione interrogativa nel dialetto alto-vicentino (On the Pertinence of Pragmatics in Grammatical Analysis an Example of the so-called Interrogative Conjugation in the High-Vicentino Dialect). In *Omaggio a Gianfranco Folena* (In Honor of G. Folena). pp. 2495–2520. Editoriale Programma, Padova.

Fava, E. (1998, October 1–3). Mood as a feature of interrogation in some Romance languages: some considerations on the descriptive adequacy of the illocutionary force devices. Talk delivered at the Conference "Fragen über Fragen," Innsbruck. To appear in *Romanistik in Geschichte und Gegenwart.*

Foulet, L. (1935–1936). L'extension de la forme oblique de pronom personnel en ancient francais (The Extension of the Oblique Form of the Personal Pronoun in Old French). *Romania*, pp. 61–243.

Friedemann, M.-A. (1995). Sujets syntaxiques: Positions, inversion et pro (Syntactic Subjects: Positions, Inversion and pro). Ph. D. thesis, University of Geneva.

Gartner, Th. (1870). *Die Gredner Mundart* (The Dialect of the Gardena Valley). Linz.

Gartner, Th. (1910). *Handbuch der Rhaetoromanischen Sprache und Literatur* (Handbook of the Rhaetoromance Language and Literature). Niemeyer Verlag, Halle A. S.

Gatti, T. (1990). Confronto tra fenomeni sintattici nell'italiano e nel dialetto trentino: Participio passato, accordo e ausiliari (Comparison between Syntactic Phenomena of Italian and Trentino: Past Participle, Agreement, Auxiliaries). Tesi di Laurea, University of Trento.

Giorgi, A., and F. Pianesi. (1991). Towards a Syntax of Temporal Representation. *Probus*, 3: 1–27.

Giorgi A., and F. Pianesi. (1997). *Tense and Aspect: From Semantics to Morphosyntax.* Oxford University Press, New York.

Giupponi, E. (1988). Pro Drop Parameter und Restrukturierung im Trentino. Tesi di laurea, University of Vienna.

Grimshaw, J. (1991). Extended Projections and Locality. In P. Coopmans, M. Everaert, and J. Grimshaw, eds., *Lexical Structure*. Erlbaum, Newark, N.J.

Grimshaw, J. (1997). Projection, heads and optimality. *Linguistic Inquiry,* 28: 373–422.

Haegeman, L. (1993). Some Speculations on Argument Shift, Clitics, and Crossing in West Flemish. In W. Abraham and J. Bayer, eds., *Dialektsyntax*, pp. 131–160. Westdeutscher Verlag, Opladen.

Haegeman, L. (1995). *The Syntax of Negation*. Cambridge University Press, Cambridge.

Haegemann, L., and R. Zanuttini. (1996). Negative Concord in West Flemish. In A. Belletti and L. Rizzi, eds., *Parameters and Functional Heads. Essays in Comparative Syntax,* pp. 117–179. Oxford University Press, New York.

Haiman, J., and P. Benincà, (1992). *The Rhaeto-Romance Languages.* Routledge, London.

Hale, K., and M. Closkey. (1984). On the Syntax of Person-Number Inflection in Modern Irish. *Natural Language and Linguistic Theory,* 1: 487–533.

Higginbotham, J. (1991). Either or. Talk delivered at the Seminario di Ricerca, University of Venice.

Hoekstra, E. (1992). On the Parametrization of Functional Projections in CP. Unpublished ms., Royal Dutch Academy of Sciences, Amsterdam.

Holmberg, A., and Ch. Platzack. (1995). *The Role of Inflection in Scandinavian Syntax.* Oxford University Press, New York.

Hulk, A. (1993). Residual Verb-Second and the Licencing of Functional Features. *Probus,* 5: 127–154.

Jaeggli, O. (1982). *Topics in Romance Syntax.* Foris, Dordrecht.

Jaeggli, O. (1986). Three Issues in the Theory of Clitics: Case, Doubled NPs and Extraction. In H. Borer, ed., *Syntax and Semantics Vol. 19, The Syntax of Pronominal Clitics,* pp. 15–42. Academic Press, Orlando, Fla.

Jaeggli, O., and K. J. Safir. (1989). *The Null Subject Parameter.* Kluwer, Dordrecht.

Johannessen, J. B. (1996). Partial Agreement and Coordination. *Linquistic Inquiry,* 27: 661–676.

Johnson, K. (1991). Object Positions. *Natural Language and Linguistic Theory,* 9: 577–636.

Jones, M. (1993). *Sardinian Syntax.* Routledge, London.

Kayne, R. (1975). *French Syntax.* MIT Press, Cambridge, Mass.

Kayne, R. (1989a). Facets of Past Participle Agreement. In P. Benincà, ed., *Dialect Variation and the Theory of Grammar,* pp. 85–103. Foris, Dordrecht.

Kayne, R. (1989b) Notes on English Agreement. *CIEFL Bulletin,* 1: 40–67.

Kayne, R. (1990). Romance Clitics and PRO. In *Proceedins of NELS XX,* vol. 2, pp. 255–302. GLSA, University of Massachussets, Amherst.

Kayne, R. (1991). Romance Clitics, Verb Movement, and PRO. *Linguistic Inquiry,* 22: 647–686.

Kayne, R. (1992). Italian Negative Infinitival Imperatives and Clitic Climbing. In L. Tasmowski and A. Zribi-Hertz, eds., *De la musique à la linguistique. Hommage a Nicolas Ruwet,* pp. 300–312. Communications and Cognition, Ghent.

Kayne, R. (1993). Towards a Modular Theory of Auxiliary Selection. *Studia Linguistica,* 47: 3–31.

Kayne, R. (1994). *The Antisymmetry of Syntax, Vol. 25. Linguistic Inquiry Monographs.* MIT Press, Cambridge, Mass.

Kayne, R. (1998). Overt vs. Covert Movement. *Syntax,* 1: 128–131.

Kemenade, van, A. (1987). *Syntactic Case and Morphological Case in the History of English.* Foris, Dordrecht.

Koopman, H., and D. Sportiche, (1992). Subjects. *Linguistic Review,* 2: 139–160.

Koster, I. (1975). Dutch as an SOV language. *Linguistic Analysis,* 1: 111–136.

Larson, R. K. (1988). On Double Object Constructions. *Linguistic Inquiry,* 19: 335–391.

Li, Y. (1990). X° and Verb Incorporation. *Linguistic Inquiry,* 21(3): 399–426.

Lightfoot, D. (1979). *Principles of Diachronic Syntax.* Cambridge University Press, Cambridge.

Lightfoot, D. (1991). *How to Set Parameters: Arguments from Language Change*. MIT Press, Cambridge, Mass.

Lurà, F. (1987). *Il dialetto del mendrisiotto* (The Dialect of Mendrisio). Edizioni Unione delle Banche Svizzere, Mendrisio-Chiasso.

Marchetti, G. (1952). *Lineamenti di grammatica friulana* (Outlines of Friulian Grammar). Società Filologica Friulana, Udine.

Massajoli, P. (1996). *Dizionario della cultura Brigasca. II: Grammatica* (Dictionary of the Briga Culture II: Grammar). Edizioni dell'Orso, Alessandria.

Mastrangelo, Latini, G. (1981). Note di morfologia dialettale (Notes of Dialectal Morphology). *Quaderni di filologia e lingue romanze* (Working Papers of Philology and Romance Languages), 3: 241–249.

Matalon, Z. N. (1977). Mari Lenghe: Grammatiche furlane (Mother Tongue: Friulian Grammar). Institû di Studis Furlans, Udine.

May, R. (1985). *Logical Form: Its Structure and Derivation, Vol. 12. Linguistic Inquiry Monographs*. MIT Press, Cambridge, Mass.

Moro, A. (1997). *The Raising of Predicates: Predicative Noun Phrases and the Theory of Clause Structure*. Cambridge University Press, Cambridge.

Munaro, N. (1995). On Nominal Wh-phrases in Some Northern Italian Dialects. *Rivista di Grammatica Generativa* 20: 69–100.

Munaro, N. (1997). Proprietà strutturali e distribuzionali dei sintagmi interrogativi in alcuni dialetti italiani settentrionali (Structural and Distributional Properties of Interrogative Phrases in Some Northern Italian Dialects). Ph.D. thesis, University of Padova.

Nicoli, F. (1983). *Grammatica Milanese* (Milanese Grammar). Bramanti, Busto Arsizio.

Obletter, A. (1991). *La rujeneda dla oma. Gramatica dl ladin de Gherdëina* (The Language of the Mother. Gardenese Grammar). Typak, Ortisei.

Ordonez, F. (1997). Word Order and Clause Structure in Spanish and Other Romance Languages. Ph.D. thesis, CUNY Graduate Center.

Ouhalla, J. (1990). Sentential Negation, Relativized Minimality and the Aspectual Status of Auxiliaries. *Linguistic Review*, 7: 183–231.

Pagani, G. Il dialetto di Borgomanero (The Dialect of Borgomanero). In *Atti dell'Istituto Lombardo di Scienze, Lettere e Arti* (Proceedings of the Lombard Institute of Sciences, Literature and Arts), vol. 51, pp. 602–611, 919–949.

Papanti, G. (1985). *I parlari italiani in Certaldo* (The Italian Varieties in Certaldo). Forni, Bologna.

Parry, M. (1989). Strutture negative nei dialetti piemontesi (Negative Structures in the Piedmontese Dialects). In G. P. Clivio and C. Pich, eds., *At del V Rescontr internassional de Studi an sla Lenga e la Literatura piemonteisa, Alba* (Proceedings of the V International Meeting of Studies of Piedmontese Language and Literature). pp. 169–177. Famija Albèisa, Alba.

Parry, M. (1994). Posizione dei clitici complemento nelle costruzioni verbali perifrastiche del piemontese (The Position of Complement Clitics in the Piedmontese Periphrastic Verbal Constructions). In G. P. Clivio and C. Pich eds. *At del VIII Rescontr internassional de Studi an sla Lenga e la Literatura piemonteisa, Alba* (Proceedings of the VIII International Meeting of Studies of Piedmontese Language and Literature). pp. 247–260. Famija Albèisa, Alba.

Parry, M. (1997a). Negation. In M. Maiden and M. M. Parry, eds., *The Dialects of Italy*, pp. 179–185. Routledge, London.

Parry, M. (1997b). Preverbal Negation and Clitic Ordering, with Particular Reference to a Group of North-West Italian Dialects. *Zeitschrift fur Romanische Philologie*, 113: 243–271.

Pellegrini, G. (1972). *Saggi sul ladino dolomitico e sul friulano* (Studies of Friulian and Central Rhaetoromance). Adriatica Editrice, Bari.

Plann, S. (1982). Indirect Questions in Spanish. *Linguistic Inquiry*, 13: 288–312.

Platzack, Ch. (1987). The Scandinavian Languages and the Null Subject Parameter. *Natural Language and Linguistic Theory*, 5: 377–401.

Poggi, L. (1983). Implicazioni teoriche della sintassi dei pronomi soggetto in un dialetto romagnolo (Theorical Implications of the Syntax of Subject Pronouns in a Romagnolo Dialect). Tesi di Laurea, University of Calabria.

Poletto, C. (1992). Complementizer Deletion in Standard Italian. Unpublished ms., University of Padua.

Poletto, C. (1993a). The Aspect Projection: an Analysis of the Passé Surcomposé. In E. Fava, ed., *Proceedings of the XVIII Meeting of Generative Grammar,* pp. 289–312. Rosenberg and Sellier, Torino.

Poletto, C. (1993b). *La sintassi del soggetto nei dialetti dell'Italia settentrionale* (The Syntax of the Subject in the Northern Italian Dialects). Unipress, Padova.

Poletto, C. (1993c). La sintassi del soggetto nei dialetti dell'Italia settentrionale (The Syntax of the Subject in the Northern Italian Dialects). Ph.d. thesis, Universities of Padua and Venice.

Poletto, C. (1993d). Subject Clitic-Verb Inversion in North Eastern Italian Dialects. In A. Belletti, ed., *Syntactic Theory and the Dialects of Italy,* pp. 204–251. Rosenberg and Sellier, Torino.

Poletto, C. (1995a). Complementizer Deletion and Verb Movement in Italian. *Working Papers in Linguistics,* vol. 5, no. 2, pp. 1–15. CLI, Venezia.

Poletto, C. (1995b). The Diachronic Development of Subject Clitics in North-Eastern Italian Dialects. In I. Roberts and A. Battye, eds., *Clause Structure and Language Change,* pp. 295–324. Oxford University Press, Oxford.

Poletto, C. (1996). Three Types of Subject Clitics and the Theory of Pro. In A. Belletti and L. Rizzi, eds., *Parameters and Functional Heads,* pp. 269–300. Oxford University Press, Oxford.

Poletto, C. (1997a). Pronominal Syntax. In M. Maiden and M. Parry, eds., *The Dialects of Italy,* pp. 137–145. Cambridge University Press, Cambridge.

Poletto, C. (1997b). Tipi di pronomi interrogativi in friulano occidentale (Types of Interrogative Pronouns in Western Friulian). *Quaderni di lavoro dell'Atlante Sintattico dell'Italia Settentrionale* (ASIS Working Papers), 1: 75–81.

Poletto, C. (1998). L'inversione interrogativa come "verbo secondo residuo": l'analisi sincronica proiettata nella diacronia (Interrogative Inversion as "residual verb second": The Syncronic Analysis projected into Diachrony). In P. Ramat and E. Roma, eds., *Atti del XXX convegno SLI* (Proceedings of the XXX SLI Conference), pp. 311–327. Bulzoni, Roma.

Poletto, C. (1999). The Internal Structure of AgrS and Subject Clitics. In H. van Riemsdijk, ed., *Clitics in the Languages of Europe, Vol 8. Empirical Approaches to Language Typology.* Mouton de Gruyter, Berlin.

Poletto, C., and A. Tomaselli (1995). Verso una definizione di elemento clitico (Towards a Definition of Clitic Element). In R. Dolci and G. Giusti, eds., *Quaderni di Linguistica del CLI* (CLI Working Papers in Linguistics), pp. 159–224. CLI, Venice.

Poletto, C., and A. Tomaselli. (1998). Tipi di verbo secondo (Verb Second Types). Unpublished ms., Universities of Padua and Verona.

Poletto, C., and L. Vanelli. (1994). Gli introduttori delle frasi interrogative nei dialetti italiani (The Complementizers in Interrogative Sentences in the Italian Dialects). In E. Banfi, G. Bonfadini , and P. Cordin, eds., *Atti del Convegno Italia Settentrionale:*

Crocevia di Idiomi Romanzi (Proceedings of the Conference: Northern Italy Crossroad of Romance Varieties), pp. 145–158. Niemeyer, Tübingen.

Poletto, C., and R. Zanuttini. (1998). Making Imperatives: Evidence from Rhaetoromance. In Ch. Tortora, ed., *Studies in honor of Paola Benincà*. Oxford University Press, Oxford.

Pollock, C. (1989). Verb Movement, Universal Grammar and the Structure of IP. *Linguistic Inquiry,* 20: 365–424.

Pollock, J.-Y. (1986). Sur la syntaxe de en et le parametre du sujet nul (On the Syntax of *en* and the Null Subject Parameter). In D. Couquaux and M. Ronat, eds., *La Grammaire Modulaire* (Modular Grammar), pp. 211–246. Editions de Minuit, Paris.

Portner, P., and R. Zanuttini. (1996). The Syntax and Semantics of Scalar Negation: Evidence from Paduan. In K. Kusumoto, ed., *Proceedings of NELS*, vol. 26, pp. 257–271. GLSA, University of Massachussetts, Amherst.

Renzi, L., and G. Salvi. (1988). *Grande Grammatica Italiana di Consultazione* (Italian Reference Grammar), vol. I. Il Mulino, Bologna.

Renzi, L., G. Salvi, and A. Cardinaletti (1995). *Grande Grammatica Italiana di Consultazione* (Italian Reference Grammar), vol. 3. Il Mulino, Bologna.

Renzi, L., and L. Vanelli. (1983). I pronomi soggetto in alcune varietà romanze (Subject Pronouns in Some Romance Varieties). In *Scritti linguistici in onore di Giovan Battista Pellegrini* (Linguistic Papers in Honor of G. B. Pellegrini), pp. 121–145. Pisa, Pacini.

Rivero, M. L. (1994). Clause Structure and V-movement in the Languages of the Balkans. *Natural Language and Linguistic Theory*, 12: 63–120.

Rizzi, L. (1982). *Issues in Italian Syntax.* Foris, Dordrecht.

Rizzi, L. (1986a). Null Objects in Italian and the Theory of Pro. *Linguistic Inquiry* 17(4): 501–557.

Rizzi, L. (1986b). On the Status of Subject Clitics in Romance. In O. Jaeggli and C. Silva-Corvalan, eds., *Studies in Romance Linguistics*, pp. 137–152. Foris, Dordrecht.

Rizzi, L. (1991). Residual Verb Second and the Wh-criterion. *Geneva Generative Papers*, vol. 2. Reprinted in A. Belletti and L. Rizzi, eds., *Parameters and Functional Heads*, pp. 63–90. Oxford University Press, Oxford, 1996.

Rizzi L. (1997). The Fine Structure of the Left Periphery. In L. Haegeman, ed., *Elements of Grammar*, pp. 281–337. Kluwer, Dordrecht.

Rizzi, L., and I. Roberts. (1989). Complex Inversion in French. *Probus*, 1: 1–30. Reprinted in A. Belletti and L. Rizzi, eds., *Parameters and Functional Heads*, pp. 63–90. Oxford University Press, Oxford, 1996.

Roberts, I. (1985). Agreement Parameters and the Development of English Modal Auxiliaries. *Natural Language and Linguistic Theory* 3: 21–58.

Roberts, I. (1991). Excorporation and Minimality. *Linguistic Inquiry*, 22: 209–218.

Roberts, I. (1993a). A Formal Account of Grammaticalization in the History of Romance Futures. *Folia Linguistica Historica* 13: 219–258.

Roberts, I. (1993b). The Nature of Subject Clitics in Franco-Provençal Valdotain. In A. Belletti and L. Rizzi, eds., *Parameters and Functional Heads*, pp. 319–353. Oxford University Press, Oxford.

Roberts, I. (1993c). *Verbs and Diachronic Syntax: A Comparative History of English and French.* Kluwer, Dordrecht.

Rohlfs G. (1966–1969). *Grammatica storica della lingua italiana e dei suoi dialetti* (Historical Grammar of the Italian Language and of its Dialects). Einaudi, Torino.

Ronjat, J. (1937). *Grammaire historique des parlers provencaux modernes* (Historical Grammar of the Modern Provençal Varieties). Sociétè des langues romanes, Montpellier.

Rooryck, J. (1992). Romance Enclitic Ordering and Universal Grammar. *Linguistic Review*, 9(3): 219–250.

Rusconi, A. (1878). *I parlari del Novarese* (The Dialects of the Novara Area). Rusconi, Novara.

Ruzzante, (1967). *Teatro* (Theater). L. Zorzi, ed. Einaudi, Torino.

Saccon, G. (1993). Postverbal Subjects: A Study Based on Italian and Its Dialects. Ph.D. thesis, Harvard University.

Salvi, G. (1988). La costruzione passiva (The Passive Construction). in L. Renzi, ed., *Grande Grammatica Italiana di Consultazione* (Italian Reference Grammar), pp. 75–98. Il Mulino, Bologna.

Santorini, B. (1989). The Generalization of the Verb-Second Constraint in the History of Yiddish. Ph.D. thesis, University of Pennsylvania.

Schwartz, B., and S. Vikner. (1996). The Verb Always leaves IP in V2 Clauses. In A. Belletti and L. Rizzi, eds., *Parameters and Functional Heads,* pp. 11–62. Oxford University Press, New York.

Scorretti, M. (1981). Complementizer Ellipsis in 15th Century Italian. *Journal of Italian Linguistics* 6(1): 35–47.

Shlonsky, U. (1990). Pro in Hebrew Subject Inversion. *Linguistic Inquiry*, 21: 263–275.

Shlonsky, U. (1994). Agreement in Comp. *Linguistic Review*, 11: 351–357.

Shlonsky, U. (1997). Clause Structure and Word Order in Hebrew and Arabic. Oxford University Press, New York.

Shlonsky, U. (1998). Subject Positions and Copular Constructions. In J. Lecarme, J. Lowenstamm, and U. Shlonsky, eds., *More Studies in Afro Asiatic Grammar.* The Hague, Holland Academic Publishers.

Signorell, F. (1987). *Normas Surmiranas: Grammatica rumantscha digl idiom da Sur-e Sotses* (Surmirans Rules: Rhaetoromance Grammar of the Dialect of Sur-e Sotses). Tgesa Editoura Cantounala, Chur.

Siller-Runggaldier, H. (1985). La negazione nel ladino centrale (Negation in Central Rhaetoromance). *Revue de Linguistique Romane* (Romance Linguistic Review), 49(193–194): 71–85.

Sorrento, L. (1912). *Lat.* modo *nel dialetto siciliano* (Latin 'modo' in the Sicilian Dialect). Madrid. Reprinted in *Revue dialectologie* Romane (Romance Dialectology Review). 1912.

Spescha, A. (1989). *Grammatica Sursilvana* (Sursilvan Grammar). Casa Editura per Mieds d'Istruczion, Chur.

Spiess, F. (1977). Di un'innovazione morfologica nel sistema dei pronomi personali oggetto nel dialetto della Collina d'Oro (The Morphological Innovation in the System of Personal Pronouns in the Dialect of Collina d'Oro). In *Problemi di morfosintassi dialettale. Atti dell'XI Convegno del C.S.D.I.* (Problems of Dialectal Morphosyntax. Proceedings of the XI C.S.D.I. Conference), pp. 203–212. Pacini, Pisa.

Sportiche, D. (1996). Clitic Constructions. In L. Zaring, and J. Roorick, eds., *Phrase Structure and the Lexicon.* Kluwer, Dordrecht.

Sportiche, D. (1997). Subject Clitics in French and Romance: Complex Inversion and Clitic Doubling. In K. Johnson and I. Roberts, eds., *Studies in Comparative Syntax.* Kluwer, Dordrecht.

Stowell, T. (1981). Origins of Phrase Structure. Ph.D. thesis, MIT.

Tomaselli, A. (1990). *La sintassi del verbo finito nelle lingue germaniche* (The Syntax of the Inflected Verb in the Germanic Languages). CLESP, Padua.

Tomaselli, A. (1995). Cases of V3 in Old High German. In I. Roberts and A. Battye, eds., *Clause Structure and Language Change*, pp. 359–369. Oxford Unversity Press, New York.

Tortora, Ch. (1996). Two Types of Unaccusatives: Evidence from a Northern Italian Dialect. In K. Zagona, ed., *Current Issues in Linguistic Theory, Proceedings of the 25th Symposium on the Romance Languages*. Benjamins, London.

Tortora, Ch. (1997). The Syntax and Semantics of the Locative Expletive. Ph.D. thesis, University of Delaware.

Tortora, Ch. (1999). Agreement, Case, and I-subjects. In *Proceedings of the 29th Meeting of the Northeast Linguistics Society*.

Tuttle, E. (1983). L'oda rusticale di Nicolò Zotti (The 'Oda Rusticale' by Nicoló 20th). In *Scritti Linguistici in onore di Giovan Battista Pellegrini* (Linguistic Papers in Honor of G. B. Pellegrini), pp. 431–464. Pacini, Pisa.

Urech, J. (1946). *Beitrag zur Kenntniss der Mundart der Val Calanca* (Contribution to the Knowledge of the Dialect in the Calanca Valley). Schuler, Biel.

Uriagereka, J. (1995). Aspects in the Syntax of Clitic Placement in Western Romance. *Linguistic Inquiry* 26: 79–123.

Vai, M. (1996). Per una storia della negazione in Milanese in comparazione con altre varietà altoitaliane (The History of Negation in Milanese in Comparison with Other Northern Italian Dialects). *Acme*, 49(1): 57–98.

Vance, B. (1989). Null Subjects and Syntactic Change in Medieval French. Ph.D. thesis, Cornell University.

Vanelli, L. (1987). I pronomi soggetto nei dialetti italiani settentrionali dal Medio Evo ad oggi (The Subject Pronouns in the Northern Italian Dialects from the Middle Ages to the Present). *Medioevo Romanzo*, 13: 173–211.

Vanelli, L. (1992). Da lo a il: la storia dell'articolo definito maschile singolare in italiano e nei dialetti settentrionali (From *le* to *il*: The History of the Masculine Singular Definite Article in Italian and in the Northern Dialects). *Rivista Italiana di Dialettologia* (Italian Review of Dialectology), 16: 29–66.

Vanelli, L. (1998). *I dialetti italiani settentrionali nel panorama romanzo. Studi di sintassi e morfologia* (The Northern Italian Dialects in the Romance Scenario Studies of Syntax and Morphology). Bulzoni, Roma.

Vanelli, L., L. Renzi, and P. Benincà. (1985/6). Tipologia dei pronomi soggetto nelle lingue romanze medievali (Typology of Subject Pronouns in the Medieval Romance Languages). *Quaderni Patavini di Linguistica* (Paduan Working Papers in Linguistics), 5: 49–66. Reprinted in Benincà (1994b).

Vassere, S. (1993). *I pronomi clitici del luganese* (Clitic Pronouns in Luganese). Franco Angeli, Milano.

Vikner, S. (1990). Verb Movement and the Licensing of NP-Positions in the Germanic Languages. Ph.D. thesis, University of Geneva.

Vikner, S. (1995). *Verb Movement and Expletive Subjects in the Germanic Languages*. Oxford University Press, New York.

Vincent, N. (1987). The interaction of periphrasis and inflection: Some Romance Examples. In M. Harris and P. Ramat, eds., *Historical Development of Auxiliaries*, pp. 237–256. Mouton De Gruyter, Berlin.

Wanner, D. (1987). *The Development of Romance Clitic Pronouns: From Latin to Old Romance*. Mouton de Gruyter, Berlin.

Watanabe, A. (1992). Subjacency and S-structure Movement of Wh-in-situ. *Journal of East Asian Linguistics*, 1: 255–291.

Webelhut, G. (1989). *Syntactic Saturation Phenomena and the Modern Germanic Languages*. PhD thesis, MIT.

Zanuttini, R. (1991). Syntactic Properties of Sentential Negation. A Comparative Study of Romance Languages. Ph.D. thesis, University of Pennsylvania.

Zanuttini, R. (1997). *Negation and Clausal Structure: A Comparative Study of Romance Languages*. Oxford University Press, New York.

Zwart, J.-W. (1993). Dutch Syntax. A Minimalist Approach. Ph.D. thesis, University of Groningen.

Zwart, J.-W. (1997). *Morphosyntax and Verb Movement*. Kluwer, Dordrecht.

Index

adverbs, 90, 95–101, 108, 124–126
agreement
  in Comp, 37, 53n.9, 55, 56, 59, 63, 68,
    71, 74, 79, 83–85
  projections, 35–40
  spec-head, 145
auxiliary, 69n.19, 116n.4
  aux to Comp, 115–117, 154, 162, 170–
    173
  do-support, 49–50

Beghelli, Filippo, 153
Belletti, Adriana, 10
Benincà, Paola, 9, 17, 23, 31, 32, 37, 41,
    43, 50, 67, 88, 108–109, 131, 132,
    151, 167

Campos, Hector, 149–150
case
  assignment, 144–147
  checking, 144–147
  subject clitics as manifestations of,
    143
Chomsky, Noam, 4, 82
Cinque, Guglielmo, 4, 17, 31, 39, 45, 95,
    96n.8, 119, 124, 147, 163n.18, 168
clauses. See exclamative, imperatives,
    interrogative
clitic climbing, 23–24 32–35
clitic doubling, 140–143

complementizer, 170–175
  clustering with subject clitics, 21–22,
    36, 84
  in declaratives, 35, 36, 118
  double complementizers, 61, 148–150
  forms, 118, 134
  in interrogatives, 35, 36 46–48, 56–65,
    82–86, 118
coordination, 9, 16–18, 24–29, 36

dialects
  list of, 7–9
  test methods, 6, 9
doubly filled comp filter, 94–95

Emilian, 16, 44, 63, 65, 135, 137n.25
  Bagnolo S. Vito, 114
  Bologna, 59, 117, 132
  Bondeno, 59
  Cesena, 117
  Forlì, 44, 132, 133
  Guastalla, 60, 69, 82
  Piacenza, 69
exclamatives, 67, 154

Fava, Elisabetta, 51
focus, 23–24, 26, 36, 95–98, 99, 101, 123
  markers, 46–48, 55, 58–59, 64–67, 80
Franco Provençal, 13n.3, 14n.4, 64
French, 18, 52, 64, 154, 164n.19

Friulian, 16, 63, 65, 137n.25, 152
  Cervignano, 26
  Cesarolo, 118
  Clauzetto, 43, 44
  Collina, 54
  Forni Avoltri, 111, 114, 116, 142
  Palmanova, 26, 111
  Remanzacco, 20, 111, 134
  San Michele al Tagliamento, 13, 25,
    59, 60, 69, 70, 72–75, 142, 151
  Sutrio, 116

Gascon, 148, 150
German, 65n.14, 88–89, 106–107, 121,
    123–124, 126, 127, 129n.18,
    131n.20, 133n.22
Giorgi, Alessandra, 37–40, 83, 129, 164,
    175
Grimshaw, Jane, 5

Hulk, Aafke, 45

imperatives, 110, 133–137, 172
  particles, 48, 67
inflected verb, 30–32, 45–55, 80, 116,
    169
interrogatives, 154–157
  and left dislocation, 91–95
  main versus embedded, 83–87, 158–
    160, 162–163

Kayne, Richard, 9, 10n.2, 16, 17, 22, 45,
    51, 174

left dislocation, 23–24, 26, 27, 91–95,
    103, 106–107, 139, 152–153, 162–
    163
Ligurian, 16, 113, 137n.25
  Alassio, 57, 142
  Borghetto di Vara, 136, 149, 165
  Carcare, 15, 136, 165
  Caserta Ligure, 56, 57, 62
  Chiavari, 84, 134
  Cosseria, 15
  Genoa, 19
  Savona, 134
Lombard, 6, 16, 31, 32, 135, 137n.25,
    169n.1
  Albosaggia, 62
  Bellinzona, 134

Brione, 111
Cevia Valle Maggia, 136, 165
Lecco, 141
Livigno, 84
Lugano, 12
Malonno, 112, 113, 117, 142
Milano, 57, 63, 109, 117, 142
Monno, 49–50, 55, 79, 85–86, 113,
    115, 142
Montagnola, 20
Vaprio d'Adda, 57, 111, 137

mood, 70, 128–129, 131, 158–163
Munaro, Nicola, 45, 52, 77–79

negation, 28, 33–34
negative markers, 11, 16, 18–20

person, 13–15, 31n.17, 37–40
Pianesi, 37–40, 83, 129, 164, 175
Piedmontese, 13, 16, 44, 64, 70, 109n.1,
    137n.25, 149
  Pra del Torno, 55
  Riva di Chieri, 136, 165
  Rodoretto di Prali, 50, 54, 153
  Turin, 20, 61, 117, 136, 142, 148, 165
Poletto, Cecilia, 5, 42, 48, 50, 53, 80,
    132, 140
Pollock, Jean-Yves, 4, 52

Renzi, Lorenzo, 10, 37–40, 53
Rhaetoromance, 6, 31, 59, 63, 69, 74,
    101n.14, 102n.15, 154, 169n.1
  Alba, 59n.12
  Campitello di Fassa, 76
  Canezei, 59n.12
  Laste, 116
  Livinallongo, 32
  Moena, 59n.12
  Pera di Fassa, 46, 55, 59, 63, 65, 66,
    67, 76, 83, 84
  San Leonardo, 32, 48, 58, 66, 67, 89–
    105
  San Vigilio di Marebbe, 104, 105
  Selva di Val Gardena, 58, 59n.12, 67,
    98n.11
Rizzi, Luigi, 4, 5, 10, 23, 42, 50, 51, 80–
    83, 88, 93, 94, 128, 144, 154–160,
    163
Roberts, Ian, 51, 71, 155n.13

Salentino, 149n.9
Sportiche, Dominique, 45, 50
subject clitic inversion, 29–30, 42–55,
     57–60, 63, 64, 112–118

Trentino, 31, 137n.25, 152
     Castello, 111
     Cles, 111, 117
     Montesover, 54, 141
     Rovereto, 44
     Trento, 137
     Tuenno, 50n.6
     Villa Lagarina, 114
Tuscan, 14n.4, 16, 131–132, 137n.25
     Colle Val d'Elsa, 38n.25, 39n.27, 131,
          137n.24
     Florence, 19, 23, 69, 71, 131
     Incisa Val d'Arno, 34–35

Vanelli, Laura, 9, 10, 31, 32, 37–40, 53
Veneto, 6, 12, 24, 65, 137n.25
     Altavilla Vicentina, 137
     Cencenighe Agordino, 116

Cereda, 42, 62, 68, 111
Cornuda, 28
Loreo, 18, 20, 21, 35, 54, 84
Padua, 20, 23, 29, 32, 43, 54, 57, 63,
     116, 151, 158–160, 161
Portogruaro, 58, 62, 63, 65, 67, 69, 80,
     84
Pramaggiore, 111
Scorzè, 43
Tignes d'Alpago, 77–78
Venice, 14, 19, 27, 28, 29, 68, 69, 70,
     141, 152, 161
Vikner, Sten, 98, 105, 107

wh-items
     doubling, 79
     interaction with subject clitics, 25, 71–
          75
     positions of, 71–83, 170
     types of, 72–75, 78, 86, 170

Zanuttini, Raffaella, 11, 15, 33n.21,
     45n.2, 48, 168